American Dream
Global Nightmare

Ziauddin Sardar · Merryl Wyn Davies

ICON BOOKS

Published in the UK in 2004 by Icon Books Ltd,
The Old Dairy, Brook Road, Thriplow, Cambridge SG8 7RG
e-mail: info@iconbooks.co.uk
www.iconbooks.co.uk

Sold in the UK, Europe, South Africa and Asia
by Faber and Faber Ltd, 3 Queen Square,
London WC1N 3AU
or their agents

Distributed in the UK, Europe, South Africa and Asia
by TBS Ltd, Frating Distribution Centre, Colchester Road,
Frating Green, Colchester CO7 7DW

Published in Australia in 2004
by Allen & Unwin Pty. Ltd.,
PO Box 8500, 83 Alexander Street,
Crows Nest, NSW 2065

Distributed in Canada
by Penguin Books Canada,
10 Alcorn Avenue, Suite 300,
Toronto, Ontario M4V 3B2

ISBN 1 84046 604 9

Typeset by Wayzgoose

Printed and bound in the UK by
Mackays of Chatham

Contents

Ziauddin Sardar is a writer, broadcaster and cultural critic. His numerous books include *Postmodernism and the Other* (1998), *Orientalism* (1999), *The A to Z of Postmodern Life* (2002), *Islam, Postmodernism and Other Futures: A Ziauddin Sardar Reader* (2003), the international bestseller *Why Do People Hate America?* (2002) and, more recently, *Desperately Seeking Paradise: Journeys of a Sceptical Muslim*. Considered one of the top intellectuals in Britain, he is known widely for his regular contributions to the *New Statesman* and national and international newspapers and magazines.

Merryl Wyn Davies is a writer and anthropologist. She is the author of a number of books, including the highly-acclaimed *Knowing One Another: Shaping an Islamic Anthropology* (1988), and is co-author of *Distorted Imagination: Lessons from the Rushdie Affair* (1990) and *Barbaric Others: A Manifesto on Western Racism* (1993). Her most recent books are *Darwin and Fundamentalism* (2000), *Introducing Anthropology* (2002) and *Why Do People Hate America?* (2002). Forever Welsh, she lives and works in Merthyr Tydfil.

Preface

Shortly after the devastating attacks of 11 September 2001, we sat down to address the question that emerged from the wreckage: 'Why do people hate America?' We were convinced that if America was to respond appropriately to that awful event, there was an urgent need for fresh understanding and debate about America's role and relations with the rest of the world. By the time we finished writing, America was already at war in Afghanistan. The subsequent events parodied the reasons and fears we outlined and analysed in our inquiry.

And yet, as the American response began to roll out a pre-determined policy geared to pre-emptive use of aggressive power in the name of self-defence and pro-active democracy-building, a tide of protest grew in America and around the world. But dissent in America or anywhere else in the world has yet to find a way to establish an alternative course. And it was the realisation that the louder and more cogently dissent emerges, the less it seems to construct an agenda for change, that led us to write this book.

The more we have followed events in America, the more we have been convinced of the existence of a deepening malaise. What we are pointing to is a cultural condition fashioned out of history, providing recurrent themes and responses through history, expressed and represented in the cultural products of American society, embedded in the self-image and definition of America as a nation – a condition that makes even rudimentary change almost impossible. The world's problems with America begin in America. We diagnose the root of the problem as the American psychosis. We do not use this term with technical, psychoanalytical exactness. But we do intend it to convey the considered meaning of a serious cultural condition, an imbalance and disorder afflicting the whole of American society.

What America does to itself, what America is incapable of achieving within its own society and culture, has consequences for people everywhere. But before there can be reasoned debate and viable change, the problem has to be made visible. We have to try to make the cultural psychosis of the American Dream visible as a Global Nightmare.

The American Dream begins with a perception that is central to American life. It is the proposition that America is different. What follows from this widely accepted, almost unconscious assumption is that America cannot be judged by the standards applicable to the rest of the world. America is exceptional. It is a cultural predisposition shaped by American history and the specific cultural narratives abstracted from that history. It is a national ethos expressed in myth. It is a view of the American national character supported by the values and moral consciousness embodied in myth, that has a profound impact on the political rhetoric of the nation. As such, it sets the limits of appropriate political debate within America. It is undoubtedly the most dangerous cultural delusion; an imminent threat to the security, peace and well-being not only of Americans but of people everywhere.

The Global Nightmare is that America has the power to impose the limitations of its Dream on the reality of everyone's life. The pursuit of the American Dream has increasingly become a substitution of fantasy for a concern for complex reality, the development of a callousness that describes itself as humanitarian concern and dedication to the noblest of human ideals. Its real consequences are death, suffering, an increasing divide between rich and poor, a squandering of the human future, and building more and more pretexts for conflict as the promise of tomorrow.

As a pervasive cultural construct, operating at home and abroad, the American Dream is embedded in American mythology. We present ten laws of American mythology that we believe are the roots of the American psychosis: cultural forces that work to make America incapable of wrestling with its own problems, of properly appraising the impact it has on the world or apprehending the scale and nature of the real problems facing America and the world. These are not immutable laws; but they do serve as a powerful tool for analysis. Each law marshals a complex of cultural effects that make America incapable of understanding its own power, that make it irresponsible with – and unaccountable for – the consequences of the uses of its power. These laws work to reassure Americans that they are a benign people, a force for good, when in fact American policy, its acts of commission and omission, is generating, fuelling and sustaining exactly the opposite effects.

We have made an analysis of films central to our argument. Hollywood is a dream factory. The dreams it fabricates are quintessentially American. They are mass-produced, commercially driven to affect, entice and resonate with the sensibilities of Americans, to mirror their preoccupations, interests and view of the world. This is what makes them such a coherent cultural force in American society, such a leading sector of the American economy and prime agent of America's interaction with the world. If movies could not speak to America at a visceral level across the diversity of American society, and through time, the entire culture of celebrity would not exist; nor would the vast array of economic activity dependent upon it. The dream factory is not all of America, but it realistically manipulates what America thinks it was, is and could be, to make a culture and economy increasingly driven by the desire to be more like the projections presented on film. This is why it is such a proper and convenient way to order an analysis of American culture. And it is a dimension of American culture familiar to people everywhere.

America, we have to conclude, is not different, not exceptional. America is imperfect, flawed, prone to error that has foul consequences, whether intended or not. Genuine change means awakening from the American Dream to confront the Global

Nightmare, and that is not an easy or hopeful prospect. But to think that just being hopeful, optimistic and positive is enough, without introducing profound change in American society itself, is to cling to delusion. America is not alone in its problems, not exceptional in its difficulties and dilemmas. Learning to see itself as part of the imperfections of an imperfect world opens the possibility of finding answers, new solutions in the struggles of many nations, peoples and worldviews, all of whom also have a vested interest in a peaceful, humane and better human future.

In writing this book, we have benefited from valuable advice and criticism from a host of our friends and colleagues. Thanks are particularly due to Sohail Inayatullah, Steve Fuller, Richard Slaughter, Tony Stevenson, Victoria Razak, John Marciano, Vinay Lal and Jim Dator. Special thanks to Jordi Serra for his expertise on comics, and Lotfi Hermi for providing invaluable service with internet searches. Once again, we are very impressed with Duncan Heath's careful editing and endless patience; and Jeremy Cox's infinite trust and belief in us. As before, Merryl Wyn Davies would like to thank her mother for continuing to endure parental neglect and being so damn cheerful about it.

London, July 2004

Introduction: The Ten Laws of American Mythology

In October 2003, the people of California voted to replace the Governor they had re-elected only a year before with the Austrian-born bodybuilder and action-film hero Arnold Schwarzenegger. The electoral victory of a Hollywood superstar, and the much anticipated poster icon of the Republican Party, was more than the triumph of a populist candidate. It was a living tableau, a commentary in action on America. The American Dream, individualism, the democratisation of everything, distrust of politicians, resentment of governance, the role of big business in society and politics, overt and covert aspects of the culture war, the racial divide, the desire for heroes and the celebrity principle, all swirled in the mix. And this was California, so the entertainment value of the whole procedure was enormous.

Candidate Schwarzenegger had neither a political action plan to get California out of its debt crisis nor much experience in politics. It was premature to answer actual questions on policy, the candidate declared; time enough for that after he was in office. In the meantime, voters should just put their trust in Arnie. And they did. What they elected to trust, and voted for, was celebrity power: the persona, cultural references and constructed celebrity of Arnold Schwarzenegger, whose manifesto was his celluloid output. His campaign buses were named after his films: *The Running Man* for Schwarzenegger's bus, *Total Recall* for the VIP bus, and *Predator* for the buses carrying representatives of the media who descended on the entertainment capital of the world in huge numbers from all corners of the globe.

In all, 135 candidates participated in the California gubernatorial election in an outpouring of democratic participation. Some candidates electioneered by participating in a *Pop Idol*-style television game show. Among the candidates was a certain Angelyne, who was famous for being, well, Angelyne. She created her fame by arresting public attention with a series of billboards that appeared all over Los Angeles featuring portraits of her in, and with, her trademark shocking pink accessories. Already a subject of scholarly dissertations,[1] she was a celebrity icon, employed in advertising and appearing on TV talk shows. There were, of course, professional politicians aplenty among the candidates, jostling with serious political wannabes as well as the various porn stars, minor actors, and other exotica. And at the heart of it all were profound issues about the nature of democracy itself.

The election took place in the aftermath of the most serious energy crisis ever in the most energy-dependent place on Earth. It was held in the aftermath of the debacle of deregulation of the energy industry, a cutting-edge policy of globalisation wreaking its havoc in America as much as anywhere else in the world. It was also a wartime election. America was at war on drugs, Aids, crime, patriotic education, and in the aftermath of 9/11, on terrorism, with troops in action in Afghanistan and Iraq. How to pay for these wars affected public finances, taxes and financial resources locally, nationally and internationally. It was an election in the wake of the Patriot Acts (legislation that integrates the work of intelligence agencies and domestic law enforcement and gives them sweeping new powers of surveillance and monitoring of suspected or potential 'terrorists'), in a state with one of the most diverse populations of a heterogeneous nation. In a nation of immigrants, migration, undocumented workers, illegal immigration and porous borders were hot issues. California has always profited from migrant workers who picked the fruit, did all the menial jobs, cleaned and scrubbed and cared for the children for pittance wages. Now they raised new questions: should they be accorded recognition and rights or were they a subversive, even ultimate, threat to the good life? More than enough weighty issues for voters to care about, especially in a state that is home to a large proportion of the productive capacity and bases of the American military-industrial complex.

In America, California is the ultimate bellwether state – the trend-setter, arbiter of the future for America as a whole. In times of trouble, Americans have upped sticks and headed en masse for the Golden State in hopes of a better future. It was the terminus of the nation's continental Manifest Destiny. It was golden because it was the strike-it-rich state of the 1849 Gold Rush. The surge across the continent to its riches led to the final destruction of the Native American tribes of the vast middle, the wild western frontier. And it propelled the nation into its most deadly conflict, the Civil War, by forcing the question of the abolition of slavery on all the territories newly carved out along the way and vying for statehood. In the awful years of the Great Depression, migrant families left their ruined dust-bowl farms and headed for 'California or bust' in the migration depicted in John Steinbeck's novel *The Grapes of Wrath*, and then the Oscar-winning movie of the same title. From this Golden State, headquarters of America's popular culture, home of cinema and television entertainment industries, has emanated America's greatest export: its vision of itself; the national story constantly narrated, recast, reconfigured, reflected upon and redefined in celluloid. In the year of the gubernatorial election there was even a feel-good movie in which California featured, playing its characteristic role in the make-up of the nation. The movie *Seabiscuit* was a retelling of history, including a narrated montage of Depression-era themes, infused with the ethos of the American Dream and the manufacture of celebrity, alive to the tensions of a bi-coastal nation, alluding to compassion but tentative of a political agenda, conservative or radical. It was a character piece reflecting on the national character of America. Was President Bush stating his own philosophy or quoting from *Seabiscuit* in his State of the Union Address of 2004 when he referred to a nation founded on the principle of a 'second chance' – the constant refrain of the film script?

California may be a glimpse of the future but it is not entire America, nor was this a national election. It was a state-wide election, premised on state legislation, a local affair. The recall election was necessary because an arcane and previously unused provision of the state constitution allows for an elected official to be recalled, forced to seek a new mandate from the electorate, if challenged by a sufficient number of citizens. It therefore straddles an old fissure of American politics: the tension between federalism, the national frame of reference, and localism, the distinctiveness and rights of the 50 states. California, for all its claims and allure, is not the whole picture, only part of the jigsaw, though hardly microcosmic. The duality of focus between the federal nation and the states is inherent in the nature of America. It is an old spectre enjoying a renaissance in American political rhetoric and policy. Is it the answer to the culture war that so deeply and acrimoniously divides America? Or is settling gay marriage – among other issues in that war – on a state-by-state basis a precursor, as it was in history, of a titanic struggle that will eventually have to be resolved by redefinition of the nature and mission statement of America? To look at the tableau is to see reflections of all that concerns America.

Scott Madnik and Kelly Kimble contested the election as candidates of the Butt Monkey Beer Party. They made no secret that their candidacy was a strategic commercial ploy to advance name recognition of their product: Butt Monkey Beer. 'If two guys who are promoting a beer company can run for the governor of the fifth largest economy of the world, this process is broken and better be fixed', Madnik told the makers of the television documentary *Schwarzenegger: The Governator*.[2]

The gubernatorial election both is and is not a referendum on the nature of America. The political rise of the 'Governator', as Governor Schwarzenegger came to be known, is part of the problematic nature of America. What it means for the future concerns the vital interest not only of Americans but of people everywhere. America is now engaged in pre-emptive democracy building in the world's hottest flashpoint to secure and establish its vision of the global future. How American democracy is understood and enacted in the United States can neither be divorced from, nor ignored by, anyone concerned with how these nation-building efforts are conceived and operate abroad. American democracy is about politics in the most general sense: it is a process formed within the ideas and culture of a nation, shaped by its history, constrained and expressed through its myths and traditions and their ritual forms. And if it ever did, America no longer stops at its own borders. Whether by virtue of its direct interventions or through the spread of its ideas and cultural products, America has long cast a global shadow.

In a sense, we are all citizens of America. Non-Americans have no choice in this; it is a necessity. America is the lone hyperpower; it is a global presence and a global reality, a determining fact that shapes the life of every person on the planet whether they acknowledge and understand it or not. To affect the condition of our lives as non-Americans we all have to learn how to engage and negotiate with the problems of America in American terms. This is the reality, not necessarily a flaw in America but the consequence of power, the meaning of empire. America has made its terms of reference global, and for America that is normal, all that needs to be or should be recognised, all that its people comprehend. So the world's problems with America begin in America as the problems of the American Self, its self-understanding, worldview, history and future vision.

In our earlier and complementary work, *Why Do People Hate America?*, we examined how America is perceived by outsiders, the non-American citizens of the globe. In *American Dream, Global Nightmare* we scrutinise how America looks at America. This is still a view by outsiders – it could not be otherwise. But there is an advantage in such examination. The advantage is not dispassionate detachment – America is too close and integrated into life everywhere for that. It is precisely the conviction that what America does to itself it does to the rest of the world – that what happens in America finds its echoes throughout the planet – that we seek to make visible and an agenda for discussion. The simple fact is that to change the conditions of our lives as non-Americans we all have to join in the American discourse. It is not possible to reject, avoid or neglect America. The question can only be how to live with America; the question must be how to live in peace with America. There can be no one-sided change. If change is necessary, it must be negotiated in concert in America as much as anywhere else in the world. Our point of view is committed to finding peaceful, life-saving and affirming ways forward. Our aim is to open a second front – beyond the tacit acceptance of malign extremes on all sides – of constructive argumentative engagement. Walt Whitman heard America singing in all its variety, and each singing what belonged to that individual and no one else. We are looking at America to help it hear the world singing in just such a way, to find the voice, the language to debate how and why the carols have become discordant and how we resolve the mutual problems of disharmony.

The constructive engagement of listening and debating is exactly what America has lacked so conspicuously. A great deal of the blame for this is placed squarely on the shoulders of President George W. Bush. As numerous commentators and writers have pointed out, his foreign policy is based on ideas formulated by the Washington-based neo-conservative think-tank, the Project for the New American Century (PNAC). The PNAC was founded in 1997 by Vice President Dick Cheney, Defense Secretary Donald Rumsfeld, Deputy Defense Secretary Paul Wolfowitz, and former Defense Policy Board Chairman Richard Perle, among others. Its openly declared policy is to establish a global American empire and subjugate all nations of the world to its will.

The Project has its origins much earlier in the aftermath of the fall of the Berlin Wall. Dick Cheney, at that time Secretary of Defense, brought together the group headed by Paul Wolfowitz to think about American foreign policy in a post-Cold War world. Colin Powell, then Chairman of the Joint Chiefs of Staff, mounted a competing (more ideologically moderate?) bid. Nicholas Lemann describes what happened next:

> Everybody worked for months on the 'five-twenty-one brief,' with a sense that the shape of the post-Cold War world was at stake. When Wolfowitz and Powell arrived at Cheney's office on May 21st, Wolfowitz went first, but his briefing lasted far beyond the allotted hour, and Cheney (a hawk who, perhaps, liked what he was hearing) did not call time on him. Powell didn't get to present his alternate version of the future of the United States in the world until a couple of weeks later. Cheney briefed President Bush [the elder], using material mostly from Wolfowitz, and Bush prepared his major foreign-policy address. But he delivered it on August 2, 1990, the day that Iraq invaded Kuwait, so nobody noticed.[3]

The Clinton administration intervened, and the Project had to be put on hold. However, with another Bush, George W., in the White House the neo-conservatives were back in business and when the spectre of '9/11' came to haunt America, found their time. When President Bush released his 'National Security Strategy of the United States of America', it was an ideological match to the policies advocated by PNAC.

The ideological stance of the Project is clearly described in its much-quoted policy paper, 'Rebuilding America's Defenses: Strategy, Forces and Resources for a New Century', published in September 2000.[4] 'At present', the Project declares, 'the United States faces no global rival. America's grand strategy should aim to preserve and extend this advantageous position as far into the future as possible.' This will require America to modernise its military, take weapons into space, increase defence spending and control the 'international commons' of cyberspace. The four 'core missions' for the American military require it to defend the American homeland; fight and decisively win multiple, simultaneous major theatre wars; perform the 'constabulary' duties associated with shaping the security environment in critical regions; and transform US forces to exploit the 'revolution in military affairs'. A clearer declaration of Pax Americana would be difficult to find.

The aggressive militaristic strategy of the neo-conservatives will have its winners and losers. William Rivers Pitt, writer and managing editor of the radical website truthout.org, sums up the consequences in these words:

> The defense contractors who sup on American tax revenue will be handsomely paid for arming this new American empire. The corporations that own the news media will sell this eternal war at a profit, as viewership goes through the stratosphere when there is combat to be shown. Those within the administration who believe that the defense of Israel is contingent upon laying waste to every possible aggressor in the region will have their dreams fulfilled. The PNAC men who wish for a global Pax Americana at gunpoint will see their plans unfold. Through it all, the bankrollers from the WTO and the IMF will be able to dictate financial terms to the entire planet ...
>
> There will be adverse side effects. The siege mentality average Americans are suffering as they smother behind yards of plastic sheeting and duct tape will increase by orders of magnitude as our aggressions bring forth new terrorist attacks against the homeland. These attacks will require the implementation of the newly drafted Patriot Act II, an augmentation of the previous Act that has profoundly sharper teeth. The sun will set on the Constitution and Bill of Rights. The American economy will be ravaged by the need for increased defense spending, and by the 'constabulary' duties in Iraq,

Afghanistan and elsewhere. Former allies will turn on us ... As the eagle spreads its wings, our rhetoric and their resistance will become more agitated and dangerous. Many people, of course, will die. They will die from war and from want, from famine and disease. At home, the social fabric will be torn in ways that make the Reagan nightmares of crack addiction, homelessness and AIDS seem tame by comparison. This is the price to be paid for empire, and the men of PNAC who now control the fate and future of America are more than willing to pay it.[5]

But is it only 'the men of PNAC', the neo-conservative Republicans, who are hell-bent on unleashing a new and virulent strain of American imperialism? Are the Democrats, and the Democratic Party, more benign, more humane and less interested in promoting imperialism and establishing an empire? Would America be all that different under a Democratic administration?

The Democratic counterpart of PNAC is the Progressive Policy Institute (PPI), an arm of the Democratic Leadership Council, which includes all the major players in the Democratic Party. In reply to the neo-conservative manifesto, the 'New Democrats' issued their own policy document under the title 'Progressive Internationalism: A Democratic National Security Strategy'. Just as President George W. Bush echoed the ideological stance of the PNAC in his foreign policy strategy, the Democratic Presidential nominee for 2004, Senator John Kerry, reflected the ideas of the New Democrats in his campaign book, *A Call to Service: My Vision for a Better America*.[6]

The PPI manifesto reaffirms 'the Democratic Party's commitment to progressive internationalism – the belief that America can best defend itself by building a world safe for individual liberty and democracy'. It is, therefore, natural for Democrats to 'support the bold exercise of American power' which is 'grounded in the party's tradition of muscular internationalism'.

Democrats, it suggests, will have nothing to do with those who 'oppose the use of force, and begrudge the resources required to keep our military strong'. Instead, they 'will maintain the world's most capable and technologically advanced military and we will not flinch from using it to defend our interests anywhere in the world'; they believe 'that America should use its unparalleled power to defend our country and to shape a world in which the values of liberal democracy increasingly hold sway' and would work at 'progressively enlarging the zone of market democracies'. This militaristic, corporate strategy would make 'Americans safer than the Republicans' go-it-alone policy'.

Beyond the rhetoric of multilateralism, the occasional nod at the rest of the world, is there not an overlap, a commonality in basic outlook between the projections of the neo-conservatives and the new democrats? Are the distinctions ones of style or substance in the consequences they would have for America, or indeed for the rest of the world? The Democrats are not challenging the neo-conservative notion of absolute American supremacy and 'full spectrum of dominance'; nor are they too worried about the Bush administration's policy of 'pre-emptive strikes' or 'regime change'. This is why, as their manifesto openly admits, the Democrats supported the wars against Afghanistan and Iraq without hesitation. They even back President Bush's plans to 'return Latin America to American leadership' by subverting democracy in Venezuela.

The opening paragraph of 'A Democratic National Security Strategy' is particularly interesting:

As Democrats, we are proud of our party's tradition of tough-minded internationalism and strong record in defending America. Presidents Woodrow Wilson, Franklin D. Roosevelt and Harry Truman led the United States to victory in two world wars and designed the post-war international institutions that have been a cornerstone of global security and prosperity ever since. President Truman forged democratic alliances such as NATO that eventually triumphed in the Cold War. President Kennedy epitomized America's commitment to 'the survival and success of liberty.' Jimmy Carter placed the defense of human rights at the center of our foreign policy. And Bill Clinton led the way in building a post-Cold War Europe whole, free, and at peace in a new partnership with Russia. Around the world the names of these Democratic statesmen elicit admiration and respect.[7]

It is a classic statement of the American perspective on history. It is a very particular kind of history, narrow in focus and short on acknowledgement of what these 'triumphs' depended on and how they were affected by the affairs of other people and nations. And, as British journalist John Pilger was quick to point out, 'New Democrats come from a tradition of liberalism that has built and defended empires as "moral" enterprises'. He argued that the Democratic Party has in fact left a longer trail of blood, theft and subjugation; its homicidal history is always justified with 'a noble mantle'.[8]

The conundrum of style or substance is not new, but goes back to America's overt entry into the business of empire. The imperial mission was first conceived by Theodore Roosevelt and his conservative coterie. The ideological justifications for empire, a homage in adaptation to the British Empire, were extensively worked out before the Republican Roosevelt became the 26th president of the United States in 1901. Empire was the logical extension of the American frontier to a global scale. It was the application of the 'strenuous life' frontier motif essential to hone the survival of the fittest to keep America vital and dominant. It was therefore a unilateral, racialist, social-Darwinian doctrine of open aggression. This vision of empire was contested by the Democrat Woodrow Wilson, the 28th president (1913–21), immortalised as the founder of the League of Nations. Re-elected on the promise of keeping America out of the bloody trenches of Europe where the First World War was raging, Wilson in fact authored the venerable Democratic tradition of taking America to war. The old adage, of course, being that Democrats start wars, Republicans end them. A devoted advocate of American exceptionalism, Wilson saw the nation as uniquely charged to bring about the 'ultimate peace of the world'. The intellectual and rhetorical foundations for an interventionist American foreign policy are contained in his war message to Congress of April 1917. America's war aim was more than the defeat of German aggression: 'The world must be made safe for democracy.' America must fight 'for the rights and liberties of small nations, for a universal dominion of right by such a concert of free peoples as shall bring peace and safety to all nations and make the world itself at last free'. Close reading of the fine print of Wilson's philosophy shows that he conceived of democracy purely for European nations, and subscribed to the conventional belief that other races had neither the civilisation nor the aptitude for democracy and therefore would not be offered access to the 'self determination of all peoples'. His rebuff of the Japanese delegation at the Versailles Conference ending the First World War, when they sought an article recognising the principle of racial equality, engendered the dynamic that eventually propelled America into the Second World War.

In practice and effect, America has alternate poles of imperial pretension, both of which can nestle within the rhetoric of a 'moral' quest. The Roosevelt militaristic vision of imperialism was:

> backed by nothing more substantial than the notion that the manifest destiny of the United States was to govern racially inferior Latin Americans and East Asians. Wilson laid over that his own hyperidealistic, sentimental, and ahistorical ideas that what should be sought was a world democracy based on the American example and led by the United States. It was a political project no less ambitious and no less passionately held than the vision of world Communism launched

at almost the same time by the leaders of the Bolshevik Revolution.[9]

William Pfaff argues that America is 'still in the intellectual thrall of the megalomaniacal and self-righteous clergyman-president [Wilson] who gave to the American nation the blasphemous conviction that it, like he himself, had been created by God "to show the way to the nations of the world, how they shall walk in the path of liberty"'.[10]

Ideology is only one element of America's impact on the world. Empire also requires the structures and processes to sustain and implement dominance. Successive Democrat presidents have played their part in laying the building blocks of American empire. It was Franklin D. Roosevelt who transformed the rhetorical motif of war into a pervasive social metaphor that has become a lasting total war psychosis. His New Deal programme, a response to the appalling social carnage of the Great Depression, saw the military as the model institution for the construction of new kinds of collaboration to address the problems of society. It was the kernel out of which the military-industrial complex emerged. A phalanx of organisations and programmes cemented new relationships between government, business and experts to mastermind mass mobilisation of the nation with military precision to combat poverty and promote regeneration. It prepared and readied the nation for total war after Pearl Harbor propelled America into the Second World War. It was Roosevelt who authorised the secret research project for the ultimate in total, mechanised war: the Manhattan Project. It was Harry S. Truman who became the only world leader to authorise the use of nuclear weapons. As inheritor of the mass mobilisation of the Second World War, it was Truman who began its transition into the national security state as he accepted the logic of moving from world war to Cold War, the psychosis of threat becoming the condition of national existence predicated on Senator Arthur Vandenberg's advice to Truman to 'scare the hell out of

the American people'. It was John F. Kennedy who first committed America to war in Vietnam. It was his successor Lyndon B.
Johnson who saw his commitment to the radical Great Society
consumed by the logic of American militarism that eventually
led to the deaths of some three million people in Indo-China.
And for all their 'muscular internationalism', it was Bill Clinton
who first subverted the negotiation of the Kyoto Treaty on
climate change, refused to support the International Court of
Human Rights, refused to sign the Landmine Treaty, bombed an
aspirin factory in the Sudan, threatened South Africa with trade
sanctions if it did not abandon plans to use cheaper generic Aids
drugs, and supported Russia in its brutal war in Chechnya.

In consequences for the rest of the world, there has been little
to choose between the war-affirming rhetoric of the new democrats and the Democratic Party and the war-mongering declarations of the neo-conservatives and their Republican mentors.
Both sides are wedded to the 'national security state' and welded
to corporate interests. Both have contributed to and participated
in the operation of American empire.

It is not that there is no difference between Republican and
Democrat, in either domestic or foreign policy, though that
argument is made with characteristic mordant wit by Gore
Vidal. America, he says, is ruled by one oligarchy with two
names: republican and democrat.[11] But there is less distinctiveness than Americans perceive. Both parties draw upon, reflect
and project a repertoire of cultural themes consistent through
American history and so pervasive as to be invisible to
Americans, so seamless and interlinked as to permit different
configurations of argument to be presented without overthrowing the consistency of the whole in its consequences and effects,
especially in America's relations with the rest of the world. The
existence of this American psyche is what makes a world of difference between Republican and Democrat for Americans and
almost no difference at all for outside observers, passive recipients of the American Way. It is the themes and meaning of this

common inheritance that we seek to examine and make visible, for it is the foundation on which the problems between America and the world have been constructed. It is the real agenda for change, for different ways of seeing the world and its problems that we urgently need to be able to debate.

The presidential election of 2004 purported to offer a clearer choice, especially in global orientation, than any in recent memory. We would not disagree. Indeed, if we were Americans, we would probably feel ourselves compelled to be Democrats as the first glimmer of making a difference. Yet, viewed from another angle, 2004's election appeared as the clearest demonstration of Vidal's oligarchy there has ever been. In the Republican corner, George W. Bush: millionaire son of a former president, founder of Zapata Petroleum, an alumnus of Yale University and its élite student society Skull and Bones. In the Democrat corner, John Kerry: millionaire son of a Massachusetts family whose involvement with politics goes back to 1600, husband of Teresa Heinz, the ketchup conglomerate heiress (his first wife was equally, fabulously wealthy), an alumnus of Yale University and Skull and Bones.

Politics and governance in America has always been the domain of a narrow élite. It was envisioned precisely in those terms by the predilections of the architects of the American Constitution, the Founding Fathers who had a horror of mob rule and pinned their democratic faith firmly on men of property. And property, or wealth, has become an essential ingredient for participation in American politics. It has been estimated that it requires at least $2 million to get elected to Congress. During the 2000 election, George Bush raised $100 million for his campaign war chest. In 2004, this figure increased to the incredible $190 million! You have to be very, very rich to play politics in America, as Ross Perot, Stephen Huffington, Steve Forbes and Michael Bloomberg, among others, made abundantly clear by bankrolling their own political endeavours. It is less talked of, less obvious that from political generation to political generation those elected to office come disproportionately from among the ranks of the possessors of inherited and transmitted wealth. In America a mere 13,000 richest families now enjoy as much income as do its 20 million poorest householders. By 1999, Bill Gates alone owned as much wealth as the bottom 40% of Americans. Meanwhile, one in three Americans earns $8 or less an hour; some 40% of American children live below or near poverty level. It is a popular myth, confounded by the institution of the family trust fund, that wealth and the noblesse oblige following from it is a constantly changing parade of new personnel. Old money does not fade on the vine, and what it takes to join the ranks of the wealthiest is a constant upward spiral.

The spirit of democratisation should be anathema to a plutocratic oligarchy in America. But throughout the layers and levels of American governance the familial and genuinely dynastic principle has applied. The trend started early and shows no signs of abating. America's sixth president, John Quincy Adams, was the son of its second president, John Adams. The Adamses were, one might say, originators of the genre. The Roosevelts were certainly noble conveyors of the tradition. The Kennedys – one president, two senators and presidential candidates, various congressmen and state officials and political activists – and the Bushes – two presidents, one senator, the father of the elder Bush (or Bush 41 as he is now commonly known), two state governors and numerous political careers in the making – show the mould is far from broken. Nothing succeeds in American politics like family connections. It was true for Al Gore. It is true in the electoral swing state of Ohio, where their governor, Robert Taft III, is the scion of the family that has seen two other Robert Tafts elected to represent the state in the US Senate, and which descends from President William H. Taft. In neighbouring Indiana there are the Bayhs. Father Birch Bayh moved through various rungs of state office before election to the Senate and a run for the presidency. He is succeeded by son Evan who also served his state, eventually becoming Governor before entering the Senate, and who is repeatedly spoken of as a coming man of potential presidential candidacy.

To sustain a modern political career requires not only family connections but corporate bankrolling and funding from the whole plethora of professional business and special interest lobbyists with money to spend for political access and influence. Key American industries and new technologies have been founded on government investment, funding of research and development, and military expenditure. The interconnection, the revolving-door exchange of personnel between military, business and government is an essential feature of the American land-scape, Democrat and Republican. It provided an underlying issue of the 2004 election in the figure of vice presidential candi-date Dick Cheney. Cheney went from politics – Senator for Wyoming and serving as Secretary of Defense – to CEO of Halliburton, a major oil industry conglomerate. Returning to politics as the most engaged and activist Vice President ever, he first oversaw a major revision of America's energy policy. When America went to war in Iraq, Halliburton was a major benefici-ary of contracts for both the military and the rebuilding of Iraqi infrastructure. These contracts were never competitively ten-dered. Halliburton was in dispute with the government for over-charging on its contracts to the military, for both the supply of fuel and feeding the troops. And all while it still had financial obligations to Vice President Cheney, whose financial severance package on returning to public office was staggered over a period of years.

Corporate America is an actor on the political scene. And corporate America has been in a mess. When Enron, the oil corporation, collapsed, its workers and average stockholders lost an estimated $25 to $50 million worth of pension funds; but the company executives walked away with hundreds of millions of dollars. There have been numerous other corporate scandals – such as WorldCom, Tyco and Xerox – mega swindles involv-ing countless billions. Qwest, for example, the fourth largest

telephone company, disclosed debt of $26 billion! The perform-
ance of corporate America has been part of what Paul Krugman
terms the 'spiral of inequality' that has overtaken America as a
whole.[12] In 1973 the typical corporate CEO received 40 times
the income of the average worker. By 2000 this disparity ranged
from 190 to 419 times average earnings. In the same period the
lowest two quintiles have seen their income actually decline. The
result of this 'unprecedented redistribution of income towards
the rich' led John Cassidy to argue that America was no longer a
middle-class society, its disparities in wealth being greater than
in any other major industrial nation. 'If anything, America with
its widening income gap, its vast, deepening divergences in
everything from education to life expectancy between rich and
poor, is less democratic today ... than in 1950', argues David
Rieff of the World Policy Institute.[13]

The rise of corporate power and concentrated wealth has
been accompanied by successive phases of ballooning public
indebtedness. This land of plenty is facing a severe public debt
problem – which brought Arnold Schwarzenegger to the fore in
California – that has produced a savagely regressive social policy. The richest nation on Earth needs a daily injection of $1.5
billion, borrowed from abroad, to sustain its deficit! And the
successive deficits were, in large part, accounted for and justified
by military expenditure, under Ronald Reagan to fund tax cuts
and the final push to win the Cold War and under George W.
Bush to fund tax cuts and pursue the war on terrorism.

Indeed, to non-Americans, America looks like a very odd
place. America seems always to be at war not just with the rest
of the world, but with itself. Its education system is in paralysis,
swinging violently between political correctness and Religious
Right. Its excessive consumer-orientated lifestyle – defended so
aggressively by both Republican and Democrat administrations
– is not only dangerously unsustainable but is actually choking
the world. Its minorities – blacks, Asians and Latinos – are marginalised and remain apart from the dominant white communi-

ties. Perpetual fear stalks its city streets, reaching pathological proportions after the dreadful atrocity of 9/11 with the emergence of homeland security, Patriot Act I, Patriot Act II, population screening and Operation TIPS – the terrorism information and prevention service, which encourages janitors, construction workers and delivery personnel to spy on their neighbours and report their actions. This paranoia is not just America's problem. It is the ailment at the heart of the global hyperpower, and all of us need to question how the condition can be survived, treated and rehabilitated to attain a sustainable future for the world at large.

Arnold Schwarzenegger's most famous screen persona is that of *The Terminator*. James Cameron's 1984 film retells the New Testament's Annunciation story. A rebel from the 21st century (Archangel Gabriel) comes back in time to warn a Los Angeles waitress, Sarah Connor (Virgin Mary), that she is to be the mother of a political Messiah who will bring salvation to the world. But if the Redeemer is to be born, she has to be saved from the Cyborg, also a product of a post-nuclear-war future, who is on a mission to kill her. The Archangel falls in love with the Virgin and impregnates her with the Messiah. Arnold Schwarzenegger plays the robot that descends from 2027 to the Los Angeles of 1984 in pursuit of a human enemy. The robot is 'part man, part machine. Underneath it is a hyperalloy combat chassis, microprocessor controlled, fully armored, very tough; but outside it's living human tissue, flesh, skin, hair, blood', making it indistinguishable from other humans. But even the outer human characteristics are controlled by a clinical logic: 'it cannot be reasoned with, it cannot be bargained with, it doesn't feel pity, remorse or fear. And it absolutely will not stop. Ever. Until you are dead.' Throughout the film, the Terminator pursues its enemy with fanatical zeal, killing or destroying whoever and whatever comes into its path, putting itself together again when bits of its anatomy are shot or blown apart. In the spectacular finale, the Terminator is blown up and burnt to cinders. Its metal skeleton rises from the ashes and carries on with its mission. The skeleton too is chopped to bits, but the individual bits come to life and continue with their goal.

American psychosis is the conceptual equivalent of the Terminator. On the outside, American society looks almost banal in its ordinariness and orderliness; but underneath it is all manufactured mythology which motivates and drives its psychosis. Like the Terminator, it is not easy to reason with America; and it pursues its military and corporate goals, the preservation of its lifestyle and the perpetual, global expansion of its empire with fanatical zeal, slaying and demolishing whatever may come or stands in its way. Like the Terminator, America seems never to understand or give up – it just goes on doing what its mythology demands. And, just as the story of *The Terminator* is wrapped around a religious fable, so the narrative of America is shrouded in a religiosity of Biblical proportions.

The psyche of America, all that defines Americana, is deeply entrenched in myth. The mythic narrative tradition of America is a particular vision of history, national purpose and the future. This mythology is shaped by ten laws which form an integral part of American consciousness, a collective inheritance that carries the nation beyond the deep, entrenched divide in its politics and society. Some of these propositions are socially and intellectually articulated while others are unstated, but all are believed with firm religious conviction. All segments of American society – Republicans and Democrats, various shades of conservatives and liberals, rich and poor – are affected by and operate under these propositions. They appeal not by being nebulous and undefined star-spangled populism but by manipulating enduring themes in American history and mythology.

Here, then, are the ten laws of Americana.

Law 1: Fear is essential

'Be afraid, be very afraid' is the American condition. To live in America is to be beset by fear, anxiety and insecurity, to be surrounded by potential harm, enemies and evil intent. And the wolf has always been at the door. A nation of optimists is the more usual self-representation of America. Repetitively, Hollywood films conclude with a resolution, a rescue, and the winners ride off into the sunset or snuggle into a warm embrace that reassures us they will live happily ever after. The formulaic ending, however, is necessary because the plot, the narrative, is founded on and propelled by fear and anxiety, the dark essential underpinning of the American condition. For America fear is an original, natural condition, the inescapable birth rite (and birth right), the inherited condition of a fragile existence that must constantly be defended. Without fear there is no America; constant recourse to fear is the motivating force that determines its actions and reactions.

Law 2: Escape is the reason for being

America was an idea before it was a country, and the country was shaped in conformity to the idea. The idea of America was created by publicity, PR and propaganda with a purpose. America was devised to be an escape route from all the ills known to the societies and nations of the Old World. It was conceived as a refuge that recruited its citizens from elsewhere – a refuge from persecution, from poverty, from unemployment and lack of opportunity – in search of room to breathe, in search of a place to recreate themselves and shape a new lifestyle free from constraints, inhibitions and restraints. So America is founded on the premise of escape from one's self; the place to recreate one's self in a more desirable, a truer, idealised form. This was overtly part of the election platform of Arnold Schwarzenegger – he was the candidate who most truly embodied the American myth, not as dream but lived reality. Escapism is America in multiple senses that have worked themselves through the cultural repertoire of American life.

Law 3: Ignorance is bliss

The greatest of all myths in the mythologising national empire of America is that of American exceptionalism. America, goes the theme, is different. Different because it was consciously created to be a departure from all that was wrong with the Old World, to be a fresh start for humanity in a virgin land. The ideology of America is the paradox of the will to individual freedom in the most nationalist of nation states. Because its ideology created a 'perfect union' with a model structure of government, America was blessed and spared the ills and pains of the rest of the world. Further, the enterprise of free citizens in a rich and spacious land of abundance made America a land of opportunity and wealth for all, the American Dream. The constant reiteration of this mantra running through American self-description and firmly embedded in the American psyche achieves the wonders of ignorance. America is honest about neither its own history nor the rest of the world. The strength of belief in American exceptionalism becomes a rationale for ignorance about the outside world and for discounting what others have to say about America. It is the great insulating ethos, the ultimate reason to glory in ignorance.

Law 4: America is the idea of nation

The Nation is the focus of American life. It is not only the vessel of myth, but essential for myth-making. The iconography of nationalism is ubiquitous in American life. Patriotism, the invocation of nationalism and pride in nation, are common reflexes expressed in personal behaviour, social events and the popular culture of America. The icons of nation are sanctified because the nation itself is invested with sacred significance. To put it another way: America is extremely nationalist. Yet Americans, for all their display of nationalism, would deny the epithet nationalist – a questionable, potentially dangerous ideology subject to manipulation for inhumane ends and purposes. Americans are proud Americans, not rabid nationalists. This blind spot occurs precisely because the concept of nation is conflated with sanctity and understood as a set of values, rights and defining characteristics, not as commitment to nation. Furthermore, this set of American values is open to, and should be sought by, all peoples everywhere. The nation that is America is full of the self-description of the values and ideals that ought to belong to all people – therefore America, as nation, is the future of all people.

Law 5: Democratisation of everything is the essence of America
Democratisation is the empowerment of the individual self – it is what America was created for. The wilderness and the frontier are the blank canvas over which each individual could inscribe themselves. The mythic narratives of America centre on the individual and their make-or-break efforts to recreate themselves. Individual liberty is the cornerstone of the enterprise of America. Each aspect of life can and should be democratised, from fast food to fast fashion, violence and gun laws to access to pornography. Indeed, the very idea of Democratisation = America.

Law 6: American democracy has the right to be imperial and express itself through empire
The peopling of America by white Anglo-Saxons was a work of imperialism. The first settlers, the paragons for and makers of mythology, the stock characters in the myth of the American nation, were the agents of imperialism, the creative force in the formation of the American nation. When Americans declared their independence, asserting their democratic rights and liberties vis-à-vis the British Empire, they constructed another mythological miasma. The nation of free citizens in fact expanded and realised their nation by the processes of empire. The relations of metropolis and periphery were, in the case of America, internal to what was made the expanding nation. America was an empire at home constructing an economy that required new inputs of land and mineral resources to serve its capital accumulation, and then new markets to service its industry. Far from being the

prototype site of opposition to colonies and empires, imperialism and empire are there in America right from its inception.

Law 7: Cinema is the engine of empire

The birth of cinema was contemporaneous with the first stirrings of off-shore American imperialism. American cinema assumed an imperial mission both at home and abroad. At home the cinema made visual and potent the mythic narratives of America for the greatest influx of new immigrants the nation had ever seen. It made the imagery of America iconic. It built the narrative tradition of America into formulaic storylines replete with stock characters. The cinema built into itself the traditions and forms of American mass culture and provided the perfect setting for formalising the mass nature of American culture. The project of America, the notion that America is the idea of nation (Law 4), was formalised and made manifest in cinema. And this standardised, industrialised, manufactured product became America's greatest export, the idea of Self it represented to the world, and through which it demonised, appropriated and brought other cultures within its own purview.

Law 8: Celebrity is the common currency of empire

The basis of celebrity is publicity, the means to grab and hold the attention of the public. The ability of American celebrities to dominate the attention of the entire world is the foundation of an empire built on and for trade and commerce. The techniques that create celebrities are the same techniques employed to market and sustain political power. Celebrities encode values and ideas that are projected on the globe and serve to enhance the power of the empire – as such, celebrity is the truly cosmic realm of American empire. The Oscars are annually broadcast worldwide. They are more than one of the highest rated television programmes. They are collective ritual where obeisance is made to the engine of empire (Law 7). The ritual performance of the Oscar ceremony is a demonstration of global power and domination that will provide headlines, column inches and immense economic rewards around the globe for the year to come.

Law 9: War is a necessity

America projects itself as a bastion of peace, a haven of democracy and concord. But the reality is radically different from the self-perception. America emerged from a war, consolidated and built the nation through war, expanded and emerged as an empire through war, and now maintains its global hegemony through war. Even before 9/11, it had waged war on over half the nations of the globe. Its economy is a war economy. Its science and technology is deeply entrenched in the military machine. It sustains and runs the most formidable war machine in history. The images and metaphors of war permeate every aspect of American society and culture – in films, television programmes, video games, fashion, children's toys, social programmes and political rhetoric. An alliance of neo-conservative ideologues, free-market right-wingers and evangelical Christians is now waging war against the social contract, the inner-city poor, pro-choice women, gays, big government and the constitutional separation between religion and the state, secular reason and religious beliefs. And to top it all we have the notion of preventive, pre-emptive war, the translation of the early-19th-century Monroe Doctrine of America's right to unchallenged secure dominance in its hemisphere into a neo-conservative policy for global domination. For America war is a necessity, for war has become its reason to be.

Law 10: American tradition and history are universal narratives applicable across all time and space

Laws 1 to 9 combine to provide the architectural framework and mythic narrative of the idea of America. But America sees this mythology, and its laws, not as local, provincial perceptions but as universal narrative. Global hegemony now becomes synonymous with the export of American history and tradition that can be applied and imposed on anyone, anywhere, anytime. After all, they *are* universal values!

Collectively these laws define the nature of the American Dream; they explain how and why America behaves as it does, and has become a global nightmare. The laws of Americana are not defined by one election – they are at work in all elections, applicable to American domestic politics, foreign policy and cultural power in general. With America now the lone hyperpower, these laws affect every citizen of every country. If this emerging course of American affairs is to be negotiated, addressed or debated, first it must be clarified and analysed.

In this book, we will elaborate the ten laws of American mythology, trace their origins and historical context and explore how they shape contemporary American politics, society and culture. The idea of America forms the upbringing of any non-American of a certain age. Anyone who grew to years and consciousness with the rise of the technology of mass communication grew up with America by just watching television. But our distinction from Americans of similar years is singularly important. We did not grow only with and through American mass popular culture; we are at least bi-cultural beings, possessors and inheritors of much more than Americana. It is this consciousness we bring to the debate. America's ethos and heroes are ours and not ours. We grew with an internal set of contradictions and debate which we now externalise because we, unlike Americans, can create the mental distance to see the connections between the embedded ideas of mass popular culture and their stranglehold on the operation of American society, in American society and on the rest of the world.

What matters about America is the way that the various strands of its own paradoxes and seeming diversity, or at least duality, of opinions and ideas find a comfortable home in its mythology and mesh together to create one universal outlook. The central representation of the nation as a set of values envelops the whole world within the ambit and proper sphere of American dominance. All human history leads to America and America leads to the human future for everyone. The laws we identify, each in their singularity and ramifications reinforce and expand the potential for empire while denying the nationalism, militarism and imperial operation of America – thus leaving the American populace to enjoy its isolationism and sense of total innocence, believing its nation to be a force for good, one that does only good deeds for fine ennobling ends, that makes the American Dream available for people everywhere. The laws work so well that Americans not only do not know but are purposely distracted, diverted and dissuaded from knowing; and everywhere prevented from framing an inquiry and debate that reasons with reality in a different way.

As laws, the ten principles of Americana have multiple layers of meaning and diverse arenas of applicability. Otherwise, why would they be laws?

CHAPTER ONE

Drums Along the Mohawk
America as Myth,
Myth of America

Drums Along the Mohawk: America as Myth and the Myth of America

To live in America is to be beset by fear, anxiety and insecurity, to be surrounded by potential harm, enemies and evil intent. America's fear and how it has expressed its desire for self-defence has become a global issue since the horrific events of 9/11, 2001. But the condition itself is not a result of the appalling attack on the World Trade Center. It is not the consequence of a new onslaught – international terrorism – breaking through the protection of the American homeland. The rationale for America's response to terrorism is shaped by history and the special terrors that inform America's sense of history. For America, fear is an original, natural condition, the inescapable birth rite (and birth right), the inherited condition of a fragile existence that constantly must be defended. Without fear there is no America. The terrible events of 9/11 struck a deep chord in the American psyche because they could be understood through familiar ideas long established in the culture and history of the nation.

Fear looms as a reality within the narrative history, myth and legends of America. It has been a driving force of American endeavour. The ferocious fearlessness of heroes in the land of the brave dominates the foreground as the official version of what the story is about. But without the terrors that tested them, heroism and bravery have no meaning. The selective process that translates history into myth is designed to emphasise enduring motifs, values and ideas extracted from particular experience. It is the special relationship between landscape and environment, the background context of history, that establishes their enduring significance. For its white settlers, America was a new world full of strange, unfamiliar dangers. It was inhabited by people who posed a constant threat to the advance of European settlement, as well as a challenge to the very idea of being human established by the natural laws that Europeans derived from their religion and history. Sustaining myths sustain because they are a response to the specific problems that lurk in the background. It is the particular kinds of fear, how they were understood and responded to in the making of America, that forms the cultural tradition of the nation.

Myth is a very specific term. Myths are narrations of origin and the creation of phenomena that are social and collective, rather than individual. Mythic narratives construct sets of values and meanings transmitted from generation to generation, forming a rhetoric, a language of ideas and relationships through which a society defines its identity, understands itself, and explains, interprets and shapes the world around it. Myth is enacted in ritual; it empowers and deploys symbols and symbolic language. Mythic stories retold with shifts of emphasis are a means to adapt to change, their motifs and ideas reconfigured not only to account for change but to extend meaning and values that manipulate the course of change. Myth is the context of understanding in which history occurs, and myth is often more potent and important than mere historic fact. People and nations can and do act as if the myth were fact and end by making myth manifest as reality. All societies have a mythic tradition. In the case of America, a land settled and a nation created in a profusion of letters and declarations, it is possible to see how its mythic tradition has been forged from its history, consciously constructed, persistently employed, widely disseminated and subject to subtle shifts over time. The mythic narratives are dramatised and populated with representative characters whose actions play out the meaning and tensions of American ideals and moral consciousness. This vibrant narrative tradition shapes and informs the American psyche. Naturally, its formulae are made into movies.

To explore the psyche of a culture there is no better place to look than at what is in plain sight. Cinema is the mass medium of America, the new technology of self-expression that drew into itself the concerns, history, myth and aspirations of the land and its people. Employing the narrative formulae of American literature; retelling the tales of the penny dreadfuls, dime novels and yellow press; visualising the scenes and stock characters of myth and legend; realising the life of a new urban population in the most realist medium of expression, made by people from this new urban population for those who were the mass of the audience: cinema is the most characteristic product of American culture, and its greatest export. The flickering nickelodeon, the silver screen in the plush picture palace, the ultimate convenience of the family drive-in cinema, the multiplex in the mall: they captivated America, gathering in the nation because what they projected was a verisimilitude of the past, present and future of America. The movies negotiated, reconfigured, expressed and amplified the American self in its past, present and future possibilities to become the cultural paradigm par excellence, *the* medium of the American mythic tradition.

And there in plain sight driving the narrative of this most narrative form is fear. It is more than a conventional dramatic device. American cinema shows us primal fears characteristic of the history of America, embedded in place and time and working through time. Pervasive and particular kinds of fear mark them as essentially American. Cinema explores the fertile taproot of the American psyche. It shows us how this complex worldview came to be, its preoccupations and how they are to be faced. Cinema cultivates and spreads appropriate attitudes and responses to fear, helpfully personified in stock characters and formulaic stories that entertain because they are so attuned to their audience.

Drums Along the Mohawk is a film epic in scope, domestic in focus, a wilderness tale. It was made in 1939, the year Hollywood revived the Western as a main feature movie genre, beginning a 30-year period when it was central to American popular culture. The film is directed by John Ford, quite simply the master of the medium and the man largely responsible for shaping our visual image of the American West. In 1939 he also made *Stagecoach*, the film that launched John Wayne on the road to stardom as the iconic cinematic embodiment of the Western hero and much else. And *Stagecoach* is the most allegoric, elegiac, genuinely mythological and visually potent Western of all. Ford also made *Young Mr Lincoln*, a fiction of the early career of Abraham Lincoln concerned with his central place in American myth, public imagination and political ideology. Each of these films is a reflection on what fascinated John Ford throughout his career: the making of myth and the importance of myth in making the idea of America.

Drums Along the Mohawk begins where America begins. The opening caption reads: '1776, the year of the Declaration of Independence.' Its final sequence is the arrival of a military contingent bearing the new flag of the new nation: 'There it is. That's what we've been fighting for. Thirteen stripes for the colonies, thirteen stars in a circle for the union.' The film is a succession of iconic scenes and images, encyclopaedic in their references, and includes all the elements integrated into the mythic tradition of how America began and the condition in which it came to be.

The domestic focus of the film is the story of Gil Martin and his new wife, Magdelana. It begins with their marriage amidst silks and finery at the home of Magdelana's parents, a grand substantial house in Albany. With proper reverence the congregation pray for the couple 'as they go forth into the wilderness'.

The ceremony over, the newlyweds climb aboard the humble wagon that will convey them to Gil's farm in the Mohawk Valley. 'It's always been like this since Bible days, each generation must make its way in one place or another', comments the parson who married them as they depart. Their place will be a small log cabin carved out of the wilderness. En route they meet the sinister Caldwell who is curious about their political affiliation. What political party do these folk belong to? 'American' is Gil's succinct answer. Caldwell responds that there are rumours the Indians will take up with the Tories, or those loyal to the British Empire and its forces. The couple arrive in their new home amidst a violent rainstorm. The first sight of her new home is a jolt for Magdelana, who from now on is known as Lana. Small and rudely furnished, the cabin is a harsh regression from the civilised life she has been used to. 'It looks fine to me because I built it; never thought it might look different to a girl raised in a big house like yours', her husband observes. As Lana sits wet, bedraggled and dejected, a door opens. She turns. There in the doorway is an imposing shape caught in deep shadow. An Indian. She screams, hysterically staggering back to cower in a corner as the Indian advances. Gil rushes in and, unable to quiet her hysterics, slaps his wife. Before them, Gil explains, is a good Indian. 'Fine friend. Good Christian. Hallelujah', says Blue Back, the Indian who has returned from a hunting trip to bring them half a deer. But Lana is not convinced; she declares she is no frontier woman: 'You had no right to bring me here, it's so awful and that horrible man, filthy Indian.'

With the utmost economy, the central elements of the American story have been set in place. The narrative of the film will balance the personal hardships and struggle of coming to terms with the wilderness with the battles to secure the land and create the community, the nation that will possess the land. The struggle to make a new life and realise the abundance of the wilderness is perpetually under threat; it will be disrupted and overthrown by savagery and secured only through violent eradication of its enemies. The triumph of the central characters, these pioneers, marches hand in hand with fear. The film script moves through a litany. After the meeting with Caldwell: 'You didn't get scared, did you – what the fella said about the Tories and the Indians?' After Lana's first encounter with Blue Back: 'You've got to get over this foolishness and stop being scared.' Finally, when Gil must make a heroic run to bring relief to the beleaguered fort, he insists: 'You're not going to be afraid. You're not going to be afraid … Say you're not afraid.' But the fear is inherent; it endures with the endurance of the central characters. Lana can say, when required, that she is not afraid and wants her husband to make his desperate bid to bring aid to the community, but she faints in fear as soon as he leaves.

This is an action film set at the most potent moment of American history as the source of myth. Its real achievement is its use of the symbolic imagery and language of myth to visualise the story in a way that relates it to both past and future. What emerges is a much larger expression of the meaning of the wilderness frontier as the mythic space in which the American character, sense of mission and characteristic response to pervasive threats were forged.

America is a nation of immigrants who escaped from the plight of the Old World. The motley accents and surnames of the characters in *Drums Along the Mohawk* are typical of the plurality of immigrant life that John Ford always included in his films, far more than his obligatory inclusion of the Irish. The making of America is a process of journeying from refined comforts and their certainties into the wilderness, a passage to the simple but ennobling primitivism of frontier conditions. The wagon used by Gil and Lana is a visual reference to the larger Consetoga covered wagons that at a later date will continue their tradition by setting off across the plains to settle the whole of America. At the most profound level, *Drums Along the Mohawk* is a journey of remaking the self. Gil is remade into the archetypal hero attuned to the land, the best possible farmer capable of making his land bear fruit in abundance. As the hero, he is possessed of innate abilities that outstrip those of the native inhabitants: he knows he can outrun his Indian pursuers, even through their own wilderness, to summon aid and secure victory. Lana too is remade. After her fearful, bedraggled arrival, we next see Lana happy and smiling, clad in simple homespun, harvesting crops and proudly displaying the blisters on her hands. She acquires strength, self-sufficiency and self-reliance in submitting herself to the wilderness experience. In the final crisis she dons a uniform to fight alongside the men to defeat their enemies. She escapes from her old life and becomes the mother of future generations who will inherit the abundance that is the fertile promise of the land. This journey of escape and regeneration is a mission cast in Biblical terms, read through Bible stories whose meaning is the necessity to bring forth a new order of society. The community comes together in the chapel for review of the personal character and behaviour of its members, to provide helpful advertisements for local business, and to underline the need for a local volunteer militia – failure to comply would result in hanging. Religion and their shared trials, their holding together in the face of the wilderness and the pervasive dangers it holds, are what shape the character of the community as a whole. This is the very idea of America.

Historically, America begins with the wilderness and the confrontation with the Other, the native inhabitants. *Drums Along the Mohawk* presents the Revolutionary War, the campaign to establish independence from the British Empire, as a distant backdrop. General Washington and the Continental Army are fully occupied elsewhere. The frontier will have to look after itself. Their conflict will be with the Indians. The Tories are making the Indians all sorts of promises, propelling a life-and-death battle, the battle between civilisation and savagery. This is the true battle to possess the land, the real meaning of making America. In all instances of battle in the film, the Tories are far outnumbered by their Indian allies. Both sides, the Tories and the Americans, are prepared to recruit the Indians to advance their cause, but both have and express equal contempt for savages. And John Ford spares nothing in the portrayal of the Indians as brutal, malevolent and murderous. He uses the most iconic, emotive image of all: when the Indians finally break into the church, the last redoubt where the women and children have taken refuge, one Indian raises an innocent mop-haired young girl above his head, ready to smash her to destruction. It is the enduring image defining the line between civilisation and savagery, with a long pedigree of recycling through history: from early reports of native America to the beastly Huns in poor little Belgium and cut-throat 'Mexican bandits', and recurring as Iraqis ejecting babies from their incubators in Kuwait. Visually the film emphasises the Indians as inhabitants of the wilderness. They are seen literally lurking behind the trees, from which they emerge, crouched like animals, when Caldwell simulates a bird call on a flute. We see in the distance the open, sun drenched clearing across which the settlers are making their desperate run for the fort from the point of view of the dark encircling forest now seething with the shapes of the Indians who burst forth from this gloom to attack. The Indians burn and wantonly destroy Gil and Lana's cabin, smashing their few homely possessions, toying with a spinning wheel as an incomprehensible curiosity before throwing it into the flames. They burn the harvest standing in the fields. The juxtaposition is direct: in the preceding sequence the settlers gathered to help Gil and Lana clear more fields to expand their farm. They set a 'fine burning' of the dead wood, a controlled exercise in making the land ready for cultivation – the origin of the concept of civilisation itself and its related ideas: cultivated, refined, educated. In contrast, the Indians burn indiscriminately, wildly, with uncontrolled destructive power to undermine civilisation at its core.

John Ford realises the Indian exactly as Richard Slotkin describes their function in American letters and ideas: 'the special demonic personification of the American wilderness.'[1]

This idea comes straight from the first reports of the Indians in the popular literature that served as recruiting publicity for the settlement of North America. 'The only God they worship is the Devil', reported Captain John Smith in his despatches on Virginia.[2] The adventurer and man on the make, John Smith, scribe of the original settlement of Jamestown, is author of far more than the Pocahontas legend. Smith, writing in the early decades of the 1600s for an English audience, was expressing conventional views, ideas of his time, the product of European history and concepts. Those he enthused, inspired and recruited to take up the challenge of America travelled with his imagery and the attitudes that formed it fresh in their minds. But John Smith was no permanent settler in America, just a trail-blazer and publicist. Those who migrated to make a new life in the New World fashioned new meanings and resonance out of the wilderness and the Other people they found there.[3]

America is the new found land, the 'New World' – *Novus Mundus*, the title of Amerigo Vespucci's widely circulated letter of 1503–4. It was a publishing sensation that, with the engine of publicity, saw his name applied to the new continent in 1507. Those who made America came out of Europe with the culture, ideas and myths of Europe. They came to a land that was wilderness with a tradition of meaning to apply to the wilderness. The forests as a place of terror, the home of an imminent threat to civilisation, is old indeed. It goes back to the Romans, from whom we derive the word 'savage', which in various European languages indicates both forest and the inhabitants of the forest. And in the end, Rome fell to these barbarians. With the empire overthrown, Rome became central to the spread of Roman Christianity and the ideal of recapturing the glories of Roman law and governance to civilise the barbarian hordes who became the European peoples. The wilderness as icon and marker of a dividing line between civilisation and barbarism became both external and internal reference overlaid by Christian ideology and teaching. Externally, people who lived in the wilds or beyond Europe were inherently barbaric and outside the natural laws as defined by Christian civilisation; internally, it was a personal, spiritual demarcation of moral teaching and upholding the natural laws of the good life. These ideas were the common inheritance of the peoples who settled America.

The fear of the wilderness, both external and internal, lived on in medieval Europe in the spectre of the Wild Man, the long-haired, club-wielding image of savagery and unnatural, demonic powers.[4] The circumscribed world of medieval Europe had little direct experience of Other – non-European – people. What it had in plenty were lively travellers' tales and iconic imagery of monstrous races, exotica, unnatural people who by their difference – physical, material and spiritual – were an ideological lesson that underlined the meaning of being civilised. The essence of civilisation was Christian identity, bounded by orthodoxy of belief and practice that defined the person, indeed the citizen, and the entire concept of natural law. The wilderness is a potent Biblical theme. Out of the wilderness the Israelites were led to the land of Canaan, the promised land of milk and honey. The wilderness was a place beyond civilisation, a place of danger and temptation. It was in the wilderness that Aaron convinced Israel to worship the false god of the graven image; it was in the wilderness that Jesus was tempted, offered mastery over all the places of the Earth by Satan. What could people formed in such tradition expect to find in the wilderness except danger, moral and physical, as well as unnatural savagery?

In America all these ideas were real, not ideological teaching devices that lived in art and books. The confrontation was direct, immediate. It is Lana's hysterical horror at her first sight of Blue Back. Old and familiar ideas out of Europe took on new meanings in the direct experience of making a life in a new environment. What reverberated through American letters was ambiguity and ambivalence as new meanings were constructed from the wilderness experience.

Settlers came to America led by imagery of the Land of

Canaan, as New Israelites. These Biblical references abound in the writings of Jamestown, the first settlement in North America, as much as in the thinking and writing of the *Mayflower* colonists, the Puritan Pilgrim Fathers who arrived at Plymouth Rock. But their land of milk and honey was the wilderness. It had to be tamed, cultivated and made to bear fruit by being brought within the laws of civilisation, consciously constructed as a garden. Success, realising the promise of a new life in a new land, however, meant not rejecting the wilderness but submitting to it, embracing the ennobling simplicity of rustic toil, in order to master it. Initially, it also meant dependence upon and appropriation from those who knew and understood this strange, different environment, the native inhabitants. In America, to possess and appropriate the land Americans have to subsume and internalise the Other; yet remain distinct. They thus have to look both ways at once.

John Ford embodies this ambivalence in the character of Blue Back. We first see him in the shadow of the doorway, truly an iconic figure. Lana's reaction is to overwrite this person with all the fears, the legends and dark imaginings out of literature. Gil's reaction is to identify Blue Back as the 'good Indian'. The function of Blue Back in *Drums Along the Mohawk* is essentially that of the aged Chingachgook in Fenimore Cooper's *Leatherstocking Tales*, the original literary works from which the Western as a genre derives. In the *Leatherstocking Tales*, Chingachgook is the adoptive father of Hawkeye who teaches him the ways and lore of the wilderness. In *The Pioneers* (published in 1823; actually the first to be written but fourth in the eventual sequence of the *Tales*), Chingachgook has become John Mohegan, the last remnant of his people, bereft of family and community. He has become a Christian, whiskey-drinking Indian – an emasculated, tamed, subservient, aberrant and almost comical figure on the fringes of settler society. In *Drums Along the Mohawk* this is exactly the role of Blue Back. He brings the newly arrived couple half a deer, clear reference to the ritual re-enactment of the myth of the 'good Indian' in America's annual Thanksgiving festival. We see Blue Back as a comic figure holding the hymn sheet he clearly cannot read and insisting on keeping his hat on as he attends church with the settlers. It is Blue Back who brings them warning of the coming of the 'savage Indians': breathlessly running to report that eight white men are leading 100 Indians on the warpath. Blue Back stands and fights with the settlers in the fort. And after the last cataclysmic battle, when the settlers are looking for the villain Caldwell, Blue Back emerges from behind the pulpit of the church and gleefully lowers the eye patch that was Caldwell's distinguishing feature over his own eye. The 'good Indian', as Hawkeye endlessly explained in his inimitable verbose Cooperian style, ever remains a member of a savage race; it is his nature. We are left to imagine what fate Blue Back meted out to Caldwell.

In casting the role of Blue Back, John Ford shows his mastery of visual imagery. He is played by the actor Chief John Big Tree, a Seneca Indian who died in 1967 and is buried at the Onondaga Reservation in upstate New York. He was genuinely an inhabitant of the region where the film is set. According to press reports, John Big Tree was one of the models for the Indian head on the nickel coin, genuinely an icon. And his casting was more than chance, for he reprised essentially the same role in Ford's later classic Western *She Wore a Yellow Ribbon*, made in 1948, where he plays the old, compliant Arapaho chief unable to command the loyalty of his young braves determined to combat the US cavalry. In the character of Pony That Walks, Chief Big Tree even reprises his lines from *Drums Along the Mohawk*: 'I am a Christian. Hallelujah. Old friends.'

The good Indian is tractable, a guide to mastering the wilderness. But submitting to the wilderness to make it into a garden is an exercise fraught with fear. America exists as a battle between good and evil on every level from the personal to the national, and its fear is holy terror. Fear is the spur to seeking saving grace; holy terror of the prospect of damnation is essential to attaining true belief and is the bulwark against giving in to the lures and pleasures of the indulgent, savage wilderness without and within.

In the pamphlets and sermons of the earliest settlers, the beginning of the publishing industry in America, the wilderness is both home and a place of constant temptation. The mission of America is to bring forth a new civilisation, to escape the failings and flaws of Old Europe and in a virgin land become an ideal community, the city on the hill, the light and model to the world. The temptation of the wilderness is indulgence, succumbing not to ennobling primitivism but coarsening lack of civilised standards, genuine regression into the savagery that is all around. One authentic reflection of this constant fear that is developed early in American literature is the captivity narrative. Captivity narratives deal with the fear of crossing the racial line, being possessed by the life of savagery. The other great theme of Puritan thought and sermons, the subject of the day books kept by the conscientious, is the personal struggle with evil, as declaimed from the pulpit in *Drums Along the Mohawk*. It is the fight for virtuous simplicity, true moral propriety. It is the resounding commandment spoken by Parson Rosenkrantz, played by the indisputably Irish actor Arthur Shields, to 'cast out the devil within'.

Arthur Shields, with his mellifluous Irish accent, is a favourite Fordian actor. John Ford was responsible for bringing both Shields and his brother, the actor Barry Fitzgerald, to Hollywood. In *Drums Along the Mohawk*, Shields provides Ford's preferred intonation for the music of scripture. And scripture, adherence to Christian morality through the trials and tribulations provided by the wilderness, is the bulwark against giving in to temptation; it is the defining possession that forms the character of America. The parson is on hand to read the sonorous words of the committal service – 'I know that my Redeemer liveth …' – the creedal definition with which the community buries its dead, but by which it must also live if it is to realise its mission. Like Chief Big Tree, Shields gets to reprise this essential set-piece in Ford's later film *She Wore a Yellow Ribbon*, in which he plays the doctor caring both physically and spiritually for the cavalry troop. In *Drums Along the Mohawk*, his booming 'Cast out the devil within' is spoken off camera, ringing in the night-time quiet to castigate one of the defenders of the fort into throwing away his whiskey jar. This is more than a moment of light relief played for laughs. It is a moment redolent with significance for the film audience of 1939 that lived through Prohibition. Temperance Leagues and moral reformers are an enduring part of American response to the wilderness. In *Stage-coach*, they are essential to the plot dynamic. *Stagecoach* begins with the whore, Dallas, the heroine who will be redeemed, and the drunken doctor and the gambler being driven out of town by the law and order league. These morally equivocal characters take the stagecoach to escape further on to the frontier, as wildness is eradicated by the victory of settled moral order. The victory over the wilderness and the devil within is by creation of law and order, the essential motif of the Western genre.

Building an ideal society, the civilising mission of America, invokes the second law of American mythology: the desire to escape the corruption, constraints and tyrannies of Europe, from which the settlers came. It is in the wilderness and against the implacable enemies it contains that victory must be achieved. Central to the action of *Drums Along the Mohawk* is the theme of military preparedness, the recourse to arms and eradication of the enemy. The fort at German Flats is the focus of this frontier community, a telling detail. The fort is an enduring feature of the Western genre, the last outpost of civilisation, the defensive heart of a community under constant threat, a bastion against surrounding savagery. Gil and Lana's first visit to the fort is both to meet the community and to attend a drill of the local militia. The militia is a democratic institution, answerable and serviceable to the community. When the Major wants to fine an absentee member he is countermanded by his troops: 'I thought that's what this war's about – not making big taxes without our say so.' This is a well armed militia. Everyone has a gun, and all are expert in using their guns, even the parson. The troops are invited to parade before the ladies to show off their military bearing. But their pride in preparedness goes much deeper: 'By thunder, I bet we can beat the whole world the way we march' is the earnest comment of one soldier.

Pride in bearing arms is one thing, but it must confront the awfulness of war. In one of the most powerful moments, John Ford captures the horror of war not through a set-piece battle scene but through the words of Gil Martin, played by Henry Fonda. Returning from battle, injured and fevered, Gil recounts the horror we do not see. Of 600 men who went to battle, only 240 remain alive. 'I killed a man', he says, 'but we won. We showed them they couldn't take this valley.' Later the line is taken up by the parson after the final battle we do witness. Sitting shocked and overcome, he murmurs: 'I killed a man.' Violence exacts a personal cost. But violence is the central act through which the regeneration of hope, the revitalisation of the dream of a new life, is achieved. Through eradication of the enemy by military might is the land secured.

In *Drums Along the Mohawk* the enemy has no motivation, no history, no reason or rationale. The enemy is pure, unmitigated savagery. The community must eradicate the enemy, drive them back into the wilderness, for 'we know only too well what will happen to us if these sons of Belial ever get over these walls'. The defenders of the fort get a graphic example of the malevolence of the enemy. Joe is the first to attempt to leave the fort to summon aid, a typical vignette performance by Francis Ford, brother of the director. Sustained by liquid courage, he crawls out of a secret passage only to be caught by the Indians and spread-eagled on a wagon loaded with hay. It is wheeled before the walls of the fort and the Indians prepare to burn Joe alive. The Indians who would perform this torture are shot by the desperate defenders. But from cover a flaming arrow is shot into the hay. It catches light. In the last extreme, Parson Rosenkrantz shoots Joe to spare him the agonies of the fire. This is the man he killed. The wilderness frontier contains an enemy without pity. This sequence is the irreducible fear underpinning not only the Western genre but also America itself. In *Stagecoach*, the final stage of the journey is the Indian attack, the archetypal scene played out against the backdrop of Monument Valley. As the small band of passengers runs out of ammunition, Hatfield, the gambler, a fine Southern gentleman, checks his derringer to ensure he has saved one last bullet for the lady, to spare her the unspeakable fate of falling prey to the Indians. This last merciful extreme is avoided only by the sound of bugles and the arrival of the cavalry to drive the Indians back into the wilderness.

The wilderness frontier experience is what distinguishes America and makes it different. It is on the frontier that all the elements that formed its essential character were shaped. With immensely subtle economy, John Ford amasses in *Drums Along the Mohawk* a mythic story of ordinary folk, the heroes and heroines of the creation of the new nation. As myth it refers, infers and evokes connections, ideas, values and meanings that link past, present and future, a film narrative that says and implies far more than appears. Ford shows us what Richard Slotkin terms 'those who tore violently a nation from the implacable and opulent wilderness'. Slotkin is paraphrasing William Faulkner's novel *Absalom, Absalom!* There could be no more fitting reference. In his magisterial study of the writings of the earliest generations of settlers of America, Slotkin argues that 'their concerns, their hopes, their terrors, their violence, and their justifications of themselves, as expressed in their literature, are the foundation stones of the mythology that informs [American] history'.[5] The wilderness frontier is a mythic space; it recurs not in one single and singular geographic location but everywhere in American experience and history. For Slotkin, the myth of regeneration through violence became the structuring metaphor of the American experience. Violence is the enduring response to fear, the requirement to defend the unique experiment in national existence that is America. But it is founded on an insecurity that nestles within the idea of America itself. For what the history and myth of the frontier establishes is that America is constantly under attack, perennially liable to assault from without and within. America has been consciously created to be different, exceptional, to provide a new beginning with new opportunity to fulfil their dreams for all its settlers. But the chance to remake themselves, to realise their dreams, means integrating the ambiguities of the wilderness. *Drums Along the Mohawk* infers this fear on the classic frontier. Faulkner's *Absalom, Absalom!* deals with another dimension of the same structuring metaphor of fear. The fear is of miscegenation – the interbreeding of races. On the wilderness frontier, the fear of miscegenation is incorporated into the captivity narrative, the need to appropriate the knowledge, skills and means to survive from the savage inhabitants while remaining separate. It is the challenge to submit to the primitivism required by the wilderness and yet remain true to the values and meaning of civilisation, to perfect the heritage of its ideals that have been brought out of the corruption and tyranny of Europe. *Absalom, Absalom!* is a novel about the violent terrors arising from miscegenation across the colour line, the ongoing consequences of slavery, the second source of savagery, institutionalised within America and present from its beginning.

The Western is the most characteristic product of the American cultural tradition because it is the defining myth extracted from the nation's history. It is myth because it is America narrating its own values and meanings to itself, and it has been retold and reconfigured to express the complexities, contemporary concerns and shifts of American culture. It is quite simply the most formative, popular and pervasive genre of American culture. It has found expression in books, magazines and comics, and on radio and television as well as in the cinema. It has had periods of varying fortune, but for 30 years from 1939 it 'was the most consistently popular and most widely produced form of action film and a significant field for the active fabrication and revision of public myth and ideology'.[6] According to John G. Cawelti, the late 1950s was one of the major peaks of popularity for the Western. In the USA in 1958, Westerns constituted 10.76% of all works of fiction published, some 1.76% of all books. In the same year, at least 54 Western feature films were made. In 1959, eight of the top ten shows on television, as measured by the Neilsen ratings, were Westerns, as were 30 of the prime-time shows. By 1967, nearly the end of the three decades, Hollywood was turning out some 37 major Western features; and during a typical week of television, some eighteen hours of prime-time viewing, 16% of the total viewing time, was devoted to Westerns.[7]

As public myth and ideology, Westerns have made their motifs and themes part of the cultural formation of Americans, as well as their vast non-American audience. But as the central location for expression of public myth and ideology, the cultural influence of the Western extends far beyond the genre itself. The western frontier is not history but an expression of ideas about the meaning of history, a genuine mythic space. It is timeless. It can accommodate the concerns of McCarthy-era anti-Communist witch hunts: *High Noon* (1952); find historic reference for and reflection on Vietnam and the Mei Lai massacre: *Soldier Blue* (1970); it can be a confection of saccharin promoting multicultural inclusion: the television phenomenon that is *Dr Quinn, Medicine Woman* (1993–); or, a rather less saccharine but equally multicultural and politically correct paean working hard to suggest historic verisimilitude: the television series *Young Riders* (1989–92). The public myth and ideology encoded and negotiated through the Western is so familiar that it can be transferred and used to structure entirely different genres. The frontier not only moved west, it expanded to be a universal frame of reference: its themes, stock characters and situations, its characteristic responses and essential concerns, are reconfigured and turn up in galaxies far, far away in 'space, the final frontier'.

Wherever the frontier motif occurs, it is always premised on fear and develops a culture of fear among the bearers of a civilising mission who are always under threat from implacable enemies. The settlers' only resort will be, and is, military preparedness, violent action or reaction to eradicate and remove their enemy. The intense drive to bring the settled moral order of law and democratic governance is premised on inherent fear of pervasive enemies who are the antithesis of all its promise. The Western was the perfect text for Cold War ideology, and the formation of the national security state in the 1950s was the pinnacle of mass production of Westerns for radio, television, cinema and comics. Children the world over grew up playing cowboys and Indians, re-enacting their mythological meanings. In America the generation that grew up on the ubiquitous Western as the dominant format of popular entertainment was the generation that also grew up to the sound of air raid sirens, doing regular drills crouching under their desks to avoid the flash of nuclear explosions: the wilderness frontier psychosis made manifest as a cultivation of fear.

The frontier of fear, like the western frontier, ever moves on. In the 1930s, when the optimistic promise of abundance and triumphalism encoded within the Western was out of tune with the mass social devastation of the Great Depression, the motif of fear found new expression. Hollywood devised the horror movie genre. And it specialised in urban Westerns, the formulaic crime dramas and shoot-outs between gangsters and the law that captured and reconfigured so much of the ambiguities of the wilderness theme, such as *Roaring Twenties*, *Little Caesar* and *Public Enemy*. And the structuring motif of fear has kept on moving on. It invests disaster movies like *The Towering Inferno*, *Earthquake* and *Volcano*. It underpins the mad scientist motif as fear of the power of science with its potential threat to de-divinise society, undermine its essential moral order, and unmake the human promise of individual freedom. There is little the scientific community can warn about that does not have resonance with a film

47

– from schlock cheap-and-cheerful to high-end prestigious movies: *Toxic Avenger* (nerd takes revenge by becoming a lethal mutant) or *The Swarm* (the killer bees are daily expected in parts of the United States) to *Soylent Green* (a pessimistic future vision that gave cinematic life to Earth Watch's preoccupation with overpopulation) or *The Day After* (a harrowing vision of the consequences of nuclear war) – lodged in our neural network as part of our visual memory bank.

Anxiety, insecurity and the complex themes of the fragility of life and civilisation have become what Barry Glassner has analysed as *The Culture of Fear*.[8] It not only lives in cinema and television as a standard formulaic narrative but has become the standard device of the culture of information, the staple, as Glassner argues, of the proliferating media of information. As information it has its own journalistic formulae and characteristic investigative structure. Most importantly, this complex has the ability to proliferate fear, to popularise fear of the wrong things and engender a false perception of the actual lived experience of the majority of American citizens. Crime, drugs, minorities, teen moms, killer kids, mutant microbes, plane crashes, road rage, carcinogens in everything – the list goes on and on. Fear is the common currency of the American media. A review of America's network evening television news programmes shows how they depend upon fear stories: scams, medicines, health, insurance, environmental fears, food scares are the standard narratives regularly revisited. The culture of fear is America; the fragility of modern affluent abundance is the recurring nightmare of a nation required to fear. To be under threat of the extinction of all that America promises is the natural condition of contemporary America. You cannot live forever, inherit the endless promise of life, liberty and the pursuit of happiness, if you are to be eaten away by gnawing cancers ingested through your food. The medical and medicinal drug culture of today's America is a lineal descendant in secularised and scientised form of the fear of the pervasive enemy, the wilderness pathology of early America. It is fear writ large in the organisation of modern consumerism.

The requirement to be afraid has been incorporated into the American psyche. It has been put to work to sustain enterprise and liberal capitalism on many fronts. Feeding the fears of ordinary Americans is now a recognised industry that takes in everything from the possibility of global eradication by asteroid impacts to mercury in fish and genetically modified crops. The public reads the sensational headline-grabbing stories. Politicians are bombarded by the plethora of schemes to investigate, evaluate and counter potent threats of an ever more complex, hazardous and precarious world. The fear industry makes work for academics eager for grants, salaries and careers, as well as for corporations in need, as they ever have been, of publicly funded research and development work as well as actual products to market. The end of the process is not security but competing doom-laden scenarios aplenty that confuse the ordinary citizen. Danger is out there. But the system works to increase anxiety without ever making it easier for the intelligent, motivated citizen to assess the quality of the information, likelihood of risk or appropriateness of the action – and spending – undertaken in their name by government.

And, of course, the anxious existence on the edge of fear propels the need to be armed in self-defence. Out of the motifs of formulaic narratives based on mythic history comes the psyche that cultivates a gun-owning culture and the intractability of debating the issue of gun control. Primal fears, mythic images of making a life in the wilderness married to particular views of the American Constitution, make the issue of gun ownership not a subject of rational debate but a visceral question of identity for the individual and the nation. Fear makes a gun-toting nation find its fulfilment, its moral purpose and its way of life regenerated, sustained and secured through possession and control of the means of violence. It is the inalienable right to have guns. It is the inalienable right to national defence that requires ever greater spending on a military equipped with ever more elaborate and sophisticated means of destruction to eradicate any and all real and potential threats.

Fear and a pervasive sense of imminent threat begin and endure with the idea of America. It lives in tension with the other central motif inscribed in the Western: the means to escape from the past and remake the self, to expand one's horizons and realise one's dreams. America begins with publicity, PR and propaganda with a purpose. Its original publicist and mythologiser, Captain John Smith, came to America as an agent of the Virginia Company, a commercial venture whose success depended on attracting settlers to develop the new lands and their products. What was sold to potential immigrants eager to escape the wars, dearth, poverty, repression and constraints of Europe was a dream of abundance and personal freedom where they could reconstruct themselves and their ideal of the good life in a wilderness ready to be made a garden. What Captain John Smith and the growing genre of published tales of the new land bequeathed to America was expansion, ever greater room and personal scope to succeed.

Escape from the failings of the Old World, the restrictions of its way of life, and the opportunity to realise the dream of the new is a basic theme of the ever moving and expanding frontier. Escape from the original settlements of America was soon added to the repertoire. Those who disliked how the early communities were developing, those who arrived too late to stake the best claim, or wanted more land, found the blank space of the wilderness a ready escape route and thus re-created the frontier further westward as the literal and literary space in which to follow their dream. The narrative tradition had breathing space, just like the land, and it was to be filled by a restless people eager to escape from anything that tied them down or constrained their dream of personal fulfilment. So escape and escapism, dream-chasing through personal reconstruction in a new setting, are conflated; they become deeply intertwined in the essence of

American ideas. America is, after all, the nation constitutionally committed to the pursuit of happiness. Escape and escapism are ideas in tension, like so many other themes within the mythic tradition of American ideas. The tension derives from inherent ambiguities. The simple ennobling primitivism of the wilderness experience contains within itself the potential promise of expanding material well-being, the accumulation of rising living standards and the comforts they can acquire. In *Drums Along the Mohawk*, Gil and Lana first lose their home and all their possessions. They face the trauma of hiring themselves out to work on someone else's land, an inferior, unpalatable but necessary alternative to the sturdy self-reliance of making one's own land flourish. But they end by acquiring more land and a finer stone-built house, inherited from Mrs McLennan, the widow to whom they came as hired labourers. They end with the means to realise the American Dream.

The escape to America is the right to pursue abundance and to become a new self-made and self-making person. Few achieve the rags-to-riches transformation. But living the dream is the idea of America, its lure and recruiting agent, the promise of 'only in America'. It has become the consumer ideal that is consistently sold and made increasingly affordable for the mass market in America. Indeed, an essential part of the expanding enterprise of America was the creation of mass production techniques to serve a mass market. The American production system, as explained by Daniel Boorstin,[9] was a characteristic response to America's escape and freedom from the traditional constraints of European labour and economic modes of operation. Only in America was the production-line Model T Ford – available in any colour as long as it was black, designed with the average citizen in mind and made truly affordable to the average citizen – possible.

Consumerism as a form of escape has been an expanding frontier of abundance that has continually moved on. It has achieved its mature development as the growth of lifestyle marketing, the idea for which America was made. It has been a process of development made through the media, by publicity and advertising. But an essential adjunct to its dissemination has been cinema and television. On one level, the public myth and ideology encoded in the films and programmes have underscored the importance of the self-making lifestyle dream. On another level, the set designs of films and especially television were consciously constructed to visualise, realise and popularise the ideal of normal life abundant in possession of things that are advertised and merchandised to the masses. And crucially, cinema and television have been the fashioners of the culture of celebrity. The stars of classic Hollywood movies were ambiguous, simultaneously signifying multiple meanings. The roles they played were embodiments of sustaining public myth and ideology. Stardom was acquired by becoming identified with the characters they played, the screen persona of the star taking on the values encoded in the characters. But, once attained, stardom includes a subtle shift by which the screen persona of the star also confers meaning on the characters they play. Stardom is far more than typecasting and a name above the title. Stardom is the acquisition of a persona that transcends a particular role, contributes to each role played and accompanies the star into daily life. A star is something more than an actor; the term 'character actor' distinguishes someone who is not a star. The greatest role played by the brightest stars in the firmament is themselves: the compound persona of celluloid and reality. And they were also real people who were the greatest embodiment of the American Dream, achievers who lived the promise of abundance. They were the centre of a media industry hungry for celebrity with an insatiable appetite and capacity to disseminate the stars as lifestyle models, paragons to be followed in the lifestyle choices of ordinary people.

The escapism of self-remaking and self-fulfilment read against the idea of the American Dream has another connotation. It is the growth of entertainment as a central factor in human experience. Neal Gabler has defined the paradigm as *Life: the Movie*.[10] Mythic narratives have emerged from the movies and become projections of self, helpfully learnt from the media and moved on to restructure reality itself. It is the rise of celebrity lifestyles as the models for ideal existence. Celebrities have become the stuff of their own genre of mythic narrative, biopic retellings in reality of the formulaic narratives of the biopic. The celebrity stories chart their ordinary backgrounds, the trials and adversities of early life, the dedication and hard work that leads to the inevitable – the big break where their charisma and star quality are revealed. The culture of celebrity merchandises the idea of replicating these celebrity lifestyles to the mass audience as a distraction from reality, but has become reality itself.

Entertainment, as Gabler argues, is the prime focus of American life, the place where values are expressed, performed, endorsed, published, taught, broadcast, ratified and mythologised in diverting ways. America is the escape into the world of possibilities. America is the place where possibilities and potential are more real, more important, than actual circumstances. The American Dream is the experience of the few endorsed and believed by the many. What sustains the impossible potential is its power to allure, its diversion from the grind of ordinary, mundane existence, its power to entertain. And in America entertainment is the medium of the masses. It is the arena of escape from the arbitration of authority and élites. Entertainment is demanded, and provided, by all aspects of social life. In America, even religion has a long tradition of serving as an entertainment. The tent revival meetings that toured the country as the medium of mass evangelism were an entertainment, and the content and structure of their evangelical procedures had a great element of entertainment. For many evangelicals, being moved by the spirit was a necessary proof of genuine religious experience that had many of the hallmarks of a sideshow – the performance of people possessed dancing wildly, speaking in tongues, and other forms of extraordinary behaviour. The political convention is another area where the ethos of giving the people a great show brings entertainment trailing in its wake.

The entertainment principle – the desire to be entertained, diverted, provided with an escape – has diversified and expanded, moved on from the fascinating realism of the first medium of mass entertainment: the cinema. But the expanding horizon now colonised by the entertainment principle carries within it what the cinema constructed: the elements, motifs and ideology of public myth. It is infused with the values and meanings narrated, negotiated and expressed by the vehicles of entertainment, the ideas of America and the American self. The public culture formed by industries of mass popular entertainment has become self-aware. It has become cynically knowing of the manipulation that is at the heart of the enterprise. The audience is educated to discuss, assess and connive with the manipulatory techniques by which celebrity is sustained. The construction of celebrity is overtly part of the show, an essential of the entertainment. To celebrity we will return in Chapter Four. Here, it will suffice to say that the more the public is aware, savvy about the means of making celebrities, the more the idea is democratised as a system everyone can participate in to make themselves celebrities. Everyone can have their fifteen minutes of fame as more and more vehicles for launching celebrities feed the voracious needs of the media for a constant stream of new personalities. The intriguing ambiguity is that while the mass audience becomes more knowing about the manipulation practised upon it, it does not necessarily become more knowing, critically informed and critical of the public myth and mythical ideology that mass popular entertainment encodes and disseminates.

Richard Slotkin argues that the western frontier that became the dominant genre of mass popular culture serves as a significant field for the active fabrication and revision of public myth and ideology. Throughout his career, says Jonathon Jones, John Ford 'made films with a deep sensitivity to how history is turned into myth. His West is a place where reality is constantly mutating into a lie.'[11] This is best illustrated by Ford's 1962 film *The Man Who Shot Liberty Valance*, and *Fort Apache*, made in 1948. 'This is the west, sir. When the legend becomes fact, print the legend', says the newspaper editor in *The Man Who Shot Liberty Valance*. The myth of the wilderness frontier, of the west, as expressed through the Western is extracted out of the historic experience of America. But it is a construct, a conscious fabrication, a myth richly overlaid with meanings, values and ideology. It is the most characteristic site of the construction and expression of the idea of America, the shaping of the American psyche. But how possible is it to investigate and debate the propensity of historic reality to constantly mutate into a lie? What are the ramifications and consequences for the public domain of a mass culture generated by this propensity? Could the constant fabrication worked around the enduring motifs of the idea of America achieve the wonders of ignorance? Which brings us to the third law of American mythology: ignorance is bliss.

Fort Apache, the first of John Ford's famed cavalry trilogy, is a eulogy to the ordinary soldier, a persuasive motif for a nation still disentangling itself from the mass mobilisation of the Second World War. Its theme is the endurance of the army as the essential institution of the nation, the force that made the nation possible. This is both a backward glance to the making of America and a forward-looking vision of the national security state founded on military strength, the army that will be necessary to realise the lessons of the Second World War. But at the heart of the film is Ford's treatment of Custer's Last Stand in the Battle of the Little Bighorn of 1876, the military disaster that overshadowed the centenary celebrations of the nation. The names and location are changed but the historic reference is unmistakable. It is Ford's variation on the theme central to Slotkin's second volume on the myth of the western frontier, *The Fateful Environment*.[12] Ford's narrative concerns how a narrow-minded military martinet with utter contempt for the Indians decides not to negotiate them onto a reservation, to remove them out of the path of the advance of the American nation, but to eradicate them by military might – a choice that results in leading his troops to certain death. In essence, the action is a classic reprise of the dictum 'C'est magnifique, mais ce n'est pas la guerre' (It's magnificent, but it's not war), Maréchal Bosquet's famed remark on the Charge of the Light Brigade by the British cavalry in the Crimean War of 1854. Both disasters became potent national myths. Slotkin sees the myth of the Last Stand as a major point for refashioning the myth of the frontier into the idea of the sacrifices necessary to sustain the expansion of empire, the fabrication of a public myth that marks the transition from the closing of the western frontier to the opening of global empire. Ford's interest is not just the making of myth but the connivance with lies. Throughout the film there has been tension between the central protagonists: Colonel Thursday, the Custer figure played by Henry Fonda, and Captain York, played by John Wayne, a soldier attuned to the frontier, knowledgeable about its conditions and Indian inhabitants, who contests Thursday's attitudes and policy. In the final sequence of the film a group of journalists visit Fort Apache eager for tales of the glorious last stand of Colonel Thursday and his men, already memorialised in an iconic painting kept at the Fort; an apt comment on the importance of the American media in myth-making, as well as the speed with which history as myth mutates into lies. Despite having disagreed with Thursday, argued against his intransigence knowing it was folly, and watched the slaughter unfold, York assures the journalists that the painting depicts just how it was: glorious and heroic. As he leaves to take his troop on patrol, York dons the military cap that had been Thursday's trademark, an early source of tension between the two men. Not only is myth more potent than history, sometimes the lie made into public myth is too powerful to permit telling the truth, and must be embraced.

The myth of the wilderness frontier is central to American exceptionalism. It is the historic source and rationale for America being different, a reason why America has been spared the ills, turmoil and troubles experienced by the rest of the world. It has become a justification for the abundance, the affluence of the American lifestyle. It is the ideological underpinning for accepting that America is and should be the pre-eminent power dominating the globe. In sum, it is the great insulating ethos, the ultimate reason to glory in ignorance. America is honest about neither its own history nor the rest of the world. The dominance of public myth and the ideology it encodes becomes a monumental natural impediment to self-scrutiny. It is a reason for the impossibility of public debate on topics of urgent public concern. It is a potent reason for ignorance about the rest of the world and for discounting what the rest of the world has to say about America. It is an impenetrable barrier to non-Americans engaging in a mutual, open and equal discourse about America and its meanings for America and the world at large.

Drums Along the Mohawk provides a neat example of how myths and lies are transformed into an ideology of ignorance. Central to the film is the local volunteer militia, the visual presentation of a well armed militia. It is not merely public myth that is realised in these sequences: it is an article of constitutional belief, strictly constructed and insisted upon with ideological rigour and political vehemence as essential to the very idea of America. To question its historicity, its accuracy and verisimilitude as what happened in history is fraught with danger. Pulitzer Prize-winning historian Garry Wills presents considerable contemporary evidence in the words of militia commanders that what Ford depicts is history turned into myth.

A captain of the New Hampshire militia reported in 1775 that 'not one-half our men have arms', and a militia officer in Virginia said that he had a stand of a thousand guns, but that none of them worked. The New York Committee of Safety refused to send troops to the field because 'they have no arms.' Thomas Jefferson, Virginia's governor, had to defend his state's militia when, lacking guns, it stole a consignment

> purchased by the Continental Army ... The new government
> promised to arm the militias. But the state of Virginia had
> been promising to do that for years, *and had never done it.*[13]

Wills poses the obvious question: if every man had a gun for
militia drill, why did so many go to battle without one? And if
the state of Virginia had been unable to provide arms for its militia, how could the new federal government so limited in its funds
expect to do so? Wills's concern is to question the relationship
between myth, history and modern times. 'There was one gun for
every ten people in the colonies. Now there is one gun for every
man, woman and child in America, with three for every adult
male of the population. Yet this later situation is justified by
appeal to the former.'[14] But to raise such questions is to stand
against the ideology of ignorance and court the wrath of everyone.

Wills cites statistics from the work of Michael A. Bellesiles.
Bellesiles's book *Arming America: The Origins of a National
Gun Culture* won the 2001 Bancroft Prize of Columbia University, New York. But the book's central thesis that guns were
much less prevalent in early America than had been generally
thought or popularly accepted, and the research methods used
to establish this argument, became a *cause célèbre*. The controversy resulted in Bellesiles's being subjected to an academic
inquiry for fraud and resigning from his post as Professor of
History at Emory University. An internet search on the subject
will lead to a plethora of claims and counter claims, including
trenchant denunciations of Bellesiles's work. In resigning his
post, Bellesiles wrote: 'I will continue to research and report on
the probate materials while also working on my next book, but
cannot continue to teach in what I feel is a hostile environment.'[15] The central controversy concerns his use of probate
records to provide statistical data on gun ownership. But as
Wills demonstrates, there is plentiful evidence from multiple
sources in the contemporary records to substantiate that gun
ownership was not universal, that arming militias, as well as the

Continental Army, was highly problematic and that militias played diverse roles at different times and different places throughout the Revolutionary War, even that commanders of the Continental Army found their efforts often troublesome. Yet, in America, the public space to debate and investigate the facts and issues of history is under constraint, profoundly involved with the power of public myth. It is not the facts that are problematic. It is the mythical ideology, with its public denouncements, public censure, and political implications that make getting the facts straight seem almost impossible. Of course, it is not just the issue of gun control that is shrouded in mythical ideology – almost no contemporary issue, from climate change to genetically modified food, the nation's nuclear weapons programme to racial profiling, can be debated in America with any openness. The ideology of ignorance is paramount; and the media ensure that Americans become good consumers rather than questioning citizens.

Cocooned in their national ethos and mythical ideology, Americans seem content or at least resigned to abide within a constructed, manufactured ignorance, a knowledgeable ignorance that embraces their own history as well as perceptions and information about the rest of the world. The consequence is an insularity of information in the most information-rich nation ever known to humanity. An inchoate world bursts upon American innocent ignorance only in times of turmoil and conflict. Or as Ambrose Bierce so pithily explained: 'War is God's way of teaching Americans geography.' America's response to danger is to fall back upon the structuring metaphors of the American experience, to rely upon the themes of its public myth: to fear, to understand its adversaries as implacable enemies, to seek a violent armed response that will eradicate the problem. The hardest argument to make is that American exceptionalism prevents Americans at every turn from understanding themselves and their relationship to the world, as much as what kind of a world is out there.

All nations have a mythic tradition. All myths can be employed by any nation as self-justification. Any country can produce examples of myths mutating into lies, commonly held with invidious consequences. But America's public space seems exceptional in its resistance to interrogating this familiar human dynamic. The American condition is the pathological conformity with which the nation holds on to its public myths and mythical ideology as values and meanings necessary for self-definition and self-description. In 1933, Franklin D. Roosevelt declared to the American people: 'The only thing we have to fear is fear itself.' His words take on a multitude of meanings and remain an enduring challenge. America has made fear essential and not reasoned or debated how to tackle fear itself. Americans are taught to fear; and they fear self-reflection and self-examination, and interrogation of a fabricated worldview where ignorance is bliss. And they are taught to escape – escape into mythology, into entertainment, into infotainment: into anything that shrouds the true facts of their history and the appalling consequences of their actions. These are the foundations of the nation. These are the lies of how the nation came to be.

CHAPTER TWO

Mr Smith Goes to Washington: America as the Idea of Democracy and Nation

Drums Along the Mohawk presents the myth of the wilderness frontier and concludes with the arrival of the flag, the symbol of the nation that is America. The nation is the vessel fashioned to carry the people shaped by the frontier experience to their destiny. And the nation too is an object of myth, invested with its own rhetoric, ritual and symbolic presence in American life, repeatedly performed to entertain with solemnity and awe. So, in 1939, the same year John Ford's movie saw the Martins set forth into the wilderness to remake themselves, cinema audiences were also entertained by *Mr Smith Goes to Washington*, a tale of America as the idea of nation, the fourth law of American mythology.

In Frank Capra's film, the hero Jefferson Smith epitomises the character produced by the American frontier: an innocent idealist. Jeff Smith comes from an unnamed western state. He teaches the young members of his Boy Rangers organisation about the natural environment and American ideals in the newspaper he produces called *Boys' Stuff*. A subtle suggestion, this: in its youth the nation existed on the frontier; now appropriating the frontier experience is necessary for young Americans to connect with their history and its values. A very Rooseveltian notion – Theodore Roosevelt, that is – recalled in the era of Franklin D. Roosevelt. Smith's selection to complete the term of a suddenly deceased incumbent Senator is urged on the state Governor by his politically astute children: 'Right now he's the finest American we've got'; 'right now he's the greatest hero we ever had. It's all over the headlines.' As the children point out, not only is Jefferson Smith a hero to 50,000 children, who each have two parents who vote, but after single-handedly putting out a forest fire he is also a popular hero. Senator Smith goes to Washington overawed by the power of its meaning, steeped in its history: 'A young patriot, recites Lincoln and Jefferson, turned loose in our nation's capital.' In the film this hero will redeem the nation by practising its meaning and values. But in his character Jefferson Smith is something more. He is the hero who integrates the two mythic cycles of America, the wilderness frontier and the nation, to explain how they belong in union, indivisible.

Jefferson Smith's arrival in Washington is one of cinema's famed sequences. 'Look! Look! There it is!' he exclaims as he stands in the foyer of the train station catching his first glimpse of the dome of the Capitol Building. And the film will return to the image of the Capitol Dome a number of times to see it lit up at night, underlining the symbolic reference: Capitol Hill – the city on a hill, the light to the nations. Captivated by the sight of the Capitol, Smith wanders off to take a bus tour with the other sightseers. This neat cinematic device provides the vehicle for a montage of images and music reprising the history of America to explain the meaning of the nation. To the strains of 'Yankee Doodle Dandy' we begin with a close-up of the words 'Equal Justice' inscribed on the Supreme Court Building; then the White House. Signposts for Constitution and Pennsylvania Avenues point the way to the Capitol Building. On a tour of the Rotunda, Jefferson Smith comes face to face with the statue of Thomas Jefferson as the music shifts to 'My Country 'Tis of Thee' ('Sweet land of liberty' in the words of its lyricist, the Reverend Samuel F.

Smith). A great bell rings and the word 'Liberty' inscribed on its base insistently and rhythmically swings into full close up. Smith arrives at the niche where the Declaration of Independence and the Constitution are kept. Images of the Trumbell painting of the signing of the Declaration of Independence, a bronze cast of the Declaration, John Hancock appending his signature, the statue of John Adams; the torch of freedom held aloft, Alexander Hamilton's statue; the handwritten words 'life', 'liberty' and the 'pursuit of happiness', are all overlaid on the ringing Liberty Bell. Then Senator Smith is off to the Washington Memorial. A bust of George Washington overlays a statue of the bald eagle as we hear the musical strains of 'The Star Spangled Banner' and the flag materialises to flutter over the eagle. The camera closes in on the stars of the fluttering banner, the music shifts to 'When Johnnie Comes Marching Home' as we see the massed armies of the Union and Confederacy in the Civil War engraved in statuary. This gives way to a memorial to the dead of '1917–1919' followed by the tomb of the Unknown Soldier at Arlington National Cemetery accompanied by the Last Post. The camera moves past row upon row of graves. Finally, reverently, Jefferson Smith mounts the steps of the Lincoln Memorial, to the dulcet playing of 'Red River Valley'. The monumental proportions of the Memorial are highlighted by the camera angles; the littleness of the lone individual before the might of history. The camera pauses on the words: 'In this temple as in the hearts of the people for whom he saved the Union the memory of Abraham Lincoln is enshrined forever', before focusing on the statue of the seated Lincoln. The music gives us the 'Battle Hymn of the Republic' merging into 'The Star Spangled Banner' before returning to 'Red River Valley' as Smith surveys the walls inscribed with extracts from Lincoln's speeches. The camera pauses on the words of his second inaugural speech – 'with malice toward none …' – before Smith leads us to Lincoln's most famous oration, the Gettysburg Address. He stands beside a young boy reading the Address to his grandfather: '… for which they gave the last full measure of devotion – that we here highly resolve ...'; we cut away to see an old black man enter and reverently remove his hat before the statue of Mr Lincoln as the boy reads: '... that these dead shall not have died in vain, that this nation under God shall have a new birth of ...'; he stumbles over the word and his grandfather, in a thick foreign accent, emphatically pronounces 'freedom'. The camera rests on the old grandfather's misty-eyed gaze and cuts to the face of the old black man. Our focus returns to the face of Lincoln as the child reads: '... and that government of the people, by the people, for the people shall not perish from the earth.' At last the music swells, the image of Lincoln merges once more with the image of the bell, and the word 'Liberty' fills the screen before a fade to black. In just three minutes of film magic we have toured the great mythic cycle fashioned out of history as the rhetoric and symbolism of the nation that is America.

The mythic narrative of the 'perfect union', as the Constitution terms itself, was established by its makers. James Wilson, a Pennsylvania delegate to the Constitutional Convention and one of the chief architects of the Constitution, speaking on 6 October 1787, praised the new government it had devised as the best 'which has ever been offered to the world'.[1] What he began, as Robert Jensen observes, has never ceased:

One of the requirements for being a mainstream American politician, Republican or Democrat, is the willingness to repeat constantly the assertion that the United States is the 'greatest nation on earth,' maybe even 'the greatest nation in history.' At a hearing for the House Select Committee on Homeland Security on July 11, 2002, Texas Republican Dick Armey described the United States as 'the greatest, most free nation the world has ever known.' California Democrat Nancy Pelosi declared that America is 'the greatest country that ever existed on the face of the earth.'[2]

The 'greatest nation on earth' has the greatest constitution on the planet. In a 1999 survey, 85% of those questioned thought the Constitution is the major reason why 'America has been successful during the last century'.[3]

Capra's montage, however, does something more than repeat the convention – it accurately conveys the veneration of history and heroes that invests the nation they founded with a messianic sanctity. Or as historian Michael Schudson puts it: 'From the time of the founding fathers there [has] been a sacred aura about the Constitution, manifest in holiday political rhetoric.' During the years between the world wars, when Capra was making his most successful films, worship of the Constitution 'acquired the trappings of a religious cult'.[4] Nor did the trend end there. Confidence in the pure and perfect original conception of the Constitution remains 'an article of faith in America's civic religion', says Daniel Lazare.[5] And the sacred can be carried even further. As former Speaker of the House of Representatives Newt Gingrich explained, for many Americans 'our nation was founded by our Creator',[6] a statement of the ultimate apotheosis where nation as civic religion is transmuted to religious icon pure and simple.

At the heart of America as nation, then, is a sacred text, the Constitution that framed its system of government. But the whole purpose of *Mr Smith Goes to Washington* is to explore a basic paradox. The film's narrative juxtaposes the sacred ideal with the grim reality of what actually happens in the nation's capital, how 'the best form of government ever offered to the world' really operates. Jefferson Smith must be a hero because politics is in hock to vested interests; machine politics operates not of, by and for the people but at the behest of moneyed bosses who own and run the politicians. Where Jeff Smith wants to build a boys' camp to teach American ideals to city children in the pure and clean wilderness, the political boss of his state, Taylor, wants government money to build an unnecessary dam on this same piece of land which he has been buying under proxy names to sell at a profit. The great climax of the film is

Smith's filibuster: 'the American privilege of free speech in its most dramatic form ... In the diplomatic gallery are the envoys of two dictator powers. They have come here to see what they can't see at home. Democracy in Action.' Smith will talk till he drops to deny the false accusation that he, not boss Taylor, owns the disputed land. But getting his message to the people beyond the Senate Chamber, faithfully recreated on the film set, is blocked. Taylor controls the local media, his hirelings use strong-arm tactics to prevent even *Boys' Stuff* speaking the truth – 'children are being hurt all over the state' – and police use fire hoses to disperse pro-Smith demonstrations. Even when this manipulation of public opinion brings sacks full of condemnation for Smith, he refuses to yield because he is fighting for a higher 'lost cause', one of the insistent themes of the film. The Senate, Smith says, needs to look at the nation through the eyes of lady Liberty who stands atop the Capitol Dome, to see 'what man's carved out for himself after centuries of fighting ... so he can stand on his own two feet free and decent, like he was created no matter what his race, color or creed ... Great principles don't get lost once they come to light. They're right here.' The resolution of the film belongs to the senior Senator, Paine, who all along has been doing Taylor's bidding, introducing the legislation on the dam knowing it to be graft, so that he 'could sit in the Senate and serve the people in a thousand honest ways'. As a result, their state has the lowest unemployment and the highest federal grants. 'But, well, I've had to make compromises ... You can't count on the people voting. Half the time they don't vote anyway. That's how states and empires have been built since time began.' Shamed by the champion of lost causes, Paine first attempts suicide and then bursts into the Senate Chamber to recant and declare that Smith has been telling the truth all along.

There is much debate among film critics about Capra's pessimism, individualism, populism and veneration of the great leader syndrome to determine exactly what constitutes the political philosophy wrapped in his sentimentality. But such earnest debate seems rather beside the point. The crux of *Mr Smith Goes to Washington* is the perennial topicality of the juxtaposition of an ideal worshipped with the trappings of religious fervour and the cynical reality it brings forth. To debate the nature of the political philosophy that can, should or ought to redeem the pure and original concept suggests that the problem lies in human nature, and misses a more fundamental question – whether the declarations, documents, institutions and process constructed at a particular time in history genuinely deserve to lay claim to being the ultimate expression of those ideals. And that is exactly the problem of America as nation. Capra makes films that endorse American nationalism, the civic religion of constitutional faith. But his subject matter is another example of history mutating into a lie, another variation on John Ford's dictum: 'When the legend becomes fact, print the legend.'

The essence of America's constitutional faith is the consensus that its ideals are so self-evident and inalienable that they never need to be critically examined. 'Freedom is a trust fund inherited at birth and certain to last a lifetime.'[7] Or as Lee Greenwood phrases it: 'I'm proud to be an American where at least I know I'm free.'[8] The mythologising of the Constitution means that ideals and reality can perpetually be at odds and never become a legitimate topic of debate. For in Capra fashion, the people are always at fault, the system perfect. As the Sterling Professor Emeritus of Political Science at Yale, Robert A. Dahl, puts it:

> Public discussion that penetrates beyond the Constitution as a national icon is virtually non-existent. Even when in-depth analysis does occur – mainly among constitutional scholars in schools of law and departments of political science and history – the Constitution as a whole is rarely tested against democratic standards in other advanced democratic countries.[9]

Or even when it is, in a useful student handbook such as John W. Kingdon's *America the Unusual*, the received civic religion is explored to vindicate the general belief which Kingdon ascribes to his students, that: '(1) the United States is the norm and (2) the United States is best.'[10] American exceptionalism, he argues, is the gift of the Constitution. The premise established at the outset by the Founding Fathers is what has delivered the conceptual and material benefits that are the nation.

But there is another way of thinking about the Constitution:

> Why should we feel bound today by a document produced more than two centuries ago by a group of fifty-five mortal men, actually signed by only thirty-nine, a fair number of whom were slaveholders, and adopted in only thirteen states by the votes of fewer than two thousand men, all of whom are long since dead and mainly forgotten?[11]

Especially when it produced a system of government fashioned not out of a coherent unified political theory but the expediency of contemporary political compromise, and characterised by being the 'most opaque, complex, confusing and difficult to understand of any advanced democratic country'.[12] Clearly this is heresy of the civic religion. All Americans know, for this is what they are taught, that their Constitution was the work of wise and honest men who examined all systems of government that had gone before. Their careful scrutiny produced a system of limited government by means of the separation of powers between co-equal branches – legislative, executive and judicial – each elected or appointed for different terms to act as checks and balances on one another and thus ensure the fundamental rights and liberties of the citizen. However, historian Garry Wills argues that the historical and constitutional evidence constantly used to justify this view 'is largely bogus'. None of the terms used to describe the Constitution actually occurs in the un-amended original document.[13] Not surprisingly, it is 'one of the most successful mythologizings of a large historical sequence that can be found in all of history'.[14]

Dahl argues that there are a number of serious problems inherent in the Constitution. It is worth exploring them in detail for the insight they provide on the constitutional conundrum that is America's idea of democracy. The Declaration of Independence of 1776 proudly proclaimed 'all men are created equal'. But the Constitution written in 1787 definitively does not incorporate that principle. Not only does it tolerate slavery, it expressly requires slaves who escape to free states to be returned to their masters, whose property they remain – the exact point made in the Supreme Court's 7–2 majority decision in the Dred Scott case of 1857: 'the right of property in a slave is distinctly and expressly affirmed in the Constitution.'[15] Slaves, according to the calculations required by the Constitution, count as three-fifths of a person for the purpose of allocating seats in the House of Representatives to white Southerners. It took the bloodiest war in American history to see the end of slavery. The combined total of battle deaths and deaths from other causes for the Civil War is 558,052, while the same figure for the US in the Second World War is 407,316. War was the necessary resolution because the Constitution provided no means by which Congress could abolish slavery.

The Constitution did not guarantee a popular democracy, the most obvious reason being that it does not guarantee the right to vote. The qualifications for voting are matters left to the individual states. This principle was reiterated by the majority of members of the Supreme Court in the case of *Bush v Gore* in 2000, when they declared that voters have no fundamental right to vote. The abolition of slavery, for example, did not automatically enfranchise African Americans. Southern states found numerous devices to prevent such an eventuality by, for example, granting a vote only to those whose grandfathers had been voters. The 'Jim Crow Laws', as these various machinations are known, were not fully overturned until the Civil Rights Act of 1964. But as the 2000 election demonstrated, the state's power to control the franchise can still reconstruct Jim Crow intentions. Many states deny the vote to anyone who has been convicted of a felony, even after they have served their sentence. Florida's drive to purge its voter register before the 2000 election led to widespread disenfranchisement of the innocent unconvicted as well as those who had convictions. It is alleged that there was a failure to check properly on the identity of those purged from the Florida rolls when names were cross-checked with lists of people convicted in other states. Near matches of names were in some instances sufficient, while in other cases plain error led to people who had never had a conviction for anything being struck off. Since America incarcerates a disproportionate percentage of African Americans, the consequence was a disproportionate number of African Americans being denied the opportunity to vote, both according to law and thanks to slipshod administrative 'mistakes'. Even more interesting, press reporting of this aspect of the Florida debacle occurred first in Britain – the story was broken by BBC TV's *Newsnight* programme – before being mentioned in America, and was never a major issue of the Florida story. True, the whole world, at the time, was fixated by the condition of chad – hanging, dimpled or pregnant – but this only demonstrates the precariousness of the most basic of democratic rights: how a vote, should you have one, is to be cast. American confidence in the perfection of their democratic freedoms is so abundant that the technicalities of how it actually works need never be a matter of concern. There is no uniform system of voting across the nation. Government funding to revamp the voting procedures is entirely dependent on state implementation. The desire for high-tech answers to the arcane Victorian concern with chads looks likely to produce ATM-style electronic voting which may leave no paper trail to enable results to be scrutinised for mechanical error or deliberate interference.

When myth becomes the medium of national discourse and self-identity, when myth assures people that their rights are self-evidently in place, questioning the mechanics of freedom becomes redundant. So, having no absolute guarantee of suffrage, nearly one third of Americans are not even registered to vote. Meanwhile, the United States ranks 139th in the world in voter turn-out in national elections since 1945, according to statistics cited by the Center for Voting and Democracy in its Claim Democracy campaign.[16] In presidential elections, voter participation hovers worryingly around the 50% mark; declining voting trends among young people suggest it is destined in time to make participatory democracy less than a half measure. Apart from presidential elections, voters have less and less chance of voting for change. In 2002, only four incumbents in the House of Representatives actually lost their seats, the lowest number ever. Far from being a ringing endorsement of satisfaction, it probably has a great deal to do with redrawing constituency boundaries to favour incumbents, a regular legislative chore. Some 40% of state legislative elections since 1996 have not been contested by both major parties; the trend of candidates returned unopposed is creeping its way to another half measure. In short, when it comes to voting, America has what the Center for Voting and Democracy terms 'a democracy deficit'.

Disregard for who votes or how their votes are achieved is the legitimate legacy of the Constitution. It provided no direct mechanism for citizens to vote for the President. This was a matter of design to insulate the chief executive from both popular majorities and congressional control. To this end, all registered Americans who actually vote in presidential elections cast their ballot for citizens who will make up the Electoral College. The Electoral College is determined on a state-by-state basis with the number of electors from each state allocated according to the state's number of seats in the House of Representatives and Senate. Since all states, no matter what their population, have two seats each in the Senate, the worth of votes in the Electoral College varies according to where a voter lives. The vote of a resident of Wyoming is worth almost four times the vote of a resident of California, and the ten smallest states choose two to three times as many electors as they would if allocated strictly in proportion to population. The system of selecting the chief executive was the last measure adopted by the Constitutional Convention, and hastily agreed without considering the implications by people anxious to leave the sweltering confines of the convention in Philadelphia. Twelve years later, in the election of 1800, the inherent flaws in this system were revealed when it looked as if nobody might be elected either President or Vice President after an inordinate number of repeated ballots in smoke-filled rooms. After more than 30 ballots, Thomas Jefferson emerged as President and his running mate Aaron Butt Vice President. A twelfth amendment to the Constitution was hastily passed, calling for separate ballots for President and Vice President. But this did not resolve the problem of the Electoral College, which continues to exist. The intention to secure an independent body to select the President succumbed to the horror of 'factions', dominance by organised political parties, that the framers so disliked. But it has not succumbed to the spirit of democracy. On four occasions the design of the system has delivered an Electoral College majority for the candidate with the least number of popular votes across the country as a whole. Before November 2000 this was the kind of permutation political commentators talked about to fill in and divert the audience during the long hours of election night broadcasts. But November 2000 was the fourth example of the framers' inability to foresee and devise a system amenable to a modern concept of democracy.

According to the Constitution, Senators were not to be chosen by the people at all. Their election was to be the concern of state legislatures. Once again, this provision was designed to insulate the members of the upper house from the passions of popular majorities and deliver a chamber responsive to the needs of property holders. It is part of what one is tempted to describe as the Cromwellian instincts of those who framed the Constitution. For all the myth of patient study of systems of governance through all history, it is hard to miss the predominant influence and example on which the framers drew. Those who settled America included considerable numbers supportive of the ideas that produced the Revolution in Britain of the 1640s. Indeed, some Americans set sail back across the Atlantic to fight in that Revolution, in support of the rights of the 'Commons in Parliament assembled' to be consulted in the decisions, especially in matters of taxation, made by the monarchy. As the British Empire in the late 18th century strove to devise means to raise revenue in America, sections of its population chafed and bridled much in the way that the English had before them, contributing to the costs of the system of governance under which they lived being as unwelcome then as it has ever proved. The English Revolution produced a cauldron of libertarian thought: the Levellers, Muggletonians, Fifth Monarchy Men and many more. The Levellers were brutally put down by Oliver Cromwell, the great upholder and uplifter of men of property, the rising yeoman class that became the middle classes who dominated British life – until the later 20th century when Tony Blair declared 'we are all middle-class now'. It was men of property, according to Ireton, Cromwell's son-in-law, who alone had a natural interest in citizenship and government. It is hard not to see this mindset at work in the deliberations of the Constitutional Convention, though it would be wrong not to notice that Philadelphia had its share of those who hankered after an upper chamber of vaguely aristocratic pretensions modelled on the British House of Lords; just as there were those who toyed with the idea of instituting a monarchy. Senators selected by state legislatures to serve for a period of six years would serve as a check on the House Representatives selected for two-year terms by popular election.

The Senate itself was designed around the nub of the Constitutional Convention's most serious problem: equal representation for small states. The issue turned on their perennial concern of how minorities were to be protected from their liberties being overwhelmed by popular majorities, confidence in majoritarian democracy not being the spirit of the Convention.

It resulted in the Connecticut Compromise, by which all states would have two representatives in the Senate no matter what their population. Dahl comments:

> Although the arrangement failed to protect the fundamental rights and interests of the most deprived minorities, some strategically placed and highly privileged minorities – slaveholders, for example – gained disproportionate power over government policies at the expense of less privileged minorities.[17]

Another endemic problem provided by the Constitution is its failure to limit the powers of the judiciary to declare unconstitutional laws that have been properly passed by Congress and signed by the President. Dahl notes: 'What the delegates intended in the way of judicial review will remain forever unclear; probably many delegates were unclear in their own minds, and to the extent that they discussed the question at all, they were not in full agreement.'[18] By virtue of this opacity, the power of the Supreme Court was established in 1803 by the case of *Marbury v Madison*. The extremely political Chief Justice John Marshall, who had formerly been Secretary of State during John Adams's presidency, issued the politically astute opinion which has ever since defined the power of the unelected judiciary, selected by the President and serving for life. Marshall declared: 'it is the province ... of the judicial department to say what the law is.' The Constitution, he argued, was a product of the people's exercise of their original right to establish the principles of their government. This 'very great exertion' could not and should not be frequently repeated. Thus, Marshall established fundamental principles of supreme authority, with the Constitution being superior to any ordinary legislative act. Judicial review was established, and its exercise in time would amount to what Dahl terms 'judicial policy making – or, if you like, judicial legislation'. For example, by its 7–1 ruling in the case of *Buckley v Valeo* of 1976, the Supreme Court established the dynamics of money politics. It ruled that the First Amendment guarantee of freedom of expression was impermissibly infringed by the limits placed by the Federal Election Campaign Act on the amounts that candidates for federal office and their supporters might spend to promote their election. Campaign finance reform is a perennial topic of discussion and legislative initiative is invoked in sober and sincere tones by politicians of all persuasions – but this has made no headway, nor dented the ever increasing amounts of money required to participate in the American democratic process. And by judicial review in *Bush v Gore* in 2000, the Supreme Court effectively appointed the President, supposedly the only official elected by the whole citizenry of the United States.

The Constitution also limited the powers of Congress in ways that prevented it from regulating or controlling the economy. On this point, Dahl observes: 'unless the constitution could be altered by amendment or by heroic reinterpretation of its provisions ... it would prevent representatives of later majorities from adopting the policies they believed were necessary to achieve efficiency, fairness, and security in a complex post-agrarian society.'[19] The introduction of income tax required a constitutional amendment in 1913. But judicial review has had wide-ranging impact on economic and social legislation. Regulation of the weekly minimum hours a worker could work was deemed by the Court in *Lochner v New York* of 1905 to be an improper interference with liberty of contract. In 1995, Chief Justice William Rehnquist authored a majority opinion that announced the Supreme Court's intention to define an outer limit on Congress's legislative authority under the Commerce Clause. And in the case of *United States v Lopez*, this principle was put into action when the Gun-Free School Zones Act of 1990 was struck down on the grounds that it did not regulate a commercial activity and did not require that a firearm be connected to interstate commerce.

The myth that has grown around the work of the 55 men who framed the Constitution is that they have given the nation something, like the Ten Commandments, that was inspired and built to last for ever. They have become the Founding Fathers – a term redolent of Biblical overtones befitting a tradition already established as part of the self-identity of those who settled America. However, the document they produced said nothing whatsoever about rights and liberties of the citizen. The Bill of Rights is contained in the ten amendments to the original Constitution, passed in 1791. So when Americans speak of their right of free speech, assembly, religion and the press, their right to a jury trial and due process and freedom from excess bail or fines or cruel and unusual punishment, they refer to changes deemed necessary to the original design of the Constitution. There have been 27 amendments to the Constitution, and various failed attempts, yet the sacred aura of immutability still settles over the document and the system it constructed to serve the society of the late 18th century.

How Americans think about their Constitution is a function of myth that constrains and limits debate about how governance should be understood and operated in the realities of society in the 21st century and beyond. The myth goes a long way to explain why Americans have so little interest in comparing the performance and development – or its lack – of their system with that of other advanced democratic societies. Take, for example, the fact that America's Bill of Rights is modelled in large part on the Bill of Rights of 1688 which became the basis of Britain's constitutional settlement in what is known as the Glorious Revolution. The seventh provision of the 1688 Bill of Rights (An Act Declaring the Rights and Liberties of the Subject and Setling the Succession of the Crowne) states: 'That the subjects which are Protestants may have Arms for their Defence suitable to their Conditions and as allowed by Law.' The US Second Amendment of 1791 states: 'A well regulated militia, being necessary to the security of a free State, the right of the people to keep and bear

Arms, shall not be infringed.' The two provisions are not dissimilar, but the legislative context and concept of governance in which they occur have served their respective societies differently over time. While scions of the aristocracy and moneyed classes in Britain possess arms to seasonally slaughter such game and wildlife as they choose, and farmers and sportspersons are licensed to own guns, the generality of the British population, especially the urban population, find gun ownership and even an armed police force unnecessary. Armed criminal activity and gun murders have regularly led to greater and greater restriction of gun ownership and increased scrutiny and supervision of those permitted to own guns. In contrast, the American restatement of the principle admits of no agreed definition of what kind of a right is established, and contains no obvious possibility of any means of preventing high-tech rapid-kill light artillery weapons being owned by teenagers. In America the issue of gun control turns not on the question of public safety, or that what may have been appropriate in the circumstances of the late 18th century is less applicable or prudent in the 21st century, but on the legitimacy of governance. Where the Constitution rules, little can be changed: the right of the electorate to determine how they will govern themselves has rather serious limits.

The Constitution has, however, been amended to answer changing perceptions of the needs of society over time. On the subject of alcohol consumption, for example, the American public made up its mind and then changed it back again – the 18th Amendment of 1919 which introduced Prohibition being overturned by the 21st in 1933 which repealed it. Not all constitutional amendments are as easy. Senators are no longer elected by state legislatures. But equal representation in the Senate for small states is a conundrum beyond the system to rectify – on the principle that turkeys are unlikely to vote for either Christmas or Thanksgiving. The majority needed in the Senate – of 67 votes – is beyond attainment among 50 variously populated states, some of whose representatives would disappear if equal representation were introduced. Legislation to abolish the Electoral College, for example, was passed with 83% of the votes in the House of Representatives (338–70) in 1989 but foundered in the Senate, succumbing to the 'democracy in action' of a filibuster. Hundreds of other such proposals have met a similar fate.

The greatest practical departure from constitutional design has been in the role, authority and influence of the presidency. It is the presidency that makes America unique among advanced democracies. The President combines the roles of monarch and prime minister, being both head of state and the chief executive. The symbolism and mystique of the presidency, the deference and veneration for the office, began with George Washington, the first president. Washington was the hero of the Revolution, the leader of the Continental Army who persevered and held his ragged force together in the darkest of days to eventually secure the independence of the nation. Washington was an iconic figure to his contemporaries, and has remained the iconic American. He is mythologised and hagiographied; and the mantle of heroic character constructed around him sets the standard for all subsequent incumbents. So the cult of the presidency is at least as hallowed as that of the Constitution. But the President is also the chief executive and increasingly a figure of combative party politics, ever since 1912 when Woodrow Wilson broke convention and became the first presidential candidate to campaign on his own behalf. Yet, according to the Constitution, the only legitimate representative of the popular will is Congress. This view was challenged by Andrew Jackson, the seventh president (1829–37) and the first to term himself simply a Democrat, the party label which endures to this day. Jackson justified his use of the presidential veto against congressional majorities on the grounds that he was the only national official elected by all the people and not merely fractions of electors in each state. Therefore, the President represented all the people, an idea easily encrusted on the symbolic meaning of the office as ritual head of state. Jackson, another war hero, ushered in the Era of the

Common Man, otherwise known as Jacksonian democracy: standing up for the little guy against the vested interests of wealth – a prototype of the Capraesque hero. But as one historian has commented, 'the common man appears to have gotten very little of whatever it was that counted for much' as a consequence.[20] Jackson's presidential activism and populism changed very little of the nation's social structure. In 1820, the wealthiest citizens of the large cities held roughly 25% of the nation's wealth. By 1850, they held 50%. Nor was there much social mobility: roughly 90% of the wealthy were descended from families of affluence and social position, only 2% had been born poor, and the wealthy were the most likely to hold public office. What Jackson did achieve was the most brutal mass violation of human rights in American history with the Indian Removal Act of 1830, designed to remove native peoples to west of the Mississippi. But the Indians were neither citizens nor created equal, propositions that the American system has had continuing difficulties coming to terms with. Jackson's assertion of the presidential mandate was bitterly attacked but became the principle followed by future activist presidents: Lincoln, Cleveland, Theodore Roosevelt, Wilson, and most conclusively Franklin D. Roosevelt. Dahl terms this development a 'pseudo-democratisation', 'little more than a myth created to serve the political purposes of ambitious presidents'.[21] It has not inhibited post-Second World War presidents from developing the 'leadership issue' as central not only to setting the agenda of American politics, but for the world itself, as de facto leaders of the free world. It has also emboldened a number of them to exercise the most awesome power of any leader and take their citizens into combat without ever obtaining an actual declaration of war; war powers, according to the Constitution, clearly being lodged in the Congress.

The iconic sacred aura of the Constitution prevents Americans from either examining its limitations or discussing its problematic attributes. So what the American people say they want is not necessarily what their democratic system can or will deliver. At which point the opacity, complexity, arcane workings and modern accretions of their system leaves the question of accountability entirely unaccountable. Is the failure to translate campaign rhetoric into legislation, policy and programme action the failure of the House of Representatives, the Senate, the presidency, the individual states, or of judicial oversight by the Supreme Court? The inability to fulfil promises or be held accountable translates into the conventional mass political participation sport of assigning blame elsewhere within the system – in the blame game there genuinely are co-equal branches to government. The system itself is the only thing never examined, blamed or called upon to descend from its mythic pinnacle of perfection, to be the subject of democratic reconsideration.

But the greatest paradox in American attitudes to their nation is neither the sacralising of the Constitution nor the endless recitation of idealised rhetoric about rights, liberties and democracy as empowering of the popular will. The greatest paradox is that the whole panoply of myth has been constructed out of arguments made *against* the Constitution by its opponents in order to advance the first law of American mythology: fear is essential, in this case fear of government. Having been presented with the best government 'ever offered to the world', Americans from across the entire political spectrum have from the outset heartily loathed the 'necessary evil' they unleashed. This attitude is as American as apple pie and, well, the Constitution itself. When it comes to governance, Americans applaud democracy with schizophrenic paranoia. Government is a zero sum game in which any operation of democratic institutions subtracts from the rights and liberties of the individual. Garry Wills describes this as 'a constant in American history – the fear of government, sometimes sensible, sometimes hysterical, but always pronounced'.[22]

It was Thomas Paine, the English jobbing radical, who termed government a necessary evil: 'Government, even in its best state, is but a necessary evil; in its worst state, an intolerable one.' Paine, born at Thetford in Norfolk in 1737, was the kind of itinerant agitprop instigator who was excellent at arguing and justifying revolution against the established order of his day, but a less than comfortable free-thinker for those who inherited the ensuing revolutions. He was a genuine inheritor of the radical ideals of the English Revolution, and it was fashionable for the ruling class in England to have the letters T and P nailed into the soles of their shoes so they could walk on Tom Paine, as well as having him tried *in absentia* for seditious libel. In France, he was imprisoned and sentenced to death by Robespierre even though he was a member of the revolutionary National Convention. In America, he articulated the common-sense propositions that led Americans to declare their independence. But he is also the Founding Father described by Theodore Roosevelt as a dirty little atheist. He was not the kind of free-thinker whose ideas sat well with the Federalist faction. He is condemned as a deist, at best, was an opponent of slavery, supporter of social security and convinced that inequitable ownership of land was the root cause of social injustice.

Why has Paine's epithet come to condition American attitudes to government? How, over time, did attacks on the Constitution become descriptions of it? And how did 'largely bogus' ideas about the Constitution come to be the received civic education and civic religion of America? 'We are pious', writes Wills, 'toward our history in order to be cynical toward our government. We keep summoning the founders to testify against what they founded. Our very liberty depends so heavily on distrust of government that the government itself, we are constantly told, was constructed to instil that distrust.'[23] According to Wills, 'the manifestations of fear of government are so numerous as to make it an American tradition (almost but not quite, *the* American tradition)'.[24]

Fear of government is as prevalent on the right as on the left of American politics. It was as much a part of the anti-war radicalism of the 1960s as the neo-conservative upsurge of the

1990s. Wills argues that it is accompanied by a characteristic set of attitudes: that government as a necessary evil should be kept to a minimum and that legitimate social activity should be provincial, amateur, authentic, spontaneous, candid, homogeneous, traditional, popular, organic, rights-oriented, religious, voluntary, participatory and rotational – or, in other words, the Jefferson Smith approach. An alternative set of attitudes about government also exists, in which government is seen as a positive good that should be cosmopolitan, expert, élite, mechanical, duties-oriented, secular, regulatory and delegative, with a division of labour. Bernard Bailyn, doyen of American historians, characterises these positions as idealist and realist respectively, and argues that they have been alternating mindsets through American history, but that America works best when they are not seen as antitheses of one another, but integrated in a balanced approach.[25] It sounds rather like suggesting that someone with bipolar disorder is fine so long as they take their medication. And if it is possible to identify periods in American history when the medication has worked, it is increasingly difficult to detect evidence of a treatable condition in the ever more stridently acrimonious and deeply divided political map of America, where both sides may fear government but fear the other side's control of government even more.

Beyond party politics – the contest for control of what kind of government is deemed evil but necessary or a positive good – America has spawned increasing numbers of citizens formed into militia bands who feel so threatened by their fear of government in the land of the free that they are prepared to take arms against it. 'The modern militia movement, far from thinking itself outside the law, believes it is the critical force making for a restoration of the Constitution.'[26] Armed groups of Americans are prepared to exercise their constitutional right to bear arms in the name of the restoration of the pure and original meaning of the document which created their form of government in the first place. And in so doing they have taken their place as a familiar plot scenario in endless series on American television. Such series as *Law and Order* and *JAG* have visited the militia mindset. The incidents at Ruby Ridge and Waco, where violent response by agents of the government created militia martyrs, have been variously rendered into television drama. The Oklahoma City bombing in which 168 people were killed is the most graphic example of how far home-grown constitutional terrorists were prepared to go, before being submerged in the greater fear of the war on international terrorism. The fear of government infringing the liberties of the citizen in the wake of 9/11, however, has shifted from the preserve of the right to the cause of the left, coalescing in their opposition to the Patriot Acts.

The rising tide of paranoia about government called forth a new breed of politician, those who participated in the electoral coup of 1994 when Newt Gingrich led a triumphant sweep to Republican control of the House of Representatives on the platform of the 'Contract With America'. It mobilised a whole new cadre with a political agenda that promised to dismantle whole agencies, undo regulatory boards, abolish long-term government service, and cut off government subsidies to the arts, to farmers, to welfare recipients. It was based on fear and loathing of 'big government' that was read back into the Constitution and offered as its only true and original meaning. So to fulfil the intent of the Founding Fathers, the adherents of the 'Contract With America' wanted amateur citizen legislators adhering to term limits, as opposed to professional politicians who simply kept on being elected again and again and were thereby tainted by Washington, lobbyists and money politics. Similarly, they wanted to abolish as much taxation as they possibly could, and strict constructionism (adherence to the literal meaning of the words and phrases of the Constitution) to limit government action and interpretation by the judiciary. Daniel Lazare saw a parallel between the Gingrich revolution and certain demonised Others:

All those Republican House freshmen in early 1995 who could be seen sporting copies of the Federalist Papers were not all that different from Iranian mullahs waving copies of the Koran. At a time when the world was changing all around them, their only response was to close their eyes, fold their hands, and trust in the wisdom of the patriarchs.[27]

The Contract With America had little success and did not last long. But the zealous fervour it unleashed survives. There is a growing clamour, not of heated political debate but intolerance of opposing views. The terms Liberal and Conservative have become terms of abuse. Are you now or have you ever been a liberal? is a question an aspiring candidate will balk at answering directly or, preferably, at all. To be a liberal is to subscribe to a vision of government activism that true constitutional faith deems untenable. And when liberalism includes being pro-choice on abortion and in favour of gay rights, it is positively a case of being asked to vote for sin. Acrimony and intolerance foreclose the possibility of debate about the Constitution, the meaning of democracy or the accountability and efficacy of governance. And faith in the Constitution, the symbols and meaning of the nation, throws up contentious issues but disturbs not at all either the fear of government or the proposition that America is the greatest nation because it has the best government ever offered to the world.

The constitutional faith in limited government makes little sense when throughout most of its history government has been the chief agent of the nation's territorial and economic advance. 'The westward course of American empire was conceived and organised as a public-works project, entirely dependent (then as now) on the government dole', argues Lewis Lapham.[28] The federal treasury funded railroads, dams, forts, river channels, mining, fishing rights, irrigation canals, as well as opening vast tracts of government land to all comers who would stake a claim. 'The West was won less by the force of independent mind than by the lying government contract, the crooked lawsuit, the worthless Indian treaty.'[29] The government has acted to protect and secure the interest of American business abroad, mobilising its forces to effectively operate the economy of foreign countries by taking charge of their customs and excise arrangements, as happened in, for example, Nicaragua, as we will examine in detail in Chapter Three. War has seen government contracts found new technologies and subsidise the birth of new industries. The American economy without the military-industrial complex would be an ailing shadow of itself, while government protection and promotion for both dying and coming sectors of industry remains as important as ever: from steel tariffs to genetically modified crops, supplied as aid to starving nations whether they want them or not and no matter what, or Aids aid so long as countries buy American-produced drugs and not generics produced in other countries. In sharp contradiction to this immense activism by government that sucks the wealth of the world like energy into a black hole and makes Americans more and more affluent, stands the fear of government, and the anti-government values it generates. These anti-government values, justified in the name of constitutional faith, produce real victims: 'the millions of poor or shelterless or medically indigent who have been told, over the years, that they must lack care or life support in the name of their very own freedom. Better for them to starve than to be enslaved by "big government". That is the real cost of our antigovernment values.'[30]

If they could look to the other advanced democratic nations, Americans would find that these countries have done much better in creating greater equality and equity, with social provision and regulation, while feeling no great loss of personal freedom. This very different concept of governance has developed and been expanded through their history of struggle against monarchy, aristocracy and even dictatorships. Complaint about taxes, bureaucracy or business regulation is not an American monopoly. It echoes with loud reverberations in every advanced democratic country. But it has not deterred the peoples who did not depart across the Atlantic from developing – through protest, conflict and mutual compromise – systems of government subject to review, renegotiation and accountability to the people. Democracy and democratisation are not just ideals of America – they have formed the history of Europe. The constitutional form of European governance has been a continuing story, no less steeped in history and having in each nation its own myth and traditions invested with national pride. But in Europe it is seen as continually perfectible with and by the exertion of the people, not perfect and immutable.

A day before James Wilson commended the Constitution to a crowd gathered in the yard of the State House in Philadelphia as the best government ever offered to the world, an article appeared in the city's *Independent Gazetteer*. It was written by Samuel Bryan and was the first of his 'Centinel' essays that were republished in newspapers in other states. 'The United States are being melted down', argued Bryan, into a despotic empire dominated by 'well born' aristocrats. The common people, Bryan believed, were in danger of being subjugated to the will of an all-powerful authority, remote and inaccessible to the people, authority of the very kind that Americans had so recently fought a war to rid themselves of. A delegate to the Massachusetts ratifying convention saw the Constitution and the form of government it instituted as the work of aristocratic politicians bent on protecting their own class interests: 'These lawyers, and men of learning and moneyed men ... that make us illiterate people swallow down the pill ... they will swallow up all the little folks like the great Leviathan; yes, just as the whale swallowed up Jonah!'[31] It seems that the predictions of these American forebears have been fulfilled.

The nation that is America began with a growing unwillingness among some settlers to accept the impositions of the British Empire of which they were increasingly provincial citizens. Without a powerful lobby in the counsels of London, their lack of representation was seen by these colonists as decision-making without consultation. At the time, the only American with Europe-wide fame and reputation was Benjamin Franklin. On 17 March 1783, Franklin wrote in a letter to his friend Bishop Shipley:

> America will, with God's blessing, become a great and happy country; and England, if she has at length gained wisdom, will have gained something more valuable, and more essential to her prosperity, than all she has lost; and will still be a great and respectable nation. Her great disease at present is the numerous and enormous salaries and emoluments of office. Avarice and ambition are strong passions and, separately, act with great force on the human mind; but when both are united, and may be gratified in the same object, their violence is almost irresistible, and they hurry men headlong into factions and contentions, destructive of good government. As long, therefore, as these great emoluments subsist, your Parliament will be a stormy sea, and your public councils confounded by private interests. But it requires much public spirit and virtue to abolish them; more than perhaps can now be found in a nation so long corrupted.

'Thus Franklin', notes Gore Vidal in his *Inventing a Nation*, 'describing England of 1783, nicely described the United States of 2003'.[32]

All nations have their mythic history and myths surrounding and encrusting their national identity. The test for any nation is how it negotiates with its tradition to adapt to changing times and the changed perceptions of how rights, liberties and the possibilities of governance by individuals and society collectively can be fulfilled. Where governance is caught in the schizophrenia of simultaneous adoration and contempt, and government itself is both the highest expression of national identity and a perennial source of fear for the individual, the nation is not just conflicted

– it is permanently divided against itself. Such a nation has more to learn from others than it can offer as a model of how an equal, accountable and efficient society can be built elsewhere.

For film critics there is something both passé and disturbing in Frank Capra's view of politics. We find it hard to escape the conclusion that *Mr Smith Goes to Washington* is a vision caught in the time warp of the 'frozen republic' – the title of Daniel Lazare's assault on the civic religion of America. The American Dream is delivering a more inequitable society with increasing poverty washing around ever more entrenched and rising islands of wealth that are associated with increasing power and influence over policy-making and government. Meanwhile, the working of the rules of American mythology have made Capra's solution more, not less, prevalent. The corruption of government has been a central American concern since the beginning of the nation. Capra's answer was to bring in a hero, an innocent idealist to purge the money changers from the temple of democracy. His view seems to have won democratic endorsement as *the* way of American politics. The basic appeal to the electorate of Presidents Jimmy Carter, Ronald Reagan, Bill Clinton and George W. Bush was that they were outsiders, idealists from beyond Washington, untainted by Washington business as usual. Once elected, all, in their own ways, have been able to play the blame game of the political, for which one should read constitutional, logjam. And in 2004 the ultimate outsider made the Capra ploy his political platform, and the citizens of California elected Arnold Schwarzenegger as their Governor. Schwarzenegger and his supporters have made no secret of their presidential ambitions. Discussing the detail of what constitutional faith in democracy brings America as the governance of the nation may be impossible. But amending the Constitution to enable a foreign-born film actor to aspire to be the next outsider to make Washington live up to its mythic ideals was the first thing political commentators discussed, even before Schwarzenegger was elected Governor. Arnie may yet go to Washington!

CHAPTER THREE

To Have and Have Not: The Imperial Expression of the American Self

Harry Morgan is a tough, independent man of the world. His main interest is making a living. So long as he can make his own way, Harry is content to let the world take care of itself. He is not so much a neutral, apolitical person as largely uninterested in the perplexities of the world at large. But when it comes to people in particular, Harry has what can only be called a good heart and an instinct for tolerance. He takes people as individuals, accepts them for what they are, letting them work out their own destiny, but nevertheless cares for even the most run-down, self-destructive, hopeless cases. There is room in Harry's world for Eddie, the rummy who once was a good man on a boat, just as his instinct for fairness justifies the dollar-a-day employment of Horatio to bait the lines on his fishing boat, even though his clients quibble at the extra expense. Harry may not be judgemental, but he is indisputably a man with a personal code of inner values that define his character. In a crisis, Harry is the kind of person people turn to. He is the resourceful, strong, resilient kind; a man who can handle himself, stare danger in the face and meet trouble with a cool head. Harry is a man the movies have made familiar: the rough diamond, the reluctant hero who is forced by circumstance to reveal his innate nobility. Harry is no idealist. He is a reluctant hero precisely because his inner strength is stirred only to defend those weaker than himself, to stand up to oppression terrorising those who cannot defend themselves. Harry does not go looking for causes. But when confronted by the abuse of decency and fairness, when tyranny, corruption and evil put themselves in his way, he cannot let them pass. Harry Morgan is the hero of Howard Hawks's 1944 film *To Have and Have Not*.

Based on an Ernest Hemingway story, *To Have and Have Not* is famous for being a character piece. Most notably, it was the first cinematic pairing of Humphrey Bogart and the nineteen-year-old Lauren Bacall, the couple providing personal chemistry both on and off the screen. The film is a sizzling exploration of sexual politics from the *auteur* director who specialised in smart, intelligent, witty films exploring the dynamics of gender relationships. From *Twentieth Century* (1934) to *Barbary Coast* (1935), *Bringing Up Baby* (1938), *Only Angels Have Wings* (1939), *His Girl Friday* (1940) and *Ball of Fire* (1942), through *To Have and Have Not*, *The Big Sleep* (1946), *I Was a Male War Bride* (1949), *Monkey Business* (1952) and *Gentlemen Prefer Blondes* (1953), strong women and sexual politics were central to his films. The son of a wealthy Midwestern family, Hawks was raised in California before studying mechanical engineering at Cornell. He served in the Army Air Corps in the First World War, about which he made seminal films: *Dawn Patrol* (1930), *The Road to Glory* (1936) and *Sergeant York* (1941). He also made notable crime dramas such as *Scarface* (1932), and Westerns: *Red River* (1948) and *Rio Bravo* (1959). He collaborated regularly with the novelist William Faulkner, as well as with many of the best writers working in Hollywood such as Jules Fuhrman, Ben Hecht, Nunnally Johnson and Leigh Brackett. And rather like Harry Morgan, Hawks has been quoted as saying: 'I *never* made a statement. Our job is to make entertainment. I don't give a damn about taking sides'; which led Robin Wood to comment:

Nowhere in Hawks' work does he show any interest in Ideas, abstracted from character, action, and situation: he has never evinced any desire to make a film on a given moral or social theme. He has always been quite free of the kind of ambitions or pretensions that most often bring directors into conflict with the commercial interests of production companies. The significance of his films never arises from the conscious treatment of a Subject.[1]

Nevertheless, or perhaps precisely for these reasons, *To Have and Have Not* is a consummate work of American mythology. The film demonstrates clearly how mythology is embedded and encoded, working beneath the surface of action, character and situation, under the radar of conscious intentions and purpose. Mythology also serves when it is not capitalised as The Big Message but diffused within the texture of normality. *To Have and Have Not* is a morality play acted out by world-weary characters with more than a hint of amorality, caught in the events of an immoral time. Its mythic narrative of the reluctant hero works so effectively because it is so entirely secondary to the pyrotechnics of the human drama; it insinuates its coherent set of ideas subliminally. We know we have been entertained. It takes more by way of conscious effort to realise what meanings accompany the entertainment.

Mythic narratives construct identity, they dramatise the set of values that define a sense of self not because they necessarily describe any specific real person but because they reflect the kind of person we think we ought to be, the sort of person we believe we should be, the kind of person we aspire to be. Myths map out grid references of good and evil, better and best, by which we locate events, find explanations and interpret what is happening. We might all like to be a superhero, but few well-balanced individuals actually believe they are or could be such wondrous life forms. But not all heroes are larger than life. It is part of the function of myth to represent the heroism of the ordinary life well lived, to extol the values and virtues that should be part of every individual to enable them in time of need to be heroic and stand for what is right. The reluctant hero is part of the repertoire of American myth, a seminal character whose presence shapes and informs the American psyche, an approachable, manageable hero, the kind of hero who makes people feel good about themselves; a realistic hero, nearer to everyday reality and therefore more human.

Harry Morgan owns a fishing boat, the kind rented out to tourists for sport fishing. The boat is registered in Florida but he plies his trade on the Caribbean island of Martinique, part of the French West Indies in America's backyard. The film begins in the summer of 1940, 'shortly after the fall of France'. Martinique is now controlled by Vichy, the collaborationist French puppet government. Harry Morgan may complain at the petty restrictions imposed by the authorities, but the fate of Europe and its dependants under Nazi control is not his concern. Harry lives at the Marquis Hotel, run by 'Frenchie', a member of the local anti-Nazi resistance who wants to hire him to smuggle key members of the Free French onto the island. 'Not a chance … I'd like to oblige you Frenchie, but I can't afford to get mixed up in your local politics', is Harry's reply. A new arrival at the hotel is Marie Browning, a young American female of dubious globetrotting background, who has ended up broke and stranded on Martinique. The only thing that bothers Harry when he sees Marie, whom he nicknames Slim, pick the pocket of an American tourist is: 'You oughta pick on somebody to steal from that doesn't owe me money.' After rebuffing another request to help the Free French, this time from a delegation of resistance leaders, Harry makes Slim return the tourist's wallet. This tourist was a client who quibbled about his bill and insisted he had to go to the bank for the money to settle up. In fact, his wallet contains enough travellers' cheques – as well as a plane ticket proving he intended to leave without paying. Harry is nobody's fool. Just as the tourist is about to sign over the money, the police turn up seeking the resistance leaders and a gun battle ensues. Amidst the flying bullets the American tourist is killed. 'He couldn't write any faster than he could duck. Another minute and those cheques would have been good', is Harry's epitaph. So now both Harry and Slim are broke, and both have to answer questions from the Vichy Gestapo.

From this point, the incandescent love affair between Harry and Marie, who refer to each other as Steve and Slim (apparently the pet names Howard Hawks and his wife used for each other), takes centre stage. It's an elegant dance with the woman taking the lead, and it culminates in cinema's most famous seduction scene: 'It's even better when you help', Slim explains, before assuring Steve that he doesn't have to act with her or do anything – except maybe whistle: 'You know how to whistle don't you Steve? You just put your lips together and blow.'

But behind the bravura, another dynamic is at work. Harry is affronted by the high-handed arrogance of the Vichy Gestapo and their mistreatment of Slim. While he can smile at her exploits in propositioning other men, he has no intention of accepting the money she offers him as a result. For the sake of buying Slim a ticket to leave Martinique, Harry agrees to help the resistance: 'I need the money now, last night I didn't.' And for Eddie's protection he plans to leave his rummy sidekick behind, but Eddie has other ideas and stows away on the boat. The mission does not go smoothly. A police patrol boat intercepts the boat on the return trip. While the Free French leader shows himself ready to surrender, Harry is busy attempting to shoot out the patrol boat's searchlight. In the exchange of gunfire the resistance leader is wounded. Harry delivers his human cargo as arranged and returns to the hotel to find that Slim has not used her ticket after all.

The wounded resistance leader has been brought to the hotel and needs medical treatment. Once again, Harry is the man everyone turns to. Then word comes that the Gestapo are plying Eddie with drink and asking him questions. Harry intervenes with a cool explanation of a night-time fishing trip and mistaking the police patrol boat for pirates. The Gestapo ask him to consider an offer of money for information and leave. Harry decides it's time they left Martinique for good.

First, he checks on the condition of the wounded resistance leader, De Bursac, who pleads with him to take over the mission that brought him to the island: freeing a 'notorious patriot' from nearby Devil's Island. 'I wish I could borrow your nature for a while, Captain', he tells Harry. 'When you meet danger you never think of anything except how you will circumvent it. The word "failure" does not exist for you.' But Harry is not to be persuaded. At last De Bursac accepts that Harry has done enough: 'This is not his fight, yet. Someday I hope it may be, because we could use him.'

While Harry is making preparations to leave, the Gestapo arrive to inform him they have Eddie in custody, and this time instead of feeding him with drink to make him talk they will withhold it. Harry is appalled: 'You know what that would do to him ... he couldn't stand it, he'd crack up.' With apparent calm, reworking the cigarette and match by-play that runs throughout the film and that serves as a metaphor for the relationship between himself and Slim, Harry gets to his gun, shoots one of the Gestapo and holds the rest at bay. At last, Harry is engaged. And he has turned the tables on his would-be persecutors. He pistol-whips the Gestapo chief who earlier had slapped Slim and now would torment Eddie, to force him to secure Eddie's release and then sign exit passes for them all. And for good measure, after turning the Gestapo over to the resistance Harry promises to complete De Bursac's mission and rescue the patriot from Devil's Island. 'Why are you doing this?' Harry is asked. 'Well, I don't know. Maybe 'cause I like you, maybe 'cause I don't like them.' But whatever his reasoning, Harry, Slim and Eddie are energised and exit purposefully and happy.

To Have and Have Not is more than a story of a man forced to choose between right and wrong by unavoidable circumstances. It is a moral drama about the inner nature, the essential character traits of the reluctant hero, however cynical, hard-boiled and apolitical he may seem. Despite his apparent disinterest, he is the centre to which everyone turns; his resourcefulness and capability is both innate and recognisable to everyone. The capacity to be heroic, however reluctantly, is in his nature. He is an American, and when push comes to overbearing oppression it is Harry who must take resolute action. And if these inner resources make Harry seem familiar, it is because he is a stock character in the Hollywood pantheon. On this occasion he was consciously summoned. The Warner Brothers studio was anxious to capitalise on the success of their 1942 picture *Casablanca*. Harry Morgan is the natural counterpart of Rick Blaine, a fact underlined, reiterated with emphasis, by both roles being immortalised by Humphrey Bogart. The narrative structure of *To Have and Have Not* is a variation on the plot themes of *Casablanca*, one of the most enduring of all Hollywood movies. *Casablanca* wore its message openly, personified in the powerful, articulate presence of Paul Henreid as the resistance leader Victor Laslo, who had to be spirited out of Vichy-controlled North Africa. But the mythic core of the film, its emotive and active centre, is Rick, the reluctant hero. Rick is the innocent American who fell in love and had his heart broken in Paris. He nurses his resentments in Casablanca until 'of all the gin joints in all the world' Ilsa walks into Rick's Place and forces him to determine events. The happiness of two people just doesn't amount to a hill of beans in a world seriously out of moral order. It is Rick who has the inner strength and presence of mind to send Ilsa off with Victor Laslo to play their part in the higher purpose of the times, while Rick turns aside to do his bit. In both films it is the reluctant hero who, once stirred to action, strikes the crucial, decisive blow for right. Both films, in their different styles, encode a portrait, a mythic narration of national character that prefigures the succinct 1998 statement of Secretary of State Madeleine Albright: 'If we have to use force, it is because we are America. We are the indispensable nation.'

To Have and Have Not is a character piece, but its most important character is the mythic persona that represents and justifies America's most favoured self-image and national story. The reluctant hero is the individual microcosm and forebear of a larger narrative: 'the myth of the "reluctant superpower" – Americans asserting themselves only under duress and then always for the noblest purposes – reigns today as the master narrative explaining and justifying the nation's exercise of global power.'[2] In its history, again and again, America sees itself acting on the world stage as Harry Morgan and Rick Blaine. The micro and the macro are unified. It is their nature, their formation in a common set of values, their adherence to founding principles, that makes America/Americans indispensable, forces them to act in a world less able to achieve, sustain and uphold universal ideals of freedom, liberty, democracy and the pursuit of happiness. Cinema echoes, encodes and makes familiar the doctrine of self-justification that transcends differences of era and political party. Like Harry, a non-judgemental, morally upright America is reluctantly forced into doing the right thing. But sometimes one myth exists to distract attention from an even more insistent Big Idea – and that Idea is Law 6 of American mythology: American democracy has the right to be imperial and express itself through empire.

People and nations can and do act as if the myth were fact and end by making myth manifest as reality. American mythic narratives are populated with representative characters whose actions play out the meaning of American ideals and moral consciousness. Justification by myth is an educative process, a conditioning in ways of looking at the world that invests circumstances with significance. But myth-making is also a selective process; what is thrown into sharp relief creates its own shadows. The more diffused, accepted and insistent the myth, the more it conditions the terms of public discourse, how events and circumstances are understood and debated. And in the shadows created lurk alternative understandings and interpretations that are not scrutinised. The myth of the reluctant hero defines and gives identity to the American psyche because it offers a coherent reading of history, the present and the future; it makes national foreign policy an extension of how Americans see themselves as individuals. It presents national character as the natural out-growth of the myth of nation, animated and embodying the same founding principles, and it places both at the centre of events, indispensable because they are motivated by and work only for high purpose, the purpose of what is right and most noble in all of humanity. When Harry Morgan or Rick Blaine enter the cause, which eventually all reluctant heroes are com-pelled to do, they are no longer looking out for number one, nor concerned for their own self-interest. Their self-evident natural nobility precludes questioning what's in it for them. In which case, the reluctant hero is the perfect vehicle for authorising and justifying the activities of empire without ever acknowledging or intimating its existence. The justification by right, individually or as a premise of national policy, relies on idealism being innate, a natural possession at the level of personal and social values, and therefore eradicates all thought of the kind of realpolitik motivating other nations and all previous empires. The reluctant hero, like the reluctant superpower, is by nature a paragon of virtues, a centre to which others turn to initiate action. Therefore any consideration of power relations or self-interest evaporates; the notion of empire passes into the shadows, falls off the agenda of legitimate debate and becomes an affront to the natural goodness of all that defines the self-identity of America. But the disclaimer contained in the myth of reluctance is belied in three distinct ways by American history itself.

First, America was an imperial construct by definition at home. The Founding Fathers of the nation had no compunction whatsoever in setting their sights on empire. They fully intended to take over the imperial mantle of the British Empire they ejected. The initial settlement of America was a work of empire in the old familiar sense – naked, aggressive possession and domination of land and peoples for national self-interest, political aggrandisement and economic enrichment. Appropriately enough, the term 'British Empire' was first coined to describe the project; and its use was justified by clever recourse to myth. Dr John Dee, who first used the term, was one of history's exotics: an advisor to Elizabeth I, a man of letters, he corresponded with all the leading cosmologists and map-makers of his day throughout Europe, as well as being mentor to the Englishmen who took an interest in voyages of exploration and settlement, and he was a notorious alchemist, a mage – a magical master – of dubious reputation. He was also Welsh, which was crucial to the cause of empire. To further the Welsh Tudor dynasty's claim to North America he revived the myth of Madoc, Prince of Gwynedd in North Wales. Madoc supposedly set sail from his native land in the 12th century, found and settled America, thus giving Britain a prior claim to the continent and the right to displace the Spanish Empire founded on the discoveries of the Johnny-comelately Columbus. The proof of this legend was supposedly contained in various reports of the language of the inhabitants of the new lands – they were speaking Welsh. The legend was acted upon as if real, and myth was made manifest as reality in the charters granted by the Crown to the merchant venture companies such as the Virginia Company that undertook settlement of the lands, thus creating the empire. At a later date, Thomas Jefferson, whose family originally came from the area around Snowdonia in Gwynedd, was much taken with the idea of Welsh-speaking Indians. As President, he financed an expedition to explore the vast interior acquired by the Louisiana Purchase of 1803 and asked Lewis and Clark to pay particular attention to finding the descendants of Madoc, reputed to live in there. The most favoured candidates, the Mandan Indians, turned out not to be Welsh-speaking, but the expedition laid the basis for exploitation and settlement of the expanded United States of America.

The justifications for empire, whether of the legendary kind or the ubiquitous belief in the natural right of Christian civilisation to dominate the Earth, conditioned the thinking of all who came to America. Those who were born and raised there under the aegis of the British Empire refashioned these old familiar ideas to appropriate their special and specific claims to the wilderness lands of milk and honey. Those who declared their independence from the British Empire did not give up the imperialist mindset in which they had been raised. It became the refashioned basis for their self-government and domination of the land and its native and dependent peoples. Only in American understanding and mythology had a watershed been crossed. In the practical process of nation-building, America continued to operate just as the ejected British Empire had done. The Revolutionary dividing line was more of an evolutionary exchange of personnel than a radical change. The ideals of self-government applied to only one class of citizens: largely white property-owners, they were a minority of the settlers of the thirteen confederated states when they formed their perfect union; certainly a minority of the population of all the territory that eventually became the continent-straddling United States of America. But the newly created governing class of the Revolutionary republic from the outset had the will, and political intent, to construct an ideology of right and self-justification to dominate the surrounding territories by imperial means. The mythology of nation, the special creation of the United States of America, forms a miasma in which the characteristics of empire become invisible by being internalised as the proper business of national purpose.

The business of laying claim to land by right of settlement, purchase – dubious or otherwise – or questionable treaty with native inhabitants, or by simple annihilation or removal of those inhabitants, is the familiar story of empires throughout history, just as it forms the bare facts of the territorial construction of the United States of America. In all these ways the new Republic continued what the British Empire had begun. The right of conquest and dominance by whatever means makes all territory the property of the state, which then devolves rights in land to its citizens. This is how settler colonies and empires have always operated everywhere; this is how the new American nation operated. Empires operate by state-controlled, -managed and -funded development of the economic exploitation of land and the commercial resources it can produce; investment in infrastructure to aid and facilitate the whole process is state business. Such, as we noted in Chapter Two, is the history of the United States of America. Free citizens in fact expanded the territory and made manifest the nation by the processes of empire. The relations of metropolis and periphery were, in the case of America, internal. Long-distance trade in primary products extracted from the land has always been the basis of empire; it is how the colonies serve the metropolis. This was the economic dynamic of the new Republic. Long-distance trade with Britain remained the foundation of its economy, the search for new long-distance trading opportunities the economic constant of its development. At home, America constructed an economy that required new inputs of land and mineral resources to serve its capital accumulation, and then new markets overseas to absorb the products of its industry. Far from being the type site of opposition to colonies and empires, America was their incarnation.

Second, when America sought to externalise its imperialism it mirrored and matched exactly the conventional ideas of empire of all the imperial powers. The first president, George Washington, saw America as a 'rising empire'. The founding generation of the new Republic had a great concern: they felt constrained and hemmed in by the existence of other imperial possessions surrounding their territory, whose presence they saw as undermining the natural rights of their destiny as a 'rising empire'. In 1778, Samuel Adams told his compatriots: 'We shall never be upon a solid footing till Britain cedes to us what nature designs we should have, or till we wrest it from her.' What, in his view, nature designed for American possession was Canada, Nova Scotia and Florida. 'The unanimous voice of the continent is Canada must be ours; Quebec must be taken', was the opinion of his cousin John Adams, second president of the Republic (1797–1801). But the ambitions of the Republic did not stop there: 'The whole continent of North America appears to be destined by Divine Providence to be peopled by one nation, speaking one language, professing one general system of religious and political principles, and accustomed to one general tenor of social usages and customs', declared John Adams's son, John Quincy Adams, in 1811 before going on to become the sixth president (1825–29). In 1786, Thomas Jefferson had gone even further, arguing that 'our confederacy must be viewed as the nest from which all America, North and South, is to be peopled'. He hoped the waning Spanish Empire would hold on 'till our population can be sufficiently advanced to gain it from them piece by piece'. The lands around the Mississippi, however, 'we must have'. For, according to Jefferson, 'this is all we are as yet ready to receive'. In fact, these lands which comprised the Louisiana Purchase had passed into the possession of the Napoleonic Empire before being acquired by the Republic and becoming what Jefferson termed an 'empire of liberty'.

The terminology and ideology were widespread. In 1789, the year the Constitution of the new Republic came into force, Jedidiah Morse's *American Geography* was published, wherein he speculated: 'we cannot but anticipate the period, as not far distant, when the AMERICAN EMPIRE will comprehend millions of souls, west of the Mississippi.'[3] At the time, the entire population of the newly confederated United States of America was a mere four million. The expansionary urge was in tension with some interpretations of the new constitutional form of government. There were those who argued that territorial expansion would undermine the goals of democratic liberty, presumably by placing the interests and instincts of imperialism before those of local control. But in practice these caveats were swept aside by the tides of 'rising empire', which served the purposes of too many vested interests to admit of serious question. Pushing forward into new lands, from the earliest establishment of the

American colonies, had been a safety valve. If local administration became too burdensome or restrictive, new settlements further out in the wilderness were established. Expanding settlement offered escape from limited economic prospects for new arrivals and the younger generations; for anyone who sought to better their chances of making it, fulfilling the American Dream, the westward frontier beckoned. And the frontier answered a profound and conflated idea at the heart of America: that to fulfil its promise and purpose as the ideal nation it should continually expand both ideologically and physically. *The Boston Herald* in 1789 described the new Constitution as 'nothing less than a hasty stride to Universal Empire in this Western World'.[4]

The classic statement of 'Manifest Destiny', the right 'to overspread the continent allotted by Providence for the free development of our yearly multiplying millions', was not made until 1845 in an article by John L. O'Sullivan. It was, obviously, not an original idea in the sense of a new thought, though most certainly it was original in the sense of being a coherent and quotable restatement of an idea that was present at the founding of the nation. It is also an inherently imperialist statement, a policy objective that could be achieved only by the processes familiar to any empire anywhere at any time in history. The fledgling Republic in its earliest years was prepared to contemplate war with the European imperial powers whose colonies surrounded the 'rising empire', even before it had an effective army or navy. It engaged in a naval war with France, was at war with Britain in 1812 and frequently contemplated war with Mexico before actual hostilities in 1846–48. In 1823, before it had fulfilled its manifest destiny, the Republic had a clear vision of its interests and security as central to events through the whole of the Americas. This was articulated in President James Monroe's seventh annual message to Congress. The 'Monroe Doctrine' views the fate of the entire western hemisphere as a 'principle in which the rights and interests of the United States are involved'. At a time when independence movements were liberating nations of South America from European empires, Monroe declared that 'henceforth' the hemisphere was 'not to be considered as subjects for future colonization by any European powers'. Any such move would be considered as 'dangerous to our peace and safety'. In effect, the United States was defining its sphere of pre-eminence and influence, marking out its own back-yard. It was a power play in conformity with the usage of the great powers that were also empires.

While in international relations America was engaged in all the activities of war, diplomacy and posturing befitting a 'rising empire', it was behaving according to the familiar pattern of colonial empires at home. In its relations with the native inhabitants, the first nations of North America, the new Republic closely followed all the established modes and developing precepts of empires everywhere. Within its own expanding boundaries America cultivated racist paternalism, benign and malign neglect alternating with bouts of ruthless annihilation, wholesale removals, consistent and continual violation of treaties and deplorable treatment of its Indian populations. All of the currents of European ideology by which the superiority of the white race over all other peoples was rephrased, reconfigured and enacted were represented in America. The Christianising mission and its social-Darwinian racist secularisation, the presumption that white learning knew more about the nature and needs of Indians than they knew about themselves – and therefore was better fitted to regulate and administer their lives – all were reflected in the shifts of policy of the government, as well as in discussion and representation of Indians in American art, letters and academia. The true exceptionalism of America was that it did not have to look overseas to hone the reflexes of the colonial imperialist mindset towards non-European people; its Others were within its own territory. America acquired its definition of self, its most basic identity, in this internal colonialism; it is an imperialist reflex inseparable from the American self, ideology and mythology. White America accepted that it was its natural right and thereby in its nature to be the 'Great Father' to its red children.

Out of its home-grown construction of national identity and practice, America developed its concept of its fitness to dominate, to be the centre of right action and high purpose. The foundation on which this construct rested was a sense of mission defined in religious terms and rhetoric. The New Israelites had a special election as a chosen race marked out by Divine Providence to be the city on the hill. When John Winthrop wrote of the new settlement of America being 'as a city on a hill', he intended to define a model community whose example would be emulated: 'the eyes of all people are upon us.'[5] The messianic nature of the early settlement of America is everywhere in the writing and rhetoric it produced. And yet before the Revolutionary war that created the new Republic, only a minority of the inhabitants of the thirteen colonies were members of a Church. Only about one in five people in New England and the Middle Colonies, one in eight in the South, were affiliated to a Church. But in the prevailing Calvinist tradition, affiliation and membership of a congregation was a matter of considerable duty and responsibility, both religious and civic. The Constitution of the new Republic specifically articulated the separation of Church and State, and in the history of American religion that made all the difference. In 1797, when the United States signed a treaty with Tripoli, it included the statement: 'The Government of the United States of America is not in any sense founded on Christian religion.' Though, as we have seen, this did not preclude the invocation of Divine Providence urging the new nation on to its manifest destiny. The treaty was written in the first flush of constitutional correctness, and before the Great Awakening swept across America in the first third of the 19th century to change the spiritual landscape. This evangelical movement, in the context of the disestablishment of any official religion, led to the formation of new denominations, a diversity of theological ideas and religious practice. In place of the stern God-centred vision of

Calvinist theology, Jesus-centred theology emerged and came to dominate the American imagination. Or as Stephen Prothero puts it, 'these evangelical enthusiasts democratized Christianity and Christianized America'. Thanks to their efforts, 'Jesus has an American history'. 'What Americans have seen in [Jesus] has been an expression of their own hopes and fears – a reflection not simply of some "wholly other" divinity but also of themselves and their nation.'[6] Revivals and the conversions or new birth they were designed to produce constructed a new Protestantism. In America, Church affiliation became the norm. The revivals, tent meetings and storytelling sermonising made preachers celebrities and the whole procedure an entertainment. The history of religion in America is complex, but increasingly it came to focus on a personal relationship with Jesus and identification with his moral teaching, which across all the niceties of theological distinction was the essence of his saving grace. Law and order spearheaded by decency campaigns spread across the nation, as did support for missionary endeavours overseas. American missionaries made the bridgehead on Hawaii, from which came justification for annexation and then statehood. American missionaries went to Africa and China. John Quincy Adams's intimation of a nation 'professing one general system of religious and political principles' came to be conflated as a unified expression of the inherent nature of national virtue. By 1892 the Supreme Court, guardian of the Constitution, could render an opinion lauding the 'Redeemer of mankind' and describe the United States as a 'Christian nation' without any sense of incongruity or radical revisionism.[7]

Thus, all of the imperatives needed to become an imperial power on the world stage were contained in and extracted from the internal history of America. An imperial policy for expansion beyond the territory of the United States was the work of conscious policy, advocated and spearheaded by Theodore Roosevelt. In Roosevelt's writings, the imperialist rationale is presented as the only way to preserve the national virtues inculcated and acquired on the western frontier when subduing the Indian inhabitants and bringing them 'thoroughly and efficiently under the control of our civilization, or (possibly more candidly confessed) under the Anglo-Saxon's commercial necessities'. The translation of the verities and virtues of the western frontier to a global frontier would serve the growth of peace and progress worldwide. Progress has been 'due solely to the power of the mighty civilized races which have not lost the fighting instinct, and which by their expansion are gradually bringing peace to the red wastes where the barbarian peoples of the world hold sway'.[8] This imperialist policy would bring 'peace by the sword', because 'On the border between civilization and barbarism war is generally normal', and the triumph of civilisation is always to be seen as both a moral and secular bettering of the world. War against savages is inherently the most righteous war. In a letter of May 1897 to the historian and strategist Alfred T. Mahan, whose writing was a major influence on his thinking, Roosevelt had a list of potential targets for America's new empire: a canal through the Central American isthmus, and annexation of Hawaii, Samoa, Cuba and whatever else could be acquired.

Roosevelt was not the only voice urging extra-territorial exertion on the United States. In 1885, Congregational minister Josiah Strong, in his popular book *Our Country*, had argued that the Anglo-Saxon is the representative of two great ideas: 'civil liberty' and 'pure *spiritual* Christianity'. 'It follows then, that the Anglo-Saxon ... is divinely commissioned to be, in a peculiar sense, his brother's keeper.' For the United States, that divine commission was a mandate to move 'down upon Mexico, down upon Central and South America, out upon the islands of the sea, over upon Africa and beyond'.[9] The Senator from Indiana, Albert Beveridge, an ideological associate of Roosevelt, presented the process of expansion as a natural consequence of the development of the nation. In a speech in Boston on 21 April 1898, Beveridge declared:

American factories are making more than the American people can use; American soil is producing more than they can consume. Fate has written our policy for us: the trade of the world must and shall be ours ... And American law, American order, American civilization, and the American flag will plant themselves on shores hitherto bloody and benighted, but by those agencies of God henceforth to be made beautiful and bright.[10]

It was in keeping with the nature and character of America to adopt imperialist policy, but what kind of imperium America would be was open to debate. The economist Charles A. Conant outlined the options in September 1898:

Whether the United States shall actually acquire territorial possessions, shall set up captain generalships and garrisons, [or] whether they shall adopt the middle ground of protecting sovereignties nominally independent ... is a matter of detail ... [What matters] is that the United States shall assert their right to free markets in all the old countries which are being opened to the surplus resources of the capitalistic countries and thereby given the benefits of modern civilization.[11]

But underlying the questions of detail was a clear understanding of utility. Conant argued: 'The United States have actually reached, or are approaching the economic state where ... outlets are required outside their own boundaries, in order to prevent business depression, idleness, and suffering at home.' If all nations practised 'commercial freedom', there would be no need for 'the exercise of political and military power'; since they did not, the United States was compelled 'by the instinct of self preservation' to engage in the imperialist game.

The bedrock of American imperialism was the 'open door' policy, outlined by Secretary of State John Hay in his two Open Door Notes of 1899 and 1900. These declared America's interest in preserving the territorial integrity of China. The ailing Chinese Empire, crumbling internally under the pressures of the Boxer Rebellion, was apparently being eyed for dismemberment by the European powers. Ostensibly the open door policy argued for anti-colonialism and anti-interventionism, with the additional implication that America was merely seeking equality and fairness in enjoying the same privileges in China as did the European powers and Japan. The appearance of disinterest was well suited to America's self-image, but its meaning in practice was quite different. As Woodrow Wilson admitted, it was 'not an open door to the rights of China, but the open door to the goods of America'.[12] America's finance and commerce, growing from its vast resource base and rapidly developing industrial system, was acquiring real advantage over other economies and nations. A level playing field worked to its natural advantage, an advantage that would just keep on growing in significance through the course of the 20th century.

When the opportunity came to put the consciously developed imperialist strategy into operation, it was given a suitably noble premise. On 11 April 1898, President McKinley sent a message to Congress proposing 'the forcible intervention of the United States as a neutral to stop the war' and to end 'the barbarities, bloodshed, starvation, and horrible miseries' happening in Cuba, where an insurrection was under way against Spanish rule and the depredations of Spain's General Valeriano (Butcher) Weyler. War fever had been rising in the United States since January of that year when the American vessel *Maine* had exploded in Havana harbour. Among the other reasons that McKinley advanced for intervention were 'protection and indemnity' of American 'life and property' and the need to prevent 'very serious injury to the commerce, trade, and business of our people'. Eight days later, a resolution recognising Cuban independence and demanding Spanish withdrawal authorised military action. Leading the charge when war came was the Assistant Secretary of the Navy, none other than Theodore

Roosevelt, commanding a volunteer regiment, the Rough Riders. They ascended San Juan Hill in the most iconic episode of the war which became a major news sensation across America. The Charge of San Juan Hill became the most popular spectacle recreated in the Buffalo Bill Wild West Show, and swiftly saw Roosevelt drafted as Vice President in that year's elections. The 'cowboy regiment' recruited and led by Roosevelt was the subject of his most popular book, *The Rough Riders* (1900), in which he presents all his arguments for imperialism as the literal translation of the western frontier to the global stage. The book served to consolidate and advance the popularity of the man destined to become the 26th president when McKinley was assassinated in 1901 by Leon Czolgosz. Richard Slotkin argues that Roosevelt also authored the idea that the military regiment is symbolic of the nation at its finest, a microcosm of the progressive order, governed by and obedient to an officer class whose place and powers are earned by native merit, and all selflessly devoted to a patriotic objective.[13]

Before setting off on his military adventure in Cuba, Roosevelt had already arranged for a second front in the Spanish American War. In his role as Assistant Secretary of the Navy, and in temporary charge of the department, ten days after the sinking of the *Maine*, Roosevelt ordered Commodore George Dewey to prepare for an attack on Manila in the Philippines should war break out. In 1896 a revolt against Spanish rule had broken out in the Philippines, just as it had in Cuba. In accordance with Roosevelt's prompting, Dewey was on hand in May 1898 to transport the exiled Filipino insurgent leader Emilio Aguinaldo from Hong Kong to Manila, where he immediately began forming a resistance army. Aguinaldo was confident; Dewey had advised him that 'the United States had come to the Philippines to free the Filipinos from the yoke of Spain' and had no territorial designs.[14] But America and its Filipino allies had different conceptions of what liberation should mean. Soon Aguinaldo and his force were portrayed as insurgents – *insurrectos* – and the whole engagement was reconfigured as the kind of savage war familiar from America's own history. Roosevelt was on hand to compare the Filipinos to the Apaches. According to the correspondent of the *Philadelphia Ledger*:

> The present war is no bloodless, fake, opera bouffe engagement. Our men have been relentless; have killed to exterminate men, women, children, prisoners and captive, active insurgents and suspected people from lads of ten and up ... Our soldiers have pumped salt water into men to 'make them talk', have taken prisoner people who ... peacefully surrendered, and an hour later, without an atom of evidence to show that they were insurrectos, stood them on a bridge and shot them down one by one ... It is not civilized warfare, but we are not dealing with civilized people. The only thing they know and fear is force, violence, and brutality, and we give it to them.[15]

Thus, America was launched on an imperialist career. Its meaning was explained in a speech by Senator Beveridge, reprinted and widely circulated by the Republican National Convention, that expounded a doctrine neatly summed up as 'where the flag once goes up it must never come down'. Reviewing the possessions gained, actual and expected – Hawaii, finally annexed in 1898; Puerto Rico; 'at the prayer of her people Cuba finally will be ours'; and in the islands of the East where coaling stations at the very least were to be America's and 'the flag of a liberal government is to float over the Philippines' – he disparaged the notion that America ought not to govern a people without their consent:

> The rule of liberty that all just government derives its authority from the consent of the governed applies only to those capable of self-government. We govern the Indians without their consent, we govern our territories without their consent. We govern our children without their consent ...

The conflicts of the future are to be conflicts of trade – struggles for markets – commercial wars for existence. And the golden rule of peace is impregnability of position and invincibility of preparedness.[16]

Woodrow Wilson, who opposed overseas expansion before the Spanish American War, invoked the reluctant hero myth for his justification. In 1900, he offered his stylistically nuanced Democrat view of the consequences in this new phase of American development, à la Harry Morgan:

We did not of deliberate choice undertake these new tasks which shall transform us ... All the world knows the surprising circumstances which thrust them upon us ... The whole world had already become a single vicinage; each part had become neighbour to the rest. No nation can live any longer to itself ... [it has become] the duty of the United States to play a part, and a leading part at that in the opening and transformation of the East ... The East is to be opened and transformed whether we will or no; the standards of the West are to be imposed upon it; nations and peoples which have stood still the centuries through ... [will be] made part of the universal world of commerce and of ideas ... It is our peculiar duty ... to moderate the process in the interests of liberty ... This we shall do ... by giving them, in the spirit of service, a government and rule which shall moralize them by being itself moral.[17]

Just seven years later, Wilson was writing:

Since trade ignores national boundaries and the manufacturer insists on having the world as a market, the flag of the nation must follow him, and the doors of nations which are closed against him must be battered down. Concession obtained by financiers must be safeguarded by ministers of state, even if the sovereignty of unwilling nations be outraged in the process. Colonies must be obtained or planted, in order that no useful corner of the world may be overlooked or left unused.[18]

But even Theodore Roosevelt, the most jingoistic advocate of imperialism, could find nuanced expression of policy that linked together the various phases, modes and moods of American empire. In his annual message to Congress as President in December 1904, Roosevelt reiterated the nation's fidelity to the Monroe Doctrine, and made friendship with America conditional on 'efficiency and decency in social and political matters' in the nation states of Latin America. But he warned that where they fell short in the scales of moral judgement, 'flagrant cases of such wrongdoing and impotence' would 'reluctantly' force America to 'exercise an international police power'. So the architect of external imperialism summoned the past to establish the present and provided the pretext from which the myth of the reluctant superpower would grow to order the future.

At the turn of the century, America had joined the great imperial game. Its debate, ideas, policy and actions were not dissimilar to those of any of the European powers. America had its jingoists, its moral theorisers, as well as its outright critics of imperialism and American actions abroad. Rudyard Kipling's poem 'The White Man's Burden' is not an exhortation to British empire, although it could be, but it expresses sentiments that were common and conventional in both countries. In fact, it was written to urge America on in the Philippines and was published on the very day the war actually broke out in February 1899:

> Take up the White Man's burden—
>   Send forth the best ye breed—
> Go, bind your sons to exile
>   To serve your captives' need;
> To wait in heavy harness,

> On fluttered folk and wild—
> Your new-caught, sullen peoples,
> Half-devil and half-child. ...
>
> Take up the White Man's burden—
> Ye dare not stoop to less—
> Nor call too loud on Freedom
> To cloak your weariness; ...

Kipling, the man of empire, was, like the American advocates of imperialism, passionate about the superior qualities of the Anglo-Saxon race and emotive and increasingly politically right-wing about empire. He was also married to an American, Caroline (Carrie) Balestier, and they spent the first four years of their married life in her home of Battleboro, Vermont, where their two eldest children were born. Kingsley Amis suggests that it was even possible Kipling might have considered becoming a naturalised American, until an acrimonious dispute between Britain and America soured the atmosphere and he returned to England.[19]

American history belies the myth of reluctant imperialism in a third way: the US introduced a novel twist to maintain the fiction of the reluctant hero. This was the creation of the 'dollar diplomacy' formula which allowed America to disclaim imperialism while acting more insidiously and malignly than any other empire. It was William Taft, Roosevelt's successor as President, who endeared himself to corporate America by promising 'to interfere with legitimate business as little as possible'. Taft set out this distinctive, exceptional development of American imperialist policy: 'The diplomacy of the present administration has sought to respond to modern ideas of commercial intercourse. This policy has been characterised as substituting dollars for bullets. It is one that appeals alike to idealistic humanitarian sentiments, to the dictates of sound policy and strategy, and to legitimate commercial aims', he declared in December 1912. Dollar diplomacy translated the economic collaboration that had underwritten the expansion of the western frontier to the global frontier. The State Department now became activist in seeking out and opening the doors for American business, especially foreign investments for bankers such as J.P. Morgan, Edward H. Harriman, Kuhn, Loeb and Company, and First National Bank. The official policy of furthering the interests of American business established close and revolving-door relations between corporate America and government at various levels. Career diplomats as well as political appointees could look forward to moving between public and private service, two realms interconnected by mutual interests. And since dollar diplomacy did not supplant but often precipitated military intervention, links between corporate business interests and the military were natural consequences of the policy. The roots of the military-industrial complex go deep into the formation of the distinctive American imperium.

The distinctive character of American empire, its exceptionalism, was the way in which dollar diplomacy enabled the creation of real power over the internal affairs of foreign nations without requiring the establishment of formal colonies. The purpose of imperialism as practised by European empires was the extraction of resources and transfer of wealth from the colonies to the metropolitan centre. Mercantile colonies where merchants were the active agents of European expansion gave way over time to complicated patchworks of direct and indirect rule. Colonial administrations served by governors, civil servants, military and legal officers from the metropolitan home nation took over the entire operation of foreign lands, with all the complexities involved in direct rule of radically different societies. Indirect rule simply meant the appointment of a 'Resident' who was the principal advisor to a local prince who remained the nominal head of state, except that the 'advice' was a polite fiction for the voice of command. Parts of India and the Malay states were under such indirect rule of the British Empire. Though this pattern of European empire most closely resembles the workings of

American dollar diplomacy, there were significant differences. The greatest of these was the conceptual distance created by dollar diplomacy, the deniability factor of being able to talk of freedom, self-determination and anti-colonialism, to have one's rhetorical cake while American business ate its fill by putting its dollars to work. The power to use power and yet appear reluctant to be directly entangled in the internal affairs of other nations and peoples, to be the centre of action, indispensable to events and decisions yet not accountable except on the corporate bottom line – a policy that Harry Morgan or Rick Blaine would have endorsed enthusiastically! The work of imperialism was in the hands of those natural and noble, democratic and freely operating principles of the market and commercial interest. It is only in the consequences for favoured recipient nations that the distinctions and exceptionalism of America's imperialism made little difference: with conventional formal colonialism, the prospect existed, however far removed, that potentially the colonial regime could be ejected; whereas, under the American variant, the mighty dollar would always be with them.

The first country to be on the receiving end of the newly fashioned dollar diplomacy was Nicaragua. It was ruled by the dictator José Santos Zelaya, who had a habit of refusing American requests for a naval base, a concession for a second canal route and proposals for new business opportunities for American firms. But the pretext for action, according to President Taft's annual message to Congress in 1909, was that Zelaya 'has kept Central America in constant tension and turmoil'. America would take an interest in Nicaraguan affairs on behalf of those beset by the troubles he created. Covertly, the secretary of an American mining company in Nicaragua duly began preparing the ground for a revolution, financing the rebels and recruiting the United Fruit Company and others to use their steamers to transport troops and supplies for the rebels – with the total agreement of the State Department. Washington broke relations with Zelaya, refused to recognise his properly elected successor, paid its custom duties to the regime established by the agent of the mining company together with General Juan Estrada, and when the rebels were defeated by forces loyal to the Nicaraguan government, landed Marines to protect the rebels while they reorganised. In August 1910 the rebels triumphed and entered the capital, Managua. After this prelude the real dollar diplomacy got under way. The State Department sent a representative to negotiate a pact with the new regime, which was signed aboard an American battleship. The pact called for a constituent assembly to be selected and for it to elect Estrada as President and Diaz, the agent of the American mining company, as Vice President, presumably for democratic form's sake. Then a commission satisfactory to the State Department was instituted to settle outstanding financial claims. Nicaragua would accept a loan from American bankers secured in part, according to a pattern that America had already perfected in Santo Domingo, against customs receipts which would be collected by a US agent. Control of customs receipts meant effective control over the entire economic life of the country, and the ability to starve it of income. Within months, the American minister in Managua noted that 'the natural sentiments of an overwhelming majority of Nicaraguans is antagonistic to the United States, and even with some members of Estrada's cabinet I find a decided suspicion, if not distrust, of our motives'.[20] The National Assembly sought to resist the provisions of the pact by amending the constitution to preclude foreign bank loans. President Estrada was forced to resign and the American minister wired the State Department that if it wished Diaz, the Vice President, to succeed him, 'a war vessel is necessary for moral effect' – which is just what happened. In June 1911, the floating of a $15 million loan from American financiers and operation of the customs houses under American supervision was agreed, while the State Department also worked out the details of the loan with two American banking houses. Most of the loan would go to settle Nicaragua's external debts to Europeans and Americans, while the banking firms would oversee the improvement of the national railways and build a new one which they would control. Not even the US Senate was prepared to acquiesce to these terms, refusing to ratify the agreement on three occasions. A new, more modest and amended agreement was then worked out, involving a participatory arrangement between a reorganised Nicaraguan National Bank and the two American banking houses; the Americans would acquire a 51% stake in the National Bank. The slimmed-down loan was to be secured by a lien on customs and a liquor tax. This time the US Senate was not asked for its consent; the arrangement was effected by executive order. An American official recommended by the two banking houses was put in charge of customs and remained in the post for the next seventeen years. Nicaragua would remain an ostensibly independent nation in America's backyard. But the various reconfigurings of America's foreign policy and global interests would, on a number of occasions in the following decades up to and including the 1980s, lead to overt and covert resort to military means and financial measures just as bizarre as the first exercise of dollar diplomacy. And the pattern that became familiar to Nicaraguans was adopted, adapted and implemented throughout Latin America. As President Taft commented in 1912, the year when US Marines were sent into Cuba: 'While our foreign policy should not be turned a hair's breath from the straight path of justice, it may well be made to include active intervention to secure for our merchandise and our capitalists opportunity for profitable investment.'[21]

Myths are abstracted from history, they are conscious constructs that present significant and relevant themes and motifs; explicitly and implicitly, they convey a body of ideas infused with a moral consciousness. Myths have their own storyline that comes complete with stock characters and familiar scenarios. The function of myth is to facilitate understanding and negotiate changing events and circumstances in the real world by reading them against its own familiar ideas, values and morals. In this way the world around us is shaped, it becomes coherent, manageable and meaningful. Myths create a sense of identity and help to identify who are the good guys, who the baddies, and why. With such information we can then decide how to respond; we have a means to relate the present to the past and choose a course of action that will lead to a desired future outcome. But as we have seen, myths, however familiar, compatible and consoling, do not represent the only possible interpretation of events. Sometimes what is abstracted from history to serve as a sustaining myth can be a lie. The myth of America as a reluctant superpower, as a nation that 'had greatness thrust upon it', as historian Ernest May argued, is a partial, self-serving and ultimately self-deluding idea. May contended that America does not act according to a pre-determined logic but reacts to circumstances, and achieved pre-eminence not by consciously seeking it but as an unintended consequence of actions taken either in self-defence or on behalf of others[22] – just like Harry Morgan. The familiar litany of the myth of the reluctant superpower begins in 1898, when the US chose war only when the continuing depredations of Spain's General Weyler in Cuba became intolerable. Then in 1914 the US remained neutral, intervening only when Germany violated US neutral rights; but it did so for altruistic purposes – to end the war and make the world safe for democracy. In 1939 the US stayed on the sidelines until provoked by Japan's surprise attack on Pearl Harbor; but it entered the conflict to pursue a crusade for democracy. The myth of the reluctant superpower does not preclude nor detract from the assertion that only by America's intervention was victory achieved and the high purpose of America as a nation fulfilled. Indeed, the myth of reluctance heightens, rather than diminishes, the feel-good factor of such a reading of history. Consistently, it is evil that is the spur to American action and intervention; therefore, the American people are reassured that their nation is good, acting disinterestedly and nobly according to its enduring values.

But, as we have shown, there is an underlying coherence of

purpose in US foreign policy – from the Founding Fathers to Roosevelt, Mahan, Beveridge and Hay through to William Taft and official endorsement of dollar diplomacy and on to Woodrow Wilson's moral charter for a global order of 'new Freedom'. The recurrences and sense of familiarity are unmistakable; they are articulated by Republicans and Democrats. And, as we shall see in Chapter Five, the enterprise was given a boost by Presidents Harry S. Truman and Dwight D. Eisenhower. The fall of the Berlin Wall in 1989 and the disintegration of Communism offered further opportunity to fulfil this vision. The administrations of George H.W. Bush and Bill Clinton revived the project with a new twist – whereas the orientation of US policy had been primarily defensive, it now became largely offensive. As Andrew Bacevich notes:

> Though garnished with neologistic flourishes intended to convey a sense of freshness or originality, the politico-economic concept to which the United States adheres today has not changed in a century: the familiar quest for an 'open world', the overriding imperative of commercial integration, confidence that technology endows the United States with a privileged position in that order, and the expectation that American military might will preserve order and enforce the rules. Those policies reflect a single minded determination to extend and perpetuate American political, economic and cultural hegemony – usually referred to as 'leadership' – on a global scale.[23]

The myth of the reluctant hero is used to camouflage the fact that the majority of Americans actually do believe that America has the right to be imperial. There is an inner fitness in America forged by its founding principles that makes it the right nation to be pre-eminent. The myth of the reluctant hero works so well because it says that it is in the very nature of America: when the circumstances arise, America will arise – just like Harry Morgan

– to do the right thing for everyone. Where there should be examination of motives and performance, the miasma of myth provides a ready assurance that natural, innate reflexes will produce the right response if and when action is needed. The myth works to anaesthetise American sensibilities to the content of the history of American engagement with the rest of the world, and the consistent principles on which it is founded and according to which it operates. More importantly, the familiarity of the myth of reluctance serves to overlay another entrenched myth from which it derives its force: the sustaining myth of nationhood, of mission, of messianic purpose – Law 4 of American mythology. If America is the very idea of an ideal nation, then it follows that American democracy has the right to be imperial and express itself through empire. These myths work to secure for Americans the most affluent lifestyles of any people in human history. Their lives are replete with commodities; their interests, attentions and concerns are absorbed and distracted by the demands of maintaining themselves in a competitive, upwardly spiralling consumer lifestyle. Along with Howard Hawks, many Americans seem to prefer just to be entertained, not to be bothered by Ideas and not to take sides in an informed debate about how their nation and their lives came to be the product of empire.

CHAPTER FOUR

The Player: Hollywood, Celebrity and Empire

As President Calvin Coolidge so memorably observed, 'the business of America is business'.[1] And as everyone knows, 'There's no business like show business'! Who could forget Ethel Merman belting out Irving Berlin's lyric in Walter Lang's 1954 Technicolor big-screen movie? The 'show business' that Merman helped give the Hollywood treatment is vaudeville, and this movie is just one in a long line of love letters to the business of entertainment made in the entertainment capital of the world. From the very beginning, Hollywood has been in love with itself and all the elements of show business that were incorporated into its business of dream-making. From the very beginning, Americans fell in love with movie stars. But most of all, it is in the movies that America itself finds love and comes to adore its own self-image. As Neal Gabler argues, America is the Republic of Entertainment; and movies are the ultimate cornerstone and weapon of this republic.[2] Cinema is both a source of escape and an instrument for shaping the mythology of escape as reason for being – what, in our topology, is the second law of American mythology. The silver screen, consciously and unconsciously, has shaped America's self-image and projected the rightness and justification of its will and claim to empire. If American empire has been a work constructed on dollar diplomacy, then the movies have been not only the shop window but also the leading export of American business. And they have direct diplomatic bearing for, in films, America imagines and shapes its imperialist relationship with the rest of the world and re-imagines and subsumes the history of other cultures and civilisations within its own worldview. In movies, America has been assured that its forces have saved the world, fought the evil enemies of freedom and human values, and won all wars in the right way, with supreme mastery of the technology of warfare. Also, the movie-going public has been reassured that American intelligence, the skulduggery of the dark side of world affairs, is efficient, all-knowing, all-seeing, and always gets the bad guys. Cinema thus serves as the driving force, the central engine, of empire – the seventh law of American mythology.

Robert Altman's 1992 film *The Player* is a hall of mirrors in which the business of movie-making plays in its own reflections. And it's about getting away with murder. The central character, Griffin Mill, is a studio executive who listens to pitches for movies, and out of the thousands he hears each year he can say yes only twelve times. At the beginning of the movie Griffin is in peril, both in his job and from death threats delivered in poison pen postcards from a disgruntled writer. With imperturbable aplomb, Mill leads us through the world of contemporary Hollywood as a business, in the business of celebrity and affirming the dreams of the American public. In this narrative journey everything is self-referential, self-absorbed, self-serving, self-loving and self-assured in its transience and insecurity. The highly personal techniques of Altman's movie-making – the naturalism of his restless camera and sound, the overlay of overheard conversation, the use of celebrity faces mostly playing themselves as celebrities – all use realism, the medium of the movies, to underline the artifice and artificiality of the dream bubble that is Hollywood.

The focus of all the action is movie-making, and what we get is a dissection of the dominant themes of the business of movies.

The pitches for new movies are all derivative, a recombinant DNA of reconfigured formulae described in Hollywood short-hand: '*The Graduate 2*', because its stars are still alive; 'a kind of *Gods Must be Crazy* except the Coke bottle is now an actress ... Sort of *Out of Africa* meets *Pretty Woman*'; '*Ghost* meets *Manchurian Candidate*'. And each pitch is presented as a package tied with the ribbon of celebrity. Each story needs a star: the names of Julia Roberts, Bruce Willis and Arnold Schwarzenegger, the bankable hot ticket names of the time, are refrains running through the entire film whenever a movie project is mentioned. The movie references are everywhere, including within the visual and technical style of the movie. It opens with the head of studio security bemoaning the modern style of film editing: 'cut, cut, cut', in contrast to Orson Welles's opening for *Touch of Evil* (1958). This famous *film noir* opened with a three-and-a-half-minute tracking shot to establish its setting and themes. The comment is contained in Altman's opening eight-minute tracking shot that establishes his setting and themes. But on another level, the darkness of *Touch of Evil* is its treatment of racism, betrayal of friends, sexual ambiguity, frame-ups, drugs and corruption of power, all of which are reflected in Altman's hall of mirrors. Mill's office is decked out with film posters, mostly for *noir* films, and there are abundant conversational references to movies such as *D.O.A.*, another classic *noir* of 1950, partially based on an earlier German film, remade in 1988 and as *Colour Me Dead* in 1969 – movies just keep on being remade. When Mill tracks down the writer, Kahane, who he believes is responsible for the poison pen postcards, Kahane is at the movies watching *Bicycle Thieves*. Vittorio de Sica's 1948 film is a classic of European neo-realism, a human story of unemployment and poverty in post-war Italy. An unemployed man gets a job – putting up posters advertising Hollywood films – but his bicycle is stolen, robbing him of his job, and he and his son set out to track down the stolen bike. Awarded an honorary Oscar in 1949, de Sica's film was the vanguard of European 'art films', the inception of the debate about movies as an art form in contrast to mass market Hollywood films as mere commercial entertainment. In a later sequence, Griffin Mill makes a speech at a glittering celebrity dinner at the Los Angeles County Museum, where his company are donating twenty of their films to the archive:

> Many people around this country and around the world have for too long thought of movies as popular entertainment more than serious art. And I'm afraid a large majority of the press supports this attitude. We want great films with long shelf lives. We want films of the new John Houston, Orson Welles, Frank Capra. We and the other film studios have a responsibility to the public to maintain the art of motion pictures as our precious mandate. Movies are art, now more than ever.

During this speech the celebrity audience chatter uninterestedly among themselves. In Altman's hall of mirrors there are reflections and distortions, reality and self-deluding illusions.

Surviving in the movie business is all about competition. Studio head Levison brings in hot shot Larry Levy to supplant Griffin Mill. Levy has a bright idea to improve the bottom line: eradicate writers from the process of making movies – the studio can simply come up with its own ideas. Any newspaper, he argues, can provide sufficient material, and they proceed to pluck potential new movies from the day's headlines as they translate them into familiar movie formulae. The fate of one movie project plays an essential role in the narrative of *The Player*, from an initial pitch to the screening of the end of the completed movie that is the penultimate scene of Altman's film. This movie within the movie is *Habeas Corpus* – helpfully explained as 'produce the corpse'. It gives a darkly satiric portrait of the movie business. What its director pitches to Mill is a film project with pretensions to be art with social consciousness and a message. And this sub-plot within *The Player* turns on the keywords of 'reality', 'innocence' and 'what happens'. *Habeas Corpus* will be about a District Attorney who believes in the death penalty but knows the reality: disproportionately, black defendants are convicted and executed. The DA vows that the next defendant he sends to the gas chamber will be smart, rich and white. 'What a hook', gushes the agent. And so it is. A wife is accused of killing her husband; the DA falls in love with the wife but puts her in the gas chamber anyway. As the execution is under way, the DA learns that the husband faked his death – the wife is innocent. The DA races to the prison, but she's dead. 'I tell you there's not a dry eye in the house', insists the director. Griffin Mill is taken aback. 'She's dead?' 'She's dead', replies the director, 'because that's the reality, the innocent die.' And he wants to make the film without stars: 'because the story's just too damned important to risk being overwhelmed by personality. That's fine for action pictures but this is special. We want real people here. We don't want people coming with preconceived notions.' His agent, however, whispers the Hollywood mantra: 'Julia Roberts', 'Bruce Willis'. But the director insists that, all in all, his concept is not even an American picture: 'No stars, no pat happy endings, no Schwarzenegger, no stick-up, no terrorists. This is a tough story, a tragedy in which an innocent woman dies. Why? ... because ... that happens.' Indeed, what a hook! Exactly the baited hook Mill needs to lure his rival Larry Levy to his doom. Mill gets the picture accepted but handed to Levy, knowing this will enable him to step in at the crucial moment to rescue the project. When we see the screening of the now completed *Habeas Corpus*, the lead roles are indeed played by Julia Roberts and Bruce Willis – playing cameo roles in *The Player*. We watch Roberts being taken to the gas chamber, strapped into the chair; the gas pellets drop, her head lolls forward. A telephone rings; down the corridor Willis charges towards the gas chamber, takes an axe to break the glass and bursts in to rescue the seemingly lifeless body of Roberts and carry her to safety – she stirs! 'What took you so long?' she asks. 'Traffic was a bitch', Willis replies. THE END. In the screening room Mill's assistant is incensed. 'You sold out. What about reality?' she shrieks. 'What about the way the old ending tested in Canoga Park?' replies the director who had made such protestations of art and meaning, reality and dead innocence. 'Everybody hated it. Now everybody loves it. That's reality!' he concludes. To which the rescued Larry Levy adds: 'This is a hit. This is what we're here for.' Yes, there's no business like show business!

In the course of *The Player*, Mill commits and gets away with the murder of David Kahane. He wrongly believes Kahane to be the sender of the death threats, and tracks him down in an attempt to buy him off with a promise of producing his film, the story of a young American in Japan. Mill is identified as the prime suspect by the police, but the only witness wrongly identifies a police officer as the man she saw leaving the murder scene. In this reality, an innocent man died and Mill walks free from the police line-up. In sum, Mill is a murderer who kills without malign intent, almost accidentally, but with presence of mind and without remorse. He is a man who loves all that is morally empty and emotionally neutered, including the lover of the man he murdered, the exotic foreign painter June Gudmundsdottir, who makes art for art's sake. He aspires to pretensions of art, but only pretentiously, for his dedication belongs solely to succeeding in the competitive world of the movie business. He defines for us what makes a movie, the irreducible ingredients underlying the recombinant DNA of movie formulae: 'suspense, laughter, violence, hope, heart, nudity, sex and, most of all, a happy ending.' He lives within a world of excess, indulgence and artificiality. He manipulates power capriciously and maliciously for his own ends. And he succeeds triumphantly. He not only rescues Larry Levy but ends up as head of the studio. And we like him. At the end of the film, as he drives from the studio his car phone rings. The call is from the writer of the poison pen postcards. Mill listens as this mystery voice pitches a movie: a studio executive commits murder and gets away with it – the plot of *The Player*. 'Can you guarantee that ending?' Mill inquires. The mysterious writer says he can. 'Then we have a deal', says Mill as he turns into a private road and pulls up before his house, a perfect house with roses around the door and an American flag proudly flying, to be greeted by his beautiful and fulsomely pregnant wife, June Gudmundsdottir. The metaphor is complete.

In Hollywood, reality is always reconfigured to conform to established formulae. It is these formulae that are its business, and its business has always been about affirmation of the American self-image and global domination. Cinema is the engine of empire metaphorically and in reality. The birth of cinema was contemporaneous with the first stirrings of off-shore American imperialism. Large-screen projection of moving images began in 1896. In America the new technology found a home in vaudeville theatres, a novelty entertainment between the variety acts, and in penny arcades and storefront theatres in working-class districts. In 1898 war fever swept the United States – 'Remember the *Maine*!' was the battle cry when an American vessel was allegedly blown up in Havana harbour, precipitating the Spanish American War. It was the war that spearheaded Theodore Roosevelt's vision of American imperialism, fabricated out of his refashioning of British imperialism and social Darwinism. The movies quickly responded to the popular mood; quite literally, movies began by going to war. Thomas Alva Edison, self-proclaimed inventor of the new medium, called one of his films *Raising Old Glory Over Moro Castle* (1899), though the iconic image was shot in front of a backcloth at his production facility in West Orange, New Jersey, not at the monument in Old Havana. As Robert Sklar observes: 'Fabrication was, of course, the point: no motion-picture films were made of the fighting in Cuba. What was important was how filmmakers responded to the challenge of reproducing the war for the benefit of vaudeville audiences.'[3]

And it was war that gave America global domination of the

movie business. Contrary to the conventional story, Edison was not the sole inventor of the technology of movies. Edison was a superb self-publicist; the celebrity inventor was considered the greatest living American. He had such a secure hold over public recognition that he was able to convince other inventors to sell him their technology because it would sell better under his name than theirs. Much of the early development of cinema, however, took place in France, and in the early years the French company Pathé Frères was a leading producer of the short one- and two-reel films that established the mass popular audience for cinema. Statistics and records of the early years of movie history are hard to come by and often confused, since movies began before copyright law existed. The first all-movie theatre opened in London in 1907; its programmes consisting exclusively of Pathé films. In 1909, figures offered by a British movie trade paper showed that French producers supplied 40% of new film releases and American producers 30% in the British market. 'There are no comparable figures for the United States, but it is likely that Pathé Frères also became the single largest producer of films shown in nickelodeons.'[4] What changed everything was the First World War, which for Europe ran from 1914 to 1918. In Europe it was a war of mass mobilisation, absorbing all the productive capacity of the major nations and producing unimaginable carnage, some of which was recorded in reality by movie cameras. A generation of Europe's young men perished in the attrition of trench warfare in Flanders fields, making the losses to the commercial film-making of France and Italy, until that time the world leaders, an unremarked casualty. Into the void stepped the American industry. Just as Woodrow Wilson led America into the war and emerged to play a dominant role in the Versailles negotiations that ended it, proposing a new world order and a new imperial vision of America's place in the world, so too, by the end of the war, the United States was producing some 85% of the films shown throughout the world, and 98% of those shown in America – a dominance it was never to relinquish. The movies became the first business of American global commercial expansion, the most successful and enduring – not least because of the structure and practices adopted by the industry in its earliest years.

Edison, the greatest living American, had a will to dominate. What he wanted was complete control of the motion picture field. To this end he tried to force his competitors to use only his camera under licence and to sell or rent films only to the exhibitors who agreed to use licensed projectors and films. He used his own applications couched in the most general terms to the US Patents Office, and the courts, to secure his position, suing competitors who failed to comply. Since few of his competitors had Edison's financial resources, successive stages of the legal process could easily mean bankruptcy, even if they won. In 1901 Edison won a case against the Biograph Company, but it was overturned on appeal. Judge William J. Wallace declared: 'It is obvious that Mr Edison was not a pioneer.'[5] He had not invented the film, or the camera capable of taking motion pictures at high speeds and precise intervals, though he had been first in the field commercially and had probably invented a successful way to make other people's inventions work. Edison repaired to the Patents Office, and further court cases followed in 1906 and 1907. In 1908 Biograph held up a white flag and called for negotiations. The result was a general settlement involving the nine major producing companies, including Edison's and two French companies – Pathé Frères and Melies. They formed the Motion Picture Patents Company; its objective was what Edison had been working towards all along: complete monopoly. The Patents Company made an agreement with Eastman Kodak, sole American producer of film stock, limiting sales to their licensed producers who would then rent their films solely to distributors and exhibitors exclusively licensed to show their films. Any distributor or exhibitor who broke the rules would be excluded, and exhibitors would pay a fee to the Patents Company for renting licensed films. Edison got a major share of these royalties, his net profits soaring to over $1 million a year. The Patents Company also worked to exclude British and Italian film producers from the American market; only one British and one French company – beyond the two French producers who were members of the Patents Company – were permitted a miniscule quota of three reels per week for both. Having established its position, the Patents Company proceeded to consolidate the vertical integration of the industry by creating its own distribution exchange, driving out or buying up its own licensees. It licensed between half and two-thirds of the 6,000 movie theatres across America.

The Motion Picture Patents Company constructed a basis for easy profits and was content with its dominance. Its complacency contained the seeds of its own demise, though it set the pattern that was to be the foundation of the movie industry until the 1950s. The Patents Company produced one-reel and then reluctantly two-reel films which it supplied to the nickelodeons, as the dedicated movie theatres that began to spread across America in 1905 were called. These theatres, crowded together in the poorest areas of town, had a voracious appetite for films and changed their programmes on a daily basis. But the Patents Company, known as the Trust, began to offer preferential terms to exhibitors who opened theatres in more well-to-do neighbourhoods or prime downtown locations where they would give movies longer runs and charge more. As Sklar notes, 'through local newspaper advertising and review and by building up a reputation for quality prints of pre-censored films, the Patents Company hoped gradually to shift the social foundations of movie patronage'.[6] In this way they left a hole in the most lucrative and loyal area of the market that allowed independent producers to thrive. The movie stage was set for a life-and-death battle from which the independents emerged triumphant. Leading the charge of the independents was Carl Laemmle, a German-born Jew who had been a clothing store manager until he opened a storefront nickelodeon. Soon he started distributing to unlicensed nickelodeons and those ill-served by the Trust, moving to production and eventually to replication of the pattern set by the Trust. As far as possible, independents like Laemmle tried to work around the Trust's restrictions, or just hoped they were not caught: camouflaging their cameras and scattering to more distant locations, including California, to evade the Trust's spies looking for violations that they could take to court. Along the way, Laemmle was the target of 289 separate legal actions that cost him $300,000.

The independents succeeded by innovation and initiative and most of all by adoption of a 'star' system. Trust producers did not identify the actors who appeared in their films. But the movie-going public quickly latched on to favourite players and began writing fan letters to those it identified with, such as 'The Biograph Girl', Florence Lawrence. Laemmle capitalised on this, hiring Lawrence away from Biograph in 1909 and giving her star billing in his own company's films. In 1910 he hired Mary Pickford from Biograph by offering to nearly double her salary. When nickelodeons changed their programmes daily, a practice that endured until the 1920s, audience recognition of star names was the most effective publicity: 'stars sold pictures as nothing else could.'[7] *The Player* is not a sorry story of what Hollywood has become today, but an accurate reflection of where Hollywood began and what Hollywood has always been about.

The movie industry began beyond the radar of the élite guardians of high culture and art and the middle-class guardians of public decency. It found its audience among the immigrants and the working classes. It created its audience often by pandering to voyeurism, with films of women undressing and nudity, a point acknowledged by the industry itself: 'in the beginning many inferior elements crowded into this business; ... the appeal was often to the morbid and the vulgar and ... some men made, and others exhibited, pictures which catered to the lowest instincts of humanity.'[8] In 1908, the year the Motion Picture Patents Company was formed, New York City moved to revoke the licence of all its 600 nickelodeons and passed laws requiring new, more expensive licences, placing films under police jurisdiction and controlling children's attendance. The industry responded quickly to this new development by offering a system of self-censorship, another pattern that was to endure and shape the development of Hollywood. But trying to disown its origins, to move away from the ghetto neighbourhoods and collaborate with the guardians of civic probity, could not save the Trust. In 1915 it was judged to be an organisation in restraint of trade under the terms of the Sherman Anti-trust Act. But by the time this axe fell on the Motion Picture Patents Company it was already losing out commercially and imaginatively to the new breed of independent producers.

The triumphant producers who made Hollywood *An Empire of Their Own*, in Neal Gabler's appropriate title,[9] succeeded because they arose from the same background as the audiences that made movies a commercial success. Apart from Laemmle, William Fox, Adolph Zukor, Jesse Lasky and his brother-in-law Samuel Goldfish (later Goldwyn) were also Jews, all from Eastern Europe. Their background was in merchandising or entertainment before entering the movie business. 'They *were* the audience. They were the same people', Gabler quotes one Jewish producer as explaining.[10] The people in question were immigrants new to America, part of the greatest wave of immigration to a nation of immigrants. Between 1870 and 1900, America received eleven million new immigrants. By 1924, some 22 million new immigrants had passed through the arrival terminal at Ellis Island. At the beginning of the 20th century, over 60% of residents in the twelve largest cities were either foreign-born or first-generation Americans. This was the principal audience for the new medium of cinema, just as it was also the background of those who came to dominate and control the development of the industry. It was through cinema that they read their life project of remaking themselves in a new and distinctive character, acquiring the narrative history and mythic story of their new identity. Cinema was the most direct medium of communication, working through visual images constructed out of reality to give the appearance of reality. Silent movies required no mastery of literary language; they told their stories through gesture and expression, not exactly a universal language but a codified system that could be mastered rapidly by anyone. American cinema's first imperial act was an imperialism of the mind. Being European Jews not only meant that the movie moguls understood the ghetto communities from many nations that were changing the face of America's cities; but also emphasised their dedication to the process that succeeded coming to America: assimilation. Assimilation had been the lodestone of 19th-century European Jewry as the only means to escape the persecution and proscription they faced. 'What united [the Jews who invented Hollywood] in deep spiritual kinship was their utter and absolute rejection of their past and their equally absolute devotion to their new country ... a ferocious, even pathological, embrace of America.'[11] Moreover:

> they would fabricate their empire in the image of America as they would fabricate themselves in the image of prosperous Americans. They would create its values and myths, its traditions and archetypes ... By making a 'shadow' America, one which idealized every old glorifying bromide about the country, the Hollywood Jews created a powerful cluster of images and ideas – so powerful that, in a sense, they colonized the American imagination. No one could think about this country without thinking about the movies. As a result, the paradox – that the movies were quintessentially American while the men who made them were not – doubled back on itself. Ultimately, American values came to be *defined* largely by the movies the Jews made. Ultimately, by creating their idealized America on screen, the Jews reinvented the country in the image of their fiction.[12]

In business terms, this new breed of movie-makers, the 'moguls', not only supplanted the Motion Picture Patents Company: they succeeded in transcending the class and cultural divide where their predecessors had failed. They did so by making more expensive and extensive films, of up to five reels or one hour in length. And they robbed the Trust of its middle-class pretensions by producing, in Adolph Zukor's phrase, 'Famous Players in Famous Plays'. It was the independents, not the Trust, that began to translate literary and theatrical culture into movies. If they changed the content of movies, they retained the will to dominate through vertical integration of the industry under single or affiliated ownership; this was re-pioneered by William Fox and became standard in the industry. Threats of anti-trust investigations and actual investigations were a recurrent feature of Hollywood history, but the axe did not fall on the new breed of movie moguls until after the Second World War. They had 33 years in which they reconfigured America's self-image and built its unassailable domination of global popular culture.

It was the new breed of movie moguls who began buying up cheap land around Los Angeles and establishing their studios in what would ever after be generically known as Hollywood. Not the least of its attractions was the lack of unionised labour in California – along with the year-round sunshine and a great diversity of landscape all within easy travelling distance. The region around Hollywood could, and did, pass muster for virtually anywhere in the world, and so in the movies became the world. And American movies were destined for the world. In 1921, *Scientific American* wrote that the movie industry had become 'infected with the new spirit of internationalism which has taken such firm root in the economic and industrial life of the country as the result of the seizure of war-time opportunities'.[13] Or more appropriately, as Edward G. Lowry commented in the *Saturday Evening Post*: 'Trade follows the film.'[14] 'The sun, it now appears, never sets on the British Empire and the American motion picture', he wrote. A member of Britain's House of Lords rose to complain that Midlands factories were forced to alter their design patterns because customers in the Middle East demanded shoes and clothes modelled after those worn by American stars. Japanese tailors attended the movies to learn how to cut the styles demanded by their Western-minded patrons. In Brazil, a 35% rise in sales of an American car followed its appearance in a Hollywood film, while architects had begun building California-style bungalows. The ability of Hollywood to promote merchandising and set popular cultural trends is another strand of global dominance original to cinema as the engine of empire. The message was not lost on Congress. In 1925 it appropriated $15,000 to establish a Motion Picture Section in the Bureau of Foreign and Domestic Commerce. Statistics published by the Bureau make it clear how dominant American cinema had become. It produced more films each year than any other country: in 1927 alone, some 700 features were made in Hollywood, while Germany made 241 and Britain only 44. Hollywood's share of total releases in most countries around the world ranged from 75% to 90%. As the *London Evening Post* commented:

> If the United States abolished its diplomatic and consular services, kept it ships in harbour and its tourists at home, and retired from the world's markets, its citizens, its problems, its towns and countryside, its roads, motor cars, counting houses and saloons would still be familiar in the uttermost corners of the world ... The film is to America what the flag was once to Britain. By its means Uncle Sam may hope some day, if he be not checked in time, to Americanize the world.[15]

The ability of movies to influence audiences has been a matter of concern from their inception. As Hollywood moved to capture middle-class audiences in middle-class neighbourhoods and become respectable, the arbiters of civic decency and taste became more, not less, concerned. As always, efforts to restrain the influence of movies centred on prurience rather than the deeper effects of its myth-making and the social and political consequences of fear, disaffection and imperial ideology encoded in and working through its narrative formulae. The system of self-censorship agreed in 1908 did not prevent some states from trying to operate more direct control by ordering the elimination of scenes or prohibiting entire films before their first public screening. Two such state laws were tested in the Supreme Court in 1915; the movie company, Mutual, claimed the protection of the First Amendment. 'We immediately feel that the argument is wrong or strained which extends guarantees of free opinion and speech to the multitudinous shows which are advertised on the billboards of our cities and towns ... It cannot be put out of view that the exhibition of moving pictures is a business pure and simple, originated and conducted for profit, like other spectacles, not to be regarded, nor intended to be regarded by the Ohio constitution, we think, as part of the press of the country or as organs of public opinion', said Justice Joseph McKenna speaking for the Court.[16] By the 1920s, the Hollywood studio system was in place, integrating production of movies with a complex hierarchical distribution system through first-run and neighbourhood cinemas owned and operated by the studios. 'As a system designed to concentrate power and as a profit-making enterprise it was without flaw, so long as one essential condition was met: ... Awesome as the power and profit of the movie moguls became in the 1920s, they never ceased to depend on their ability to please the public.'[17] But Hollywood did not just depend on the American public – it was a global business. Overseas sales accounted for more than a third of the industry's total income during the 1920s. It was the vital margin for the high profits, high salaries and extravagant lifestyle of the moguls and stars. The world was the icing on Hollywood's cake.

The era of silent movies established the principal genres of movie-making. Hollywood took its stories from theatre, from the literary fiction of America through to dime novels, as well as from newspapers and the unsolicited scenarios that began to deluge the studios. Hollywood was where stories went to be refashioned into what Roland Barthes terms 'collective representations'. But as the movies became the centre of cultural myth-making, the stars who sold the pictures grabbed and held more and more attention from the public. Fan magazines, newspaper stories and gossip columns devoted to the private lives of the stars emerged before the First World War and accompanied the rise of Hollywood to global domination. Projecting, preserving and protecting the public image of the stars became an industry in itself, a public relations industry that served as a shop window for the product the stars sold: movies. The culture of celebrity begins with the rise of Hollywood. How the stars lived, loved and enjoyed themselves, as much as how an ordinary girl or boy could become a star, became a staple interest of the public.

In 1921, headlines screamed the news that Roscoe 'Fatty' Arbuckle was charged with the murder of a young actress. Virginia Rappe had been one of the many pretty girls at a party that lasted over the Labor Day weekend, accompanied by copious amounts of bootleg booze. When the party ended she was discovered in a bedroom, her clothes torn and seriously ill. She died soon after in hospital. Arbuckle was charged with murder and later indicted for manslaughter. There were three trials; two ended with hung juries before he was acquitted at the third. While the Arbuckle case was winding to the destruction of his career, other scandals hit the headlines and began to make the private peccadilloes and sins of the stars as shocking to the guardians of civic morality as the movies themselves. The rising crescendo of alarm at the influence and effect of movies and the culture of celebrity was reflected in newspapers, books and academic studies by earnest sociologists. 'Our children are rapidly becoming what they see in the movies',[18] wrote Norman E. Richardson in 1921. In a 1926 edition of a prestigious political science journal entirely devoted to movies, Donald Young, a sociologist at the University of Pennsylvania, suggested that movies 'introduce and spread personal and social attitudes far beyond the reach of most of us'.[19] In the same issue, Wilton A. Barrett described the movie as a 'purveyor of ideas, symbols and secrets'; and 'it could narrate facts to the great majority and offer suggestions, which the jealous minority did not intend, as it never has intended, the humble servants of humanity and an exploiting civilization to know'. Writing in 1916, Hugo Münsterberg, Harvard professor of psychology, explained the complex influence of movies as follows: 'Depth and movement alike comes to us in the moving picture world, not as hard facts but as a mixture of fact and symbol.'[20]

Hollywood responded to these various statements of its power and influence by the old method of offering self-censorship, and a new initiative asserting its power for good. A new trade organisation, the Motion Picture Producers and Distributors Association, was formed. As its president, the industry hired the Postmaster General, former chairman of the Republican National Committee and Presbyterian elder, Will H. Hays. His task was to promote a new sense of gravitas for the movies through a whole range of public relations activities, including behind-the-scenes lobbying in Washington. Motion pictures, he argued, had infinite promise as the 'Esperanto of the Eye' that broke down all barriers of language, spoke to all nations and peoples and eventually would clear up all misunderstandings among nations and thus abolish war. And while Hays was promoting his version of the civilising mission of the movies, the Hays Office was developing a production code for self-censorship standards covering the issues of taste and decency. The text of the 1930 version of the code was written by Catholic layman and motion picture trade publisher Martin Quigley, in collaboration with Jesuit priest Daniel A. Lord. It too explicitly cast self-censorship in the context of a civilising mission: 'If motion pictures present stories that will affect lives for the better, they can become the most powerful force for the improvement of mankind.' And this mission was expressly a global mission:

'Motion picture producers recognize the high trust and confidence which have been placed in them by the people of the world and which have made motion pictures a universal form of entertainment. ... Hence, though regarding motion pictures primarily as entertainment without any explicit purpose of teaching or propaganda, they know, that the motion picture within its own field of entertainment may be directly responsible for spiritual or moral progress, for higher types of social life, and for much correct thinking.'[21] In other words, Hollywood would much prefer to have it both ways – it was only entertainment, it was only business, but it was an important and ennobling business. The content of the code prescribed standards and requirements in depicting crime ('the sympathy of the audience should never be thrown to the side of crime, wrong doing, evil or sin'), sex, profanity, dances, costume, religion and national feelings, declaring that 'the history, institutions, prominent people and citizenry of other nations shall be represented fairly'. In 1934, when the Catholic League of Decency began flexing its congregants to boycott films that the Church considered indecent, Hays offered stricter enforcement of self-censorship through the Production Code Administration, headed by the former Irish-Catholic Philadelphia journalist Joseph I. Breen. The Breen Office, as it became known, was the enforcer with the power to approve, censor or reject movies made or distributed by Hollywood studios.

In 1927 the world of Hollywood changed. In October of that year a movie theatre on Broadway showed *The Jazz Singer*, the first talkie. It was an appropriate vehicle for this new departure by the Empire of Hollywood. Leslie Halliwell in his annual film bible describes it as an 'archetypal Jewish weepie'.[22] It is the story of a cantor's son who finds show business fame as a blackface singer in the genre of the American minstrel shows. It made history: 'You ain't heard nothin' yet.' And momentarily it raised fears that the global dominance of Hollywood might be threatened by the diversity of the world's languages as opposed to the universal language of silent film. With 30–40% of gross revenues coming from foreign markets, this was a concern. But the allure of Hollywood, as well as its hold on ownership of theatres and distribution networks around the world, were too strong. Its share of the German and British markets fell less than 10% between 1927 and 1931, and less than 15% in France. Elsewhere in the world, Hollywood continued to supply between 60% and 90% of all films shown, and even a third or more in markets such as India and Japan which had their own highly developed mass-production film industries. The profitability of the global empire of cinema continued, adapting to the language barriers by dubbing, subtitling and for a time even utilising the opportunities of the studio system and the presence of foreign actors to make simultaneous foreign language versions of films.

With the addition of sound, movies became more potent than ever. Movie moguls accepted and promoted their role as moral guardians of America along with their stock in trade: the affirmation of American values as they defined, reconfigured and projected them through their cultural myth-making. So, in 1941 Darryl F. Zanuck could argue convincingly before a Congressional hearing that Hollywood had produced 'pictures so strong and powerful that they sold the American way of life, not only to America but to the entire world'.[23] Louis B. Mayer, founder of the MGM studio, according to his grandson, saw his characteristic films of small town America as 'artefacts of Americana and really saw them as shaping the taste of the country. One part of life in Communist Russia he would have admired if he had stayed behind was the way in which art is focused to shape society ... He wanted values to be instilled in the country and knew how influential films could be and very much wanted to capitalize on it.'[24] Jack Warner, one of the Warner Brothers, the company that made *The Jazz Singer*, expressed a general sentiment when he told a reporter: 'More and more is the realization growing that pictures can and do play an all-important part in the cultural and educational development of the world.'[25]

In the 1930s and 40s, the so-called 'Golden Age', Hollywood

was dominated by the studio system, the enormous economies of scale of mass production that allowed Hollywood to keep turning out the huge quantity of product to satisfy the demand of audiences worldwide. Each studio was headed by a self-made scion of the new immigrants. The films made by each studio answered to the personality and psyche of the head of the studio, who presided over his empire with total command. The studios were repositories of their hopes and dreams and how they saw America. So the civilising, Americanising mission became, and has remained, part and parcel of the mantle of cinema. The imprint the movies bore was that of American empire. 'Out of this mix of energy, suspicion, gloom, iconoclasm, and liberalism', writes Gabler, 'came not only a distinctive kind of film, but also a distinctive vision of America – particularly urban America. It was an environment cruel and indifferent, one almost cosmologically adversarial, where a host of forces prevented one from easily attaining virtue. It was a world that daunted and dared – a world where one's only hope and only meaning lay not in higher morals, not in love, not in family, not in sacrifice, but in action leavened by a vague sense of honour.' This vision found an echo with the under- and working classes of Depression-ridden urban America, 'who felt their own sense of betrayal, suspicion, and anxiety and for many these films came to frame their experience'.[26] And at the end of the day in the cosmology of Hollywood, as in all myth, it is the lone man, the single individual who is the focus, the meaning and the message. The remaking of self is what the movies have always been about.

Films built out of reality and attuned to the psyche of reality became more real than reality. It is not the case that all Hollywood films are triumphalist documents of America and therefore direct and unmediated tools of empire. Rather, films are nuanced expressions of America for America, and work to insulate and isolate the American psyche as the totality of reality. They present America with an image of itself, but they also present America with an image of the world. And then they sell this vision to the whole world. Just as America is depicted in coded stereotypes, stock characters in formulaic narratives that explore cultural myths and legends to represent an idealised nation, so too the world has been encoded in the playbook of Hollywood. The peoples and history of the world have also been reconfigured as stock characters and formulaic narratives, the myths and legends of all the world integrated into the recombinant DNA of Hollywood story-telling.

There is a remarkable consistency to Hollywood's view of the world, which can best be described as the 'Columban vision'. The movies have reacquainted the world with motifs, themes, ideas and symbols that travelled in the backpack of Christopher Columbus, the man who 'discovered' America. Conventional history makes Columbus a 'modern' man, a rationalist man of science opening the way for the advance of Europe and its imperial civilising mission. In constructing this portrait, history airbrushes out all that sits uneasily or contradicts this image. In particular, history pours derision on the well-thumbed, carefully annotated books that Columbus chose to take with him on his voyage. These expressed his vision of the world, what he expected to find when he arrived in the east by travelling west, and he used their conventions to describe everything he found on his arrival. Far from being 'modern', Columbus was a thoroughly 'medieval' man, and his vision of the world was shaped by the *Travels of Sir John Mandeville* and the *Imago Mundi* of Pierre d'Ailly, the books he took with him.[27] These medieval bestsellers presented the world beyond Europe as a place of marvels and wonders, filled with grotesque peoples who defied natural law and who lived beyond the rules of Christian life that defined the values, modes and normality of real life for all Europeans. Far from being fables, fairy tales and proof of the blinded credulity of the medieval mind, the worldview of the books Columbus read, and how he thought, was a well-ordered ideological view of everything. And it provided Columbus, and Europe, with exactly the will to dominate that was the making of imperialism. And what is more it made good stories, archetypal stories that affirmed what Europeans needed to know: they were the true, real people, the centre of the universe; and all Others, all non-Christian and non-European people, were in varying ways and degrees unnatural, wedded to superstition and the works of the Devil, or were agents of the Devil himself and there to be dominated, tutored, conquered and possessed. This ideology was a clear division between right and wrong, Us and Them, friend and enemy, an adversarial vision of the world described in sharply moralist terms with clear imperial meaning. And this 'medieval' ideology informed all the travellers' tales that delighted the reading public long after mere rationalist scientific information was available. In the 20th century this old tradition of the myths and legends underpinning imperialism came to rest in Hollywood, the place where all good stories went to be recast as part of an American ideology of empire.

When Columbus made landfall in the Americas, the people he and his crew found fell into two simple, old and familiar categories: the peaceable, innocent children of nature ready to be taught and tutored in civilisation; and the cannibals beyond the pale of all civilisation, the enemies who had to be annihilated. In Hollywood terms: the good Indian, the loyal scout, the tractable squaw; or the bloodthirsty, the hostile, barbarous, murderous scalping Indian who had to be defeated, had to be eradicated. America is a nation and a mythic culture built on the foundations of the Columban worldview at home. It was a nation founded with slavery within. In Hollywood terms again, there are the house niggers, the mammies – Hattie McDaniel or Butterfly McQueen in *Gone With the Wind* – the Steppin' Fetchits, the Rochesters, the tractable blacks; and there are the bad-ass blacks, the ominous, evil, lurking menace that at any moment could rise up and rape innocent white women in their beds and overthrow all order – a convention begun with *Birth of a Nation* (1915) that lived on to the blaxploitation movies of the 1970s such as *Shaft*. Racism comes included in the foundations of

America and works its way through the language of Hollywood. Whether Indian or Negro, these Others that were part of America were caught in a pre-modern mind: superstitious, easily duped by witchdoctors, ghosts, spirits, mumbo jumbo of any and all kinds, and in awe of the wonders that the white civilised world could create.

Columbus, like all the other explorers who opened the world up for Europe, set sail for the Indies. 'The Indies' was a generic term for all that was not Christian Europe, whether east or west. What would be found there would be part of the generic ideological world picture that the explorers had been taught; they took it with them and inscribed it upon all the people they found. The same is true of Hollywood. They had their natives at home, and the conventions of the Western could simply be transferred anywhere in the world that the storyline required. In the early 1930s, when the reality of the Depression slackened the audience for 'A' feature Westerns and their optimistic, triumphalist nationalism, Hollywood relocated to the Indian frontier of the British Empire. *Lives of a Bengal Lancer* (1934), *Gunga Din* (1939), based on a combination of Kipling's *Soldiers Three* and his best-known poem, and *Wee Willie Winkie* (1937), based on a Kipling short story, were all essentially Westerns set in the East. *Lives of a Bengal Lancer* was such a model of the Columban Indies that it was remade in 1939 as *Geronimo*, the Afghans reconfigured into Apaches in a reworked script using convenient locations on the Hollywood backlot that could be anywhere in the world. Even *The Charge of the Light Brigade* in Michael Curtiz's 1936 version is given a backstory that explains the military debacle in the Crimean War as a revenge punishment for Surat Khan, the evil Afghan assisting the Russian enemy! Africa enters the movies through the *Tarzan* genre. There have been no fewer than 34 Tarzan pictures since the first talkie, *Tarzan the Tiger*, in 1929; and Tarzan too has travelled the Indies, making his appearance in India (1962), having gone to New York in 1942. All the conventions of the Dark Continent have been given Hollywood form in the remakings of *King Solomon's Mines* (1950 and 1985) and the other Ryder Haggard staple, *She* (1935). In the movies, Africans are immersed in the barbaric mindset of animist paganism, an antithesis to all that is civilisation. The Chinese are either evil, as is the case with Ming, the adversary of Flash Gordon (in the Universal Studios serials, 1936–40), or barbarians, dead to humane virtues like the people of *The Good Earth* (1937). The yellow peril and the land of the geisha had their cinematic stock representations, of the past, present and future – and they are all effete, cruel, fanatical and soulless in their opposition to the all-American heroes. The Middle East was essentially the land of the Arabian Nights. Its first Hollywood outings were in Rudolph Valentino's sensuous *The Sheik* (1921) and *The Thief of Baghdad* (1924), with its thousand and one nights of stories spawning a multitude of Hollywood incarnations for Aladdin and Sinbad in a timeless land of allure, marvels and evil villains – before the real villains, the terrorists, arrived to dominate Hollywood's vision and provide the stock plot-line for innumerable films. As far as Hollywood was concerned: the Middle East is either a distant fantasy or a current dark reality, with nothing in between. When Valentino was not alluring in romantic Bedouin mode he embodied the Latin Lover, a generic idea that inscribed the world beyond America as lands of passion. Or there was Mexico, the land of peons, villains, banditos, endless revolutions and gross racial stereotyping. The point, of course, is that racial stereotyping is the function of the Columban worldview, giving easy potted portraits of the lands and their peoples, familiarising the film-going audience with easy footnotes of stock characters – effete, sensual, venal – and formulaic storylines that occur then, now and always in a history of the world channelled through foreign villains and all-American heroes. It is an ideological vision of a world ready for, and needing, the civilising mission of America. In the Columban vision of Hollywood, the hero takes up the white man's burden and wins the day. The unique potency of cinema as empire derives from the structural necessity of the narrative form – every film has a last reel, a denouement, a climactic resolution; and that resolution underlines American power and dominance. In short, the good guys win, and in the movies of course, that means America wins.

This was the empire made on film stock by the Hollywood studio system. It survived the arrival of radio and served the nation during the Second World War, gathering its greatest audience and sustaining its worldwide dominance. But it was overthrown by the same anti-trust laws that broke the Motion Picture Patents Company. 'What remains is a spell, a landscape of the mind, a constellation of values, attitudes, and images, a history and a mythology that is part of our culture and consciousness. What remains is the America of our imaginations and theirs. Out of their desperation and their dreams, they gave us this America', Neal Gabler says of this world.[28] But by the time the axe fell on the studio system, Hollywood was already losing audiences to the new kid on the block: television. The studios adapted in part by recycling their system and their 'B' movies, the familiar genres with their in-built worldview, messages and mythic formulae, using their production facilities to make television programmes. The empire was divided and reconfigured and yet maintained its hold. Movie audiences and profits were in decline in the 1950s through to the 70s, but Hollywood was alive and well. The mechanics of worldwide market dominance established from the early years, honed and developed through the studio era, remain in place. As Costa-Gavras, the Greek-born film-maker, explains:

When *Jurassic Park*, *The Fugitive* or any other big film comes to Paris, the American distributors dictate the terms: 'You can have *Jurassic Park* for 10 or 15 weeks, but to have it you must take another four or five American films to run along with it for two weeks each'. This is called a train – a locomotive film with cars that follow along. No matter how well the secondary films do, they stay for the number of weeks stipulated in the contract. Of course, the exhibitor agrees because he won't be able to get another *Jurassic Park* to pull in the audience. This means there is little room for French or other European titles in any given cinema.[29]

The supply of American television programmes and shows works on similar lines. Hollywood shows are sold in packages, which include a couple of hit shows but also a great deal of other material; and the whole package may be tied with corporate sponsorships. So, while foreign markets are kept open for American films and television products, there is virtually no traffic going the other way – there are hardly any openings for locally produced English, French or Asian films to be shown in American cinemas or for non-American television shows to be broadcast on American television networks. American films now dominate around 70% of the French market, 85% of the Italian market, 90% of the German market and nearly all of the British market. The figures are not too dissimilar for most Asian and Latin American countries. Even in India, which has an acclaimed and thriving local film industry, American films have a substantial slice of the market. While Hollywood movies account for less than one-tenth of the world's annual production of feature-length films, American films account for more than 70% of box office receipts worldwide. 'Anything so big and with so much power over the minds of men', notes Costa-Gavras, 'is dangerous to the democratic spirit'.

Hollywood movies did not fully recover from the collapse of the studio system until the 1980s, when a new system and new technologies offered fresh opportunities in a globalising world for a return to old-fashioned astronomical profits. Instead of the old hierarchical system of first- and second-run movie theatres, Hollywood latched on to mass blanket marketing, the same film in every available cinema opening on the same day. This was the distribution system that gave birth to the blockbuster as a global phenomenon. Hyped, advertised and publicised through every available vehicle of radio, television, newspapers and magazines, and impossible to ignore in its grasp of public attention, when such a film succeeded, it succeeded very big indeed. And picking up the threads laid early in movie history, the blockbuster developed into a vehicle for merchandising: records of the soundtrack, posters, T-shirts and memorabilia of all kinds became the must-have accessories for kids and adults everywhere to add to the health of the bottom line. What made a blockbuster was often nostalgia, a return to the motifs, formulae, ideas and themes that had enabled Hollywood to flourish in its studio heyday. Pastiche was in. Indiana Jones, the Spielberg hero who dominated the box office, was self-consciously a pastiche of 1930s genre pictures, and the 1980s version included all the racial stereotyping of other peoples and the incarnation of the perennial evil enemy in the guise of the Nazis. Then, in another return to the formulae that made Hollywood, came the superheroes recycled from comics: Superman, Batman, Spiderman and many more. The arrival of video cassettes, cable, satellite television, and the internet all provided new leases of life for Hollywood films, new and old. They provided new sources of profit from the back catalogue, new openings for re-showing old films to ever wider audiences, ever more opportunities for a more enveloping grasp of public attention everywhere. The empire, in the words of the quintessential 1980s blockbuster, most definitely struck back to continue its reign and dominance as the pre-eminent force in globalised mass popular culture, whose centre is the Hollywood of the American Dream.

Hollywood entrenches the American Dream and reinforces the dynamics of American mythology, and serves as handmaiden to empire, in four distinct ways. First, it breeds fear and paranoia. Fear surrounds and envelops the settlers who made America, as every Western re-emphasises. Then there are all the villains: the land barons, the speculators, the gunmen, the bankers, the railroad magnates, unscrupulous adventurers and mountebanks of all kinds, crooked politicians and judges, and the systems built on unscrupulous power such as prisons, political machines and industrial corporations – all of which can eat up the innocent little guys, the ordinary citizens beset by powers beyond their strength. And when earthly powers lose their audience appeal, Hollywood recombines the DNA of villainy to produce nasty aliens attacking peaceful American communities. During the Cold War they personified the fear of Red Communists, taking over the United States in such films as *Invasion of the Body Snatchers* (1955). No wonder 45% of Americans believe that intelligent aliens have visited the Earth and are hell-bent on abducting them! National scares, which occur with mundane regularity, about invasive plant and insect species, such as 'Africanised killer bees' and 'South American fire ants', are regularly given film treatment: *The Swarm* (1978), *They Live* (1988), *Tremors* (1989, with its sequel in 1995); or the first explicit, and arguably the best, eco-drama: *The Birds* (1963). At times of crisis, Hollywood always had a new genre, from the horror movies of the 1920s, the space and alien sagas and the monster movies, through to the schlock horror blood-and-zombie movies of the 1970s such as Tobe Hooper's *The Texas Chainsaw Massacre* (1974) or John Carpenter's *Halloween* (1978), which their directors openly acknowledge reflect the trauma of Vietnam.[30] All these films have the same subtext: harmless, peace-loving Americans, and their flora and fauna, are under threat, constantly in danger of being attacked and overwhelmed by more aggressive foreigners.

Second, Hollywood appropriates the narratives and histories of Other cultures, and promotes ignorance and prejudice about Other people. Quite contrary to the strictures of the production code, it is the racial stereotype, the Columban worldview, that Hollywood projects and inscribes over the rest of the world. Third, American movies promote the ideals of the American Dream and American values as something that every person on the planet should aspire to. Fourth, American cinema projects the idea of America as a universal nation with a natural right to domination. The war movies and the spy movies have imagined American dominance, to which all other nations are mere subsidiaries and bit players. In the movies, America has always been the 'leader of the free world' because that is the original ethos that America appropriated for itself.

To a very large extent, these functions of cinema are supported and fuelled by celebrity, the most common currency of empire – the eighth law of American mythology. Celebrity, the star system, is the force that made Hollywood, the mechanism that sold its product to audiences at home and around the world. The first global superstars were the stars of the silent movies: Chaplin, Mary Pickford, Fairbanks and Valentino. Audience rapport with the stars transcended their roles in a particular film. Stars invested their persona into the roles they played in various films. The carefully managed image, the public relations idea of their persona off and on screen, was constructed by the studios to sell their movies. And the star system created whole new industries that lived in a symbiotic relationship with Hollywood: fan magazines, gossip columnists, the endless acres of newsprint on the lifestyles, loves and doings of the stars that fed the ever more voracious appetite of an ever growing and diversifying media industry. In hard currency, it is difficult to know whether the movies or the stars are the highest grossing asset of the Hollywood Empire. What is certain is that the stars are essential to the global domination of American ideas and culture, goods and products, and patterns of consumption, as well as an essential vehicle for promoting the American Dream on a planetary level. Celebrities, recognisable names that are perpetually in the news for one reason or another, or for no reason at all, are made by cinema and television. As American film and television production dominates the planet, most global celebrities are American. Celebrities are both an extension of the American entertainment industry and self-contained entertainment themselves, with their very own globally-broadcast 24-hour cable and satellite channel, the E Channel. And they come in all varieties – indeed, 'there are as many different kinds of celebrities as there are animals in the zoo'.[31] The ranking of celebrities has become an industry in itself. Journalists use a graded system: A-list, B-list, C-list. The American business magazine *Forbes* issues an annual list of the top 100 celebrities, ranked according to their earning power, press and television appearances and website hits. 'Hot lists' of celebrities are published regularly. Every other year, a magazine like *Time* publishes a list of 'the world's most influential people', ranked – unashamedly – according to their contribution to American culture and its dominance.[32] There are weeklies such as *People* and *Hello!* that are devoted totally to celebrities and their lifestyles; and newspapers and magazines like *Vanity Fair* that regularly devote long sections to nothing more than photo portfolios of celebrities; not to forget television programmes that endlessly promote the hagiography of celebrities – including the Biography channel, which endlessly recycles uncritical fodder about American film and television stars. There's an industry within the celebrity industry, the industry that grooms and manages and helps fabricate and sustain celebrities – the world captured in *America's Sweethearts* (2001), a lame attempt at satire focusing on Hollywood's love of self. *America's Sweethearts* takes pot shots at obsequious attendants, cut-throat publicists and snaffling movie junketeers. But there are also 'portrait photographers, make-up artists, hairstylists, dress makers, talent scouts, publicity and marketing departments; the managers, drug dealers, press agents, psychotherapists, plastic surgeons and lawyers employed by major celebrities; the image consultants, speech writers and "spin doctors" … Assistants are essential to busy celebrities and are now called Celebrity Personal Assistants (CPAs) or Celebrity Assistants (CAs) and in the United States, there are agencies that specialise in supplying them.'[33]

In maintaining the dominance of America and its empire, celebrities perform three vital, interrelated functions. First, they create and maintain a market. The ability of American celebrities to dominate the attention of the entire world is the foundation of an empire built on and for trade and commerce. The techniques that create celebrities are the same techniques that are employed to market and sustain political power, or to market and popularise a new consumer product. Indeed, celebrities are commodities; and 'are manufactured, just like cars, clothes and computers', and have a 'commercial value'.[34] On the surface level, as we see in *America's Sweethearts*, celebrities have an obvious commercial value to manufacturers and corporations eager to promote their products. But at a deeper level, celebrities create a market for the endless desire of all things American. Everything they do, everything they wear, everything they surround themselves with becomes important and generates a market. In the final analysis, the market that celebrities create is a market for the American Dream. That's why celebrities play such a crucial role in maintaining and expanding the empire.

Second, celebrities perform the function of attracting attention in a world where it has become increasingly difficult to hold anyone's attention. Celebrities grab and hold the attention of the international public so it can be manipulated and shaped to the dictates of the empire. They are known simply for being known, and have the appeal of instant recognition. As a special class of people, they are granted instant access to television shows and given acres of press coverage. When a film is released, or a new television show hits the small screen, celebrities go on the road to bring the new product to the attention of the world. But this attention is not limited to the new product. Celebrities also bring attention to the empire: what is happening in America and to Americans. So the message of America is relayed constantly through the mouths of people admired and imitated by most of the inhabitants of the planet.

Third, celebrities serve as a rallying call for the ideology of American empire. Celebrities draw and hold people's attention not simply to generate markets for American goods and services

– they also create desire and operate as a magnet for seduction. What celebrities actually sell is psychological desire and social need for their lifestyle, what they personify and what they represent. Celebrities encode values and ideas – it is part of the story that is contained in their publicity material, and is the service that American celebrities offer to the commercial and marketing nexus they work for. Millions of people around the world measure their success or failure by using American celebrities as a yardstick. What they are actually doing is imbibing the encoded norms and values, nursing the manufactured desire to be consumed by the American Empire. The celebrities' symbolism is of success measured by the ultimate test of being the proper model for how life can and should be lived. Celebrities are the American Dream not as lifestyle but as identity, as image and symbol of the American Self. Billy Wilder relates an anecdote about Louis B. Mayer, founder of the film factory MGM. Wilder observed Mayer holding Mickey Rooney, the child star of the 1940s, by the lapel and screaming: 'You're Andy Hardy! You're the United States! You're the Stars and Stripes. Behave yourself! You're a symbol!'[35] So celebrity is the ideology of America writ large on the global scale.

In these three ways, celebrity and the culture of celebrity function in a truly globalised realm of American empire. The Oscars provide just one illustration of both the power of American cinema and the global reach of American celebrity. The star-studded ceremony is broadcast to the globe and generates endless coverage on television, radio, press and the internet. The saga of a particular celebrity like Michael Jackson is relayed to a captive world audience as it unfolds, minute by minute. The private lives of celebrity couples, such as Jennifer Aniston and Brad Pitt, their sexual exploits and marital upheavals, are conveyed, blow by blow, to planetary spectators. These are not simply newsworthy events, although even as news they demonstrate the global power of American celebrities. They are rituals that mythologise the power of America and pay homage to the engine of empire.

Thus, celebrity is a special kind of mythology, as well as being an integral part of the overall system of American mythology. There are three words that thread American popular culture into a universe of myth: hero, star and celebrity. Mythic narrative is, we are informed by the experts, always built around the exploits of heroes. In the epics, sagas and stories, it is the heroes as human archetypes who mediate with enduring values in complex ways for the instruction and edification of the masses. Heroes, individuals who stand for something bigger than themselves, acquire fame by doing exceptional deeds, by demonstrating their courage, intelligence or leadership. Heroes become heroes by undertaking an epic journey that leads them to overcome insurmountable odds and evaluate their own self. In American mythology, stars of film and television are accorded the status of heroes simply for undertaking the journey to become an entertainer. On the other end of the spectrum, minor celebrities, particularly American sports celebrities, seek to become stars. It is cinema that ultimately provides the shine of a true celebrity. So, while 'the hero was distinguished by his achievement', notes Daniel Boorstin in *The Image, or What Happened to the American Dream*, the star/celebrity has nothing more to offer than 'his image or trademark. The hero created himself; the celebrity is created by the media. The hero was a big man; the celebrity is a big name.'[36]

Just as stars are mythologised as heroes, so heroes are mythologised as stars. John Walker illustrates the point by relating the life story of Audie Murphy (1924–71). Murphy was an orphan of a modest household in Texas. A crack shot, he joined the army, fought in the Second World War, and emerged as one of the most decorated soldiers of America. Celebrity life led to a career in the movies; most notably, Murphy played himself in the 1955 film version of his autobiography, *To Hell and Back*. Murphy made many 'B' Westerns, usually playing a gunfighter. So, 'Murphy was a real war hero who became a Hollywood star playing heroic roles even though his acting skills were limited and his boyish features made him an unconvincing tough-guy'.[37] The film star and hero suffered from post-traumatic stress and died in a plane crash at the young age of 46. But his story does not end with his death. The American artist Richard Krause memorialised and confirmed the mythic status of Murphy in 2000 by painting seven portraits of the star, which he donated to the Audie Murphy Research Foundation. The myth of Murphy is kept alive by the Foundation through its website and news-letter and a fan club. Murphy is also commemorated in Oklahoma City's National Cowboy Hall of Fame.

American history is replete with heroes of this kind. As we discussed in Chapters One and Two, the historic narrative of America itself is woven through the telling of the deeds of such heroes. The heroes are real people – George Washington, Thomas Jefferson, Daniel Boone, Andrew Jackson, Davy Crockett, Kit Carson, Buffalo Bill, and anti-heroes like Jesse James and Billy the Kid. We know they are heroes because that is how they have been made famous, and their fame is secured by being enveloped in myth, the subject of popular narrative genres built on their lives and deeds. But the really interesting thing about American history is not that it is enveloped in myths of heroes, stars and celebrities, but its contemporaneity, the simultaneous occurrence of deed and mythologising. It is a narrative lived less in the light of history than of serialisation, yellow journalism, the television mini-series, the celluloid hagiography and ultimately the movies. In a genuine sense, America conflates and simultaneously consumes history and myth through manipulating the public's fascination with heroes as stars.

The question is not unpicking reality from myth. Nor is it a question of demystifying fact from fiction. The point is understanding how the manufacture and manipulation are operated. And from the first stirrings of the star system there is a format to star celebrity. It is the self-same format that constructs the narrative structure of the film biopic, the movie of the life story of a famous person. It begins with humble origins, the early struggle for recognition of talent, the overnight success that is the product of hard work and dedication but which turns on innate talent that is unstoppable. After that there are a variety of scenarios, from troubled life and personal tragedy through to installation in the hearts of millions as the star is constructed as an icon, the living embodiment of the American Dream. In his study of fame, Leo Braudy argues that in the ancient world – indeed through most of history – fame was a way of honouring 'what aspired to be permanent in human action and thought, beyond death and all of life's accidents'.[38] In contrast, 'popular culture in democratic societies serves as a form of collective emotional memory, which supports the creation of our social identities, not because we owe allegiance to the state and its institutional occasions, but because we connect the stages of our lives to public people and their doings'.[39] And, as Braudy also notes, money has a great deal to do with the manufacture and manipulation. It also has consequences on the possibilities and potential for political debate in America. Increasingly, politicians are presented, packaged and marketed in parody of stars. The biopic of the candidate, using the conventions familiar from Hollywood films, trailing implications of heroism, has become a necessity of every campaign. Image is a political growth industry while substance in political debate withers. To be a celebrity appears to be the surest route to political success. At the centre of the American psyche is a fascination with heroes – a natural enough phenomenon across all cultures. But American desire is for specific heroes, heroes who are stars, and stars who have global presence. This historic pattern has become intertwined with the rising culture of celebrity, weaving film, celebrity, politics and empire in one complex whole.

As the frontier was being lived it was mythologised, and as mythology it passed swiftly into the realms of popular culture. This pattern keeps on recurring. A basic source for narratives of movies and television is newspapers, just as Larry Levy insists in *The Player*: the boiler-room of celebrity culture. News is not the stuff of celebrity culture so much as a modern perversion. In America, news has always been the bedrock of the largest and most pervasive industry there is: celebrity. Cases in the law courts, the based-on-a-true-story syndrome, not only feed the insatiable appetite of films and television for storylines – they make celebrities of criminals. If myth is a realm of negotiation and film and television are the arena of mythologising, it is hardly surprising that whatever happens in America gets encapsulated in its films and television. It is not simply that America now lives itself through television, that events become events when they are watched live on television. That is only half the story. The more significant other half of the story is that there is virtually no time lag between the event in reality and the entry of the event into mythologising and mediation in the medium of television drama and films. The trauma of 9/11 and what happened afterwards provides an illustration. Within weeks, the event became the subject of the first television mediation in the special edition of *The West Wing*.[40] As soon as the Washington snipers – who terrorised the suburbs around Washington, DC with random shootings – had been caught, they became a television film. Indeed, the film was broadcast before the jury had reached its verdict! In the television series *JAG* (about the Judge Advocate General service), the military trial of suspected terrorists was being portrayed almost as quickly as the administration was preparing for real trials. The military lawyers, who in reality supervise the denial of human rights in such places as Guantánamo Bay to the contravention of international law, were being portrayed on television as shining examples of the scrupulous fairness, balance and integrity of America. They track, vanquish and bring to justice terrorists with aplomb, style and unerring success. *The Agency*, another television series, provides an obvious example of how the process of instant mythologising has proceeded, and the bizarre, counterfactual counterpoint that television offers to reality. Advertised as the first series to actually film in the precincts of the CIA headquarters, it was upstaged by reality. Its storylines, prepared in advance, showed an organisation tackling events that became real, and it had to be shunted from the schedules as a result. But more importantly, given that the war in Iraq was founded on totally faulty intelligence, *The Agency* is relentlessly hyped as a demonstration of the omniscience and unerring success of the organisation designated as fall guy for that war. Real events are mythologised, even before they are digested by Americans themselves or the people of the world. And this tendency is accelerating, collapsing the future on the present to produce a homogenised continuum of past, present and future. This is not mere entertainment; it is not just propaganda or astute public relations. It is a political act with political consequences, because it is the operation of a coherent ideology: we don't just see life as a movie – we live within a movie of our lives, where the opportunity to stop and debate what is happening, why it is happening, and whether anything can be done is becoming ever more rare. Serious debate of anything is being drowned out by the dictates and clamour of a celebrity culture that is no longer background noise, but life itself.

In the opening tracking shot of *The Player*, Japanese executives wander the studio precincts and the son of a Wall Street investor mooches around the offices of the studio's top executive looking for a celebrity date. The connections between Wall Street, celebrity and cinema are neatly made. The proliferation of celebrity culture as the global life medium of the 21st century, and the power of global corporations, has consolidated the American entertainment industry in the hands of fewer and fewer corporations. Almost everything we see and hear is now under the economic clout and cultural sway of mega-corporations such as AOL Time Warner, Disney, General Electric, News Corporation, AT&T, Viacom, and Sony. The integration, the search for monopoly and complete control that marked the birth and then the rise and rise of Hollywood, has reconfigured itself for a new technological era. But the Leviathan itself keeps getting bigger and more influential, sucking in more space and time, turning every aspect of our lives into some form of infotainment. And, in the end, it reduces audiences the world over into standardised units of consumers of empire. 'The real impact of these vertical integration mergers', notes Benjamin Barber, 'is going to be the gradual homogenisation of culture on a planetary scale and the choking off of difference. This will not come as a result of overt censorship, tyranny or even the monopolistic intent of a small group of media owners, but rather as a consequence of market forces that tend to give popular majoritarian culture the edge. Imitation and competition for that majoritarian market will squeeze out anything too innovative or different.'[41] Barber describes this tendency as 'totalistic'; others have labelled it 'totalitarian'. Either way, cinema and celebrity work not just to expand and enhance the empire but also to colonise the imagination and future of all other cultures. All those things that are outside the purview of the empire, the reality of Other people and other cultures, can exist only on the margins. The wiring of every individual on the planet into the warm embrace of cinema and celebrity leaves little room to imagine other possibilities, other ways of knowing, being and doing. We no longer know how to imagine because Hollywood imagines for us all: 'it has *become* our imagination, it has *become* our power to envision, and describe.'[42] The business of show business is the business of empire is the business of colonising all minds and undermining all imaginations.

CHAPTER FIVE

Sands of Iwo Jima: The Psychosis of War

'A lone and outnumbered, they had one thing in their favour ... the American Dream': so runs the promotional tagline for *Sands of Iwo Jima*. At the climax of the film, Marines struggle in the strong winds atop Mount Suribachi. Straining together, six men raise aloft the Star Spangled Banner, Old Glory. The film reconstructs an actual 1945 event photographed by Joe Rosenthal: 'In that moment, Rosenthal's camera recorded the soul of a nation.'[1] Images in the midst of war; images captured in the moment and used to serve the war effort. Images recreated for the movies to cement the relationship between the cinema and the military. And these images have lived on as an iconic statement of a nation under the shadow of war; they not only serve the causes of war but also help sustain the military-industrial complex of the national security state. National security is the rallying cry that has cultivated a war psychosis and made America a pre-eminent power – the greatest accumulation of power there has ever been in human history, and at greater material cost than human imagination can easily comprehend. If the moment on Iwo Jima encapsulates the American Dream, its consequences are global nightmare.

Iwo Jima, or Volcano Island as it is named on maps, is a speck of rock in the Pacific. A Japanese possession strategically located some 600 miles south-east of Tokyo, in 1945 it was a fortified airfield, a necessary stepping stone, an essential war objective. It was the site of one of the bloodiest battles of the Pacific theatre in the Second World War. The assault on Iwo Jima has been described as 'throwing human flesh against reinforced concrete'. US Marines fought an enemy so well dug in they hardly ever saw a live Japanese soldier. In 38 days of fighting there were 25,851 American casualties, of whom 6,821 died, a one in three casualty ratio of the expeditionary force. One company of Marines, Easy Company, suffered 75% casualties: of the 310 men who landed on the island only 50 boarded ship after the battle. Virtually all the 22,000 Japanese who held the island died. The facts of Iwo Jima seem more like the carnage of the First World War. Yet it is not the facts of Iwo Jima but the image it produced that is so potent.

On 23 February 1945, after four days of fighting, five Marines of Easy Company and one Navy Corpsman raised the American flag on Mount Suribachi, the volcanic cone of Iwo Jima. Marine Sergeant Bill Genaust filmed the event and Associated Press photographer Joe Rosenthal took the still picture: 'It has every element ... It has everything ... It's perfect: the position, the body language ... You couldn't set anything up like this – It's just so perfect', photographer Eddie Adams says of this picture.[2] Ongoing controversy alleges the picture was staged. It has become one in the lexicon of images used to demonstrate that in war, truth is the first casualty. Rosenthal has consistently defended and vindicated his claim for the veracity – vérité – of his picture. The power of the image itself has never been in doubt. Within two days of Rosenthal's picture being published the US Senate was discussing turning it into a monument. President Franklin D. Roosevelt decided on a more pragmatic use. He selected it as the symbol for the seventh Bond Tour to raise the money to pay for America's war effort. Soon the image was everywhere – in a million retail store windows, 16,000 movie theatres, 15,000 banks, 200,000 factories, 30,000 railroad stations and 5,000 billboards across America – and there was a nationwide tour by the three surviving members of the group that raised the flag, recalled from the Pacific expressly for this purpose. It raised $24 billion.

In 1949 Hollywood returned to this most potent of images, faithfully recreating the event in Allan Dwan's film *Sands of Iwo Jima*. There were cameo appearances by the three survivors of the actual flag-raising – John Bradley, René Gagnon and Ira Hayes – prominently trailed in the opening credits. As a whole, the film intercut actual combat footage from Iwo Jima with scenes filmed at Camp Pendleton, the Marine Corps base in California. *Sands of Iwo Jima* is more than a cinematic homage to an icon. It confirmed the stardom of another icon: John Wayne. And it consolidated the movie cliché of the tough, hard-bitten sergeant sternly, even mercilessly, preparing his troops for the rigours of combat. Wayne's character might die on Iwo Jima, but his stardom would live on to become another icon of the American Dream and be forever identified with the military prowess, preparedness for war and power of the nation.

The Second World War was a war of mass mobilisation, a war in which Hollywood too did its bit. Stars such as James Stewart, Tyrone Power, Eddie Albert, Robert Montgomery, and the brightest luminary of all, Clark Gable, enlisted and saw distinguished service. They served not just on the front line. Ronald Reagan spent the war making training films before earning his honourable discharge from the Navy. Frank Capra offered his services to the War Department and directed a whole series of documentaries, the first of which, *Prelude to War* (1942), won an Oscar. The series, known as *Why We Fight*, was described by Winston Churchill as the most perfect 'statement of our cause'. Capra's films were seen by every enlisted American serviceman. John Ford spent the war in the Field Photographic Branch of OSS, the Office of Strategic Services, forerunner of the CIA. Ford's *The Battle of Midway* (1942) also won an Oscar. Walt Disney turned his studio into a plant producing films for the war effort. 'The call went out to all of us to get busy, to roll up our shirtsleeves and get things moving', John Wayne is quoted as saying of the aftermath of Pearl Harbor.[3] The statement is perfectly accurate and exactly what one expects John Wayne to say. Except, as is well known, John Wayne was conspicuous as one who never enlisted, making what Garry Wills describes as a 'career choice': remaining in Hollywood to seek the stardom that had so far eluded him by evading the call of the draft board.[4] Wayne's campaign brought a victory more decisive, more potent than any other. When he died in 1979, a Japanese newspaper headline simply read: 'Mr America Dies.'

World war produced its own necessity. It created a strategic collaboration between government and Hollywood. A tax on the ticket price made going to the movies seem patriotic. It delivered to Hollywood its greatest audiences, a peak of 90 million people a week, some two-thirds of the American population. And despite Hollywood's concern about loss of overseas markets, the war generated the most profitable era of movie-making until the 1980s. In movie theatres people could see newsreels of what was happening 'over there'. The newsreels were only part of the programme the ticket bought – newsreel, cartoon, second and main feature, as well as adverts. And all, by design, delivered a concentrated message supportive of the war effort.

The strategic elements of collaboration were various. Before the war, in 1938, the government had filed an anti-trust suit intent on breaking the studios' monopoly of the film-making process through the vertical integration of production, distribution and exhibition. It was abandoned for the duration as a quid pro quo for Hollywood's demonstration of patriotism. As international tension grew in Europe in the 1930s, many perceived Hollywood as pro-Britain, and war films such as *A Yank in the RAF* (1941) and the Oscar-laden *Mrs Miniver* (1942) strengthened this perception, while America was still firmly isolationist. Hollywood was a haven for European refugees and émigrés, and the major studios were conspicuously owned by Jews. During the years of the Depression, Hollywood liberals embraced both social activism and anti-fascism, sentiments they were criticised for including in their movies. When war broke out in Europe in September 1939, Franklin D. Roosevelt told the American people: 'I hope the United States will keep out of this war. I believe it will.' The Democratic platform on which he campaigned for re-election in 1940 was unequivocal on not taking America to war – except in case of attack. When the attack came at Pearl Harbor everything changed. Roosevelt's covert support for Britain became all-out effort against Hitler, and Hollywood had the opportunity to place itself at the heart of the nation's efforts. Washington formed the Office of War Information to mobilise propaganda. It offered Hollywood government assistance in the form of technical advice, archival battle footage, uniforms, extras, tanks, planes and ships for making war films. In return it required script approval before shooting, removal of material deemed unpatriotic, and close monitoring of plot-lines. Hollywood also had its own informal system of regulation through the Hays Office, which monitored its own voluntary Production Code, the play-book of what should and could not be said or shown.

From this strategic collaboration came an outpouring of films, not solely war films, with considerable consistency of form and ideology. The specifics of the war film can clearly be seen in *Sands of Iwo Jima*. The military becomes the microcosm of America, the institutional vessel of the American Dream of democracy, fighting for liberty and freedom to achieve the purpose of the nation. *Sands of Iwo Jima*, like so many others, concentrates on a platoon made up of the diversity of America. The focus is on the ordinary soldiers who come from different backgrounds – rich, poor, urban, rural, college kids and the barely educated; indeed, many wartime films displayed a level of integration which was true of neither the forces at the time nor the nation as a whole. War films aimed to explain what the troops were fighting for – the ideals of America, their defence and expansion across the globe. They also required a radical simplification of all complexity; war films were about the confrontation of good and evil, the fight against an enemy that was cruel, remorseless and barbaric. In this context, the platoon becomes the agent of good and decency, the metaphor for family, for collective endeavour, and ultimately serves as the collective experience, memory and memorial for the audience and the nation.

While *Sands of Iwo Jima* bears all the hallmarks of wartime strategic collaboration and its essential message, the film has strategic significance in another sense. It stands at the point where the propaganda ethos of wartime mobilisation was being read back into history and cast forward to shape the coming Cold War.

In the films John Wayne made during the Second World War, many of them war films, he was most often cast as second banana, the dissonant element whose role is to underline the fact that victory required not following individual passion and thus detracting from the collective effort necessary for effective action. This is his role in John Ford's 1945 film *They Were Expendable*. Wayne's stardom was a post-war phenomenon, beginning with Howard Hawks's *Red River* (1948) and confirmed by the John Ford cavalry trilogy – *Fort Apache* (1948), *She Wore a Yellow Ribbon* (1949) and *Rio Grande* (1950). The stern, hard-bitten, unbending father figure, the prototype for Sergeant Stryker in *Iwo Jima*, is there in *Red River*. The consummate professional soldier is his role in the cavalry trilogy. Ford's trilogy is a paean of praise to the common soldiery. As we have seen, *Fort Apache* concludes with the national necessity of making legends, even from military disaster, to serve the cause of military preparedness. *She Wore a Yellow Ribbon*, made in the same year as *Sands of Iwo Jima*, takes the theme even further in its opening and closing narration. The scene is set with a remarkable falsification of history. 'Custer is dead. And around the bloody guidon of the immortal 7th Cavalry lie 212 officers and men. The Sioux and Cheyenne are on the warpath', we are told. The news is telegraphed across 'the lonely miles' of the west. Its effect is fear in settlements and homesteads 'under threat of Indian uprising'. Then the outrageous claim – 'Pony Express riders know that one more such defeat and it will be a hundred years before another wagon train dares to cross the plains.'! The Indians are joining in common cause, 'making war against the US cavalry'. In fact, the narrative of the film is highly topical: it locates President Truman's Cold War stance, the doctrine of containment of Communism, in the 19th-century American West. The climax of the film is a daring raid in which the cavalry run off the war ponies of the Indians and thereby forestall a war. The hostiles are to be herded back to their reservation, humiliated, under the watchful eyes of the cavalry. The final sequence shows a troop of cavalry riding the land they have now secured. As the narration tells us: 'So here they are, the dog faced soldiers, the regulars, the 50 cent a day professionals, riding the outposts of a nation … They were all the same, men in dirty shirt blue and only a cold page in the history books to mark their passing. But wherever they rode and whatever they fought for, that place became the United States.'

In different films, stars inform and expand the references encoded in the narratives. Not only do these films make the military central to the history, national purpose and future of America, they embody complex symbolic ideas in the screen persona that became John Wayne. And in all three pictures – *Fort Apache*, *She Wore a Yellow Ribbon* and *Sands of Iwo Jima* – the character who is the ardent, sometimes questioning but ultimately convinced apprentice who learns the necessity of war and military preparedness, is played by the same actor – John Agar. These three films came at a turning point in history when the ideals taught as *Why We Fight* were not being demobilised but reconfigured to serve preparedness for a different kind of war, a Cold War that would place the military and war at the centre of national life. To be ready, the military had to be trained, had to be hardened. The motif of Marine training would recur again and again, and eventually attain a sinister meaning as a cinematic cliché.

War and military preparedness were the making of the United States. This is not mere Hollywood cinematic licence; it is a constant motif running through the entire course of the nation's history. America begins with taking up arms against 'savage' native inhabitants. The earliest instructions to the personnel of the Virginia Company licensed them to use force and cautioned them never to permit the savages to see a dead white person, lest their military invulnerability be called into question. King Philip's War, 1675–77, set the pattern for so many later conflicts in which attack on the native inhabitants was reported as response to aggression, an act of self-defence. In time, the colonists took up arms against the British Empire and established their independence through war. The Continental Army was the foundational institution through which America came to be a nation.

Nations themselves are narrations, a product of historical narratives that provide a sense of shared experience, a platform for solidarity and a reservoir of national symbols. *The Making of a Nation*, a popular 'collector's edition' history published by *US News and World Report*, provides a handy list of '100 Milestones That Define America', documents brought forward from the National Archive 'to further the public's appreciation of our nation's civic legacy'.[5] The bulk of these documents are directly or indirectly related to war. As *The Making of a Nation* shows, the Declaration of Independence – the call to war – and the Gettysburg Address – a memorial to one of the bloodiest battles of the bloodiest war – are powerful symbols that shaped the story of the American community. Through such symbols, the collective memory of America filters its past, manages its present and envisions its future. While the Declaration of Independence symbolised America's separation from the British Empire, it was the War of Independence which turned that separation into a reality. But it was unlike any other war of independence fought around the world against colonial rule. 'The first successful anti-colonial war in the modern period', notes David Ryan, 'it also represents one of the most advanced forms of white colonial expansion ... Independence facilitated the process of future white expansion across the continent. Unlike the processes of decolonisation that characterised the rise of the nation-states in the late twentieth century, in which the indigenous populations rejected the foreign occupants, in America the foreign occupants were there to stay.'[6] The revolutionaries, quickly canonised and turned into Founding Fathers, were expansionists who saw war as a necessary means to achieve their goals – their ideas and exploits produced the ninth law of American mythology: war is a necessity.

What American history offers is a repertoire of themes and reflexes, a set of motifs providing an insight into the American psyche. The Bush administration has been blamed extensively for creating a culture of perpetual war, from the language of 'Infinite Justice' and imposing democracy to the idea of pre-emptive war on Iraq and threats of similar actions against Syria and Iran, to its rejection of the Nuclear Test Ban Treaty and the International Criminal Court. But there is nothing really new in the war-mongering, divisive political outlook of the Bush administration. The defensive impulse, the scare-mongered mindset, the need to justify aggression as defence, and the illiberal tendencies these fears unleash domestically and abroad, all recur in American history – as does the political rationale for expansion justified in terms of spreading benevolent democracy and free markets that in practice serve to advance the cause of American commerce. Even the most specific actions of the Bush administration, such as the USA-PATRIOT Act ('Uniting and Strengthening America by Providing Appropriate Tools Required to Intercept and Obstruct Terrorism') and the suppression of scientific results that undermine its policies, have strong precedents in American history. The use of the military as a metaphor for society began right at the beginning – with America itself.

During the American Revolutionary War, France was the ally of the fledgling Republic, contributing money, munitions and men to the war effort which, historians argue, made the decisive contribution to its success. The Statue of Liberty was the symbolic gift to America from France memorialising this alliance. The French fought to achieve liberties for Americans they themselves did not possess. The alliance was sealed by two treaties of 1778, written by Benjamin Franklin, which stipulated that France would drop its claims to Canada – opening the way for it to be made the fourteenth state of the Republic, long to remain a foreign policy objective of the new nation – while the new Republic 'guaranteed the present possessions' of France in the western hemisphere, such as its eleven islands in the West Indies, 'from the present time and forever' – the terminology so evocative of all the treaties the new nation would make with its native inhabitants, and which were to meet the same fate.

France had its own revolution in 1792, to acquire for French citizens the liberties they had secured for Americans. Fourteen years of independence, however, had made quite a difference to the American outlook. Britain and France were soon at war, and that concentrated minds wonderfully across the Atlantic. Although the American Republic was now independent, most of its trade was still with Britain. The old empire moved swiftly to seize American shipping in furtherance of its blockade of France; American seamen were shanghaied to serve in British ships, and in various other ways Britain offered ample grounds for America to side with its treaty partner France. But that was not at all what the new 'rising empire' had in mind. In 1793 President George Washington issued a Neutrality Proclamation, while the conservative faction, led principally by Alexander Hamilton, began strategising for something more useful to the American purpose.

As the European conflict progressed, Hamilton won approval for an increase in the American army, the construction of a navy, the flotation of a war loan, and wartime taxes. Hamilton was appointed Inspector General, second-in-command, of the new forces. 'Besides eventual security against invasion, we ought certainly to look at possession of the Floridas and Louisiana and we ought to squint at South America', Hamilton wrote to Secretary of War McHenry. As war fever spread in a poisoned atmosphere of dissension within America, a series of four legislative measures were introduced to contain and punish dissent. The Naturalization Act raised from five to fourteen years the residence requirement for those seeking citizenship. The Alien Enemies Act empowered the President to arrest, jail or exile any alien of an enemy state. The Alien Act gave the President authority to order any alien judged 'dangerous to the peace and safety of the United States' out of the country; this was aimed principally against radical-minded Irishmen. The Sedition Act made it a 'high misdemeanour' subject to a $2,000 fine and a jail term of up to two years for anyone to publish 'false, scandalous and malicious writing' against the government, Congress or President. Anyone opposing enforcement of federal law or advising 'insurrection ... or combination' was liable to up to five years' imprisonment or a $5,000 fine. Twenty-five people were tried under the provisions of the Sedition Act; ten Republican journalists or printers were convicted. David Brown was sentenced to four years' imprisonment for persuading people in New England to erect liberty poles bearing the sign:

NO STAMP ACT, NO SEDITION, NO ALIEN
BILLS, NO LAND TAX, DOWNFALL TO THE
TYRANTS OF AMERICA, PEACE AND
RETIREMENT TO THE PRESIDENT, LONG
LIVE THE VICE PRESIDENT AND
THE MINORITY

The Federalist press sought to create the right mentality to support war and contain dissent. 'Take care you sleepy southern fools. Your Negroes will probably be your masters this day twelve month and your matrons and young girls will be defiled', wrote William Cobbett, editor of the *Porcupine Gazette*, elaborating the consequences of Jacobin liberty under which guns bought in the French West Indies would soon be used in Virginia and Georgia. Fisher Ames, the 'sage of Dedham', urged the administration to 'wage war, and call it self defence'.

Preparations for this undeclared war against France threw into relief the deep divisions among the American public. Vice President Thomas Jefferson retired to compose a series of resolutions, which he hoped would be passed by each state legislature, including opposition to the Alien and Sedition Acts. They were passed, in watered-down form, by only two states. In this context of public division, President Adams began to rethink his position and opened diplomatic channels to France. The result was the 1800 pact with Napoleon resolving shipping and commercial matters. Hamilton found himself head of an army for territorial expansion with nowhere to go. But territorial expansion there was. With a pact in place and Napoleon master of Spain, the stage was set for the Louisiana Purchase of 1803 by which the by now President Thomas Jefferson acquired 828,000 square miles of American real estate for $15 million.

The notion of interfering in the internal affairs of other countries, of subverting and undermining legitimate and representative rulers, also emerged in the formative phase of American history. The war of 1801–05 against Tripoli aroused little interest among the populace. It was, argues Sidney Lens, the first example of a situation where 'Uncle Sam sponsored, organised, led and paid for an internal revolt against a recognised regime'.[7] Lens is referring to the scheme that William Eaton proposed to President Thomas Jefferson and his Secretary of State, James Madison. Jefferson had misgivings about interfering in the internal affairs of another state. But Madison argued that the principle of non-intervention should be countermanded by the principle of 'just war'. The scheme called for backing Hamet Karamanli in overthrowing his brother Yusuf as Pasha of Tripoli to secure a leader who would be more compliant to the interests and protection of US shipping. The costs of America's intervention were to be borne by Hamet out of a $20,000 tribute that he would levy on the Swedes, the Danes and the Dutch (the other nationalities who often served as flags of convenience for European shipping in North African waters), once installed on his throne courtesy of American military backing. The whole military endeavour, led by a motley crew, was a debacle. The scheme was upstaged by intervention of the American consul in Algiers, who negotiated a settlement by which Yusuf would keep his throne on the pledge of not molesting American shipping.

Throughout the 1800s, war and preparation for war served the expansion of America to secure new territories and fulfil its manifest destiny to 'overspread the continent' and reach far beyond in search of markets. The Union expanded westwards. American citizens, with the tacit support of government and politicians, poured into Texas, still a province of Mexico. They banded together and took up arms against the revolutionary government in Mexico City. The Battle of the Alamo in 1836, the iconic resistance to the last man, memorialised in cinema by John Wayne (*The Alamo*, 1960), was a sacrifice in service of war preparedness for land-grabbing newcomers to territory that was not part of the United States of America. By their efforts Texas became an independent republic, only later, in 1845, added to the US. But the Texan adventure prepared the stage for the wars of 1846–48 which annexed half the territory of Mexico, all the land west of Texas to California, to the United States. In the Mexican War, the young West Point graduates who would become the leading commanders of the Civil War served together and learned their battle craft. The West Point class of 1854 is the theme of the film *Santa Fe Trail* (1940). While the 'class' was completely inaccurate in placing eight future generals of the Civil War as contemporaries at West Point, it was right in general principle – any class from the 1820s to the 1860s produced general officers who fought on each side. Intriguingly, *Santa Fe Trail* puts the strongest arguments for defence of the

Union and the importance of the military as the central institution of American society into the mouths of J.E.B. Stuart (hero of the film, played by Errol Flynn) and Jefferson Davis, then Secretary of War of the United States but later to be President of the Confederate States of America, leader of the South.

The Civil War was the second greatest military mobilisation in American history, and in its aftermath the military was systematically used to eradicate the native inhabitants of the vast western territories of America: 'wherever they rode and whatever they fought for, that place became the United States.' And the expansion beyond the continent began, driven by desire for stepping stones to the markets of China. Hawaii was occupied in 1867, the trail blazed by missionaries who were the forefathers of landowning sugar planters and pineapple growers. Alaska was purchased from Russia the following year. The Custer debacle in 1876, far from being a threat to this process, was one last flicker of victorious defiance for the native peoples in the midst of a coordinated military campaign. Custer was one element of a three-pronged manoeuvre for the eradication of 'hostiles'. After his defeat the other contingents moved swiftly to subjugate the tribes. The retribution was the prelude to Wounded Knee, the last horror of the Indian Wars. In 1890, Chief Big Foot's small band of Minniconjou Sioux were mown down by troops using Hotchkiss machine guns, the wounded left to die in the snow. The iconic photograph of the body of Chief Big Foot contorted and frozen is the memorial of the closing of the American frontier and the opening of global imperialism. In the doctrine of imperial expansion advanced by Theodore Roosevelt in his 'Expansion and Peace' (1899), he argued that 'peace' could be imposed on 'barbarian races' only by armed force of a superior race. The meaning of the doctrine became evident in the Spanish American War. As we saw in Chapter Three, America claimed the Philippines, another stepping stone to China. When Filipinos failed to recognise this liberation and began an insurgency against American forces, their action was read as provocation justifying a 'savage' war: the resort to the tactics, methods and consequent atrocities of the home-grown Indian wars against 'savages'. The conflation of imperial wars with these domestic wars is explored in detail by Richard Slotkin in *Gunfighter Nation*.[8] As Slotkin points out, the exploits of the military, in wars domestic and foreign, were simultaneously revised and fabricated into public myth and ideology in popular literature and entertainment. The triumph of American arms was recycled as a symbolic statement of national purpose in such spectacles as Buffalo Bill's Wild West Show. Huge audiences in cities across America, and internationally, visited the shows to see and experience the cavalry charges, the Indian fights, and in time the Rough Riders taking San Juan Hill in Cuba (1898), the other theatre of the Spanish American War. And those who could not get to Buffalo Bill's extravaganza could see moving pictures of the Rough Riders in the new nickelodeons. Of course there were no film cameras on site in Cuba to record the taking of San Juan Hill. The movie version was reconstructed on film lots in New Jersey.

The Rough Rider sequence proved to be the most popular attraction for both the Wild West Show and the new nickelodeons. But the military metaphor, the willingness to appropriate the idea of war as a pervasive social concept, has a longer and deeper hold on the American psyche. Slotkin argues that it begins with the Civil War, the conflict that not only embraced all of America but reconfigured and remade the idea of the nation. We have seen the symbolic importance of the Gettysburg Address. It was a subtle reshaping of the mission statement of America – 'a new birth of freedom' – one that remained problematic in terms of the Constitutional order. The carnage of the war was transmuted into nostalgia and idealised as a call to high purpose, both of which served to disseminate the idea of the nobility and efficacy of military organisation. One only has to think of the 1993 film *Gettysburg* with its intense and sympathetic portraits of both armies to grasp how all-embracing and all-pervasive the battle made both war and the military in American consciousness. The producer Ted Turner felt so passionate about the project that he insisted on having a role as one of the ordinary Confederate soldiers. The first great landmark of cinema is D. W. Griffith's *Birth of a Nation* (1915), a battle epic that demonstrated the technical and emotional possibilities of cinema, but one dedicated to unabashed racism. And the most enduring cinema epic is *Gone With the Wind* (1939) – the only movie, apart from Disney cartoons, made before 1960 to feature on the all-time list of highest grossing films – a eulogy to the ante-bellum South in which war is a central character. The ability of the military to mould social solidarity to set all hands working towards a noble goal begins with the Civil War. As America grew richer, more divided and nakedly acquisitive and corrupt in the aftermath of war, it was 'retrospectively idealised, producing such formulations as William James' call for a "Moral Equivalent of War" to mobilise patriotism and Edward Bellamy's utopian vision of a society built around the just and efficient workings of an "Army of Industry"'.[9]

Nineteenth-century America bequeathed to 20th-century America multiple traditions and motifs of war as a necessity, understood as idealised patriotism and social metaphor. And the necessity of war is the military. The Second World War saw the mass mobilisation of American society, the only experience comparable to the Civil War. The ratio of military participation to total population for both sides in the Civil War was 11.1%; the figure for the Second World War was 12.2%. We have seen how Hollywood played its part in fashioning a vision of ideological purpose in the Second World War. But VJ Day did not bring demobilisation to Hollywood as it did to the rest of America. The strategic collaboration formed between the cinema and military outlasted that war to be retooled, reconfigured to play its part in the transition to Cold War. In service of Truman's call for rearmament and his tireless work to frighten Americans with the prospect of the 'red menace', Hollywood found new use for war films and new themes for movies attuned to the times and national purpose.

Peter Biskind's complex reading of the war films of the 1950s shows how subtle and diverse the genre became, and yet how consistent in basic premises.[10] He examines *Strategic Air Command* (1955), a domestic war drama in which a baseball player is recalled to the air force and becomes a pioneer of a new generation of jet fighters. *Twelve O'Clock High* (1949) and *Flying Leathernecks* (1951) both return to the Second World War. In *Flying Leathernecks* John Wayne is again the stern commander, this time honing his flyers for the rigours of combat. *From Here to Eternity* (1953) and *The Court Martial of Billy Mitchell* (1955) both deal directly with the military as an organisation. Under the shadow of a new kind of war, a Cold War that is permanent and pervasive, preparedness becomes both a state of mind and a practical necessity. Preparedness becomes a cultural condition that finds expression in all aspects of social life. War films could be made with conservative or liberal orientations, even with radical intent. They could, in the words of critic Julian Smith, 'rekindle the romance by making the cold war as warm and appealing as the war that had given us the best years of our lives'.[11] But whatever point on the political spectrum they represented, there was a consistency at their core. The military remained a metaphor for society, and the essential battle was often an inward, self-absorbed concern about contending principles for organising American society. The conservative concern for individualism within a society based on corporate structures could generate tensions; just as the liberal concern for self-sacrifice for the common good that generated conformism produced its own tensions.

But in whatever variant, whichever inherent tensions drove the plot-line, the overriding message was clear: the military is necessary for national purpose, and science, the development of technology, is the way to achieve national security, to make war as self-defence. When the military becomes the central agent of society, the most pressing issues of society become themes of war films.

The themes of authority, conformism, the domestication of war, the tyranny of the organisation, individualism and corporatism, as well as idealised patriotism and the military as the vessel of national purpose, could even be read across genres. We have seen how such ideas could be anchored in history, set on the western frontier as the story of how the nation came to be. They could also be cast in terms of futuristic threats from outer space, for the 1950s was the expansionary era of science fiction movies. Aliens as the savage barbaric enemy, the total and pervasive threat to human civilisation, were an easy metaphor for the lurking red menace. Such films as *Invasion of the Body Snatchers* (1956), *The Day the Earth Stood Still* (1951), *It Came From Outer Space* (1953) or *The Thing* (1951) all deal with different aspects of paranoia and menace. But more interestingly, in countless science fiction films when the aliens appear, dealing with them falls to just two agencies: the military or the scientists; civil society, government by civilian authority, is noticeable by its absence. Security and self-defence look to a strong military and investment in scientific development: the creation of better, more sophisticated and potent weapons.

What gave the American war engine the edge, and eventually made it the most formidable force in history, was scientific and technological research. Throughout the 20th century, American science was shaped and directed by the military; and its institutions of higher learning and research served as handmaidens for its military machine. The success of particular projects conducted by academic researchers during the Second World War, such as the Manhattan Project that produced the atomic bomb, and radar development, cemented the relationship between the Department of Defense and the universities. A complex organisational structure evolved in which the military set Research and Development (R&D) priorities and administered research funds. Institutions like MIT and Stanford University reaped rich rewards from doing military research. But the military, with its own extensive network of research institutions, such as the RAND Corporation, supported research not just in universities but also in industry. For the weapons industry, the military was the sole customer – and a customer that made pressing and changing demands. Weapons manufacturers were increasingly forced to specialise and pool their resources through mergers and subcontracting to ensure the necessary capital and expertise to undertake long, expensive and technically complex research programmes. The outcome was the emergence of huge defence-orientated corporations with a high degree of specialised technical knowledge and no semblance of competition. By the 1950s, some 70% of American science was funded and sponsored by the military, both in industry and in the universities. The distinction between military and civilian science had all but evaporated. As F.A. Long put it in a seminal paper: 'Military R&D is embedded in and derivative of civilian science and technology.'[12]

The dangers inherent in the close relationship between industry, universities and the military were spelled out by President Dwight D. Eisenhower in his farewell address on leaving office on 17 January 1961. He began by insisting that war was a necessity for America: 'Our arms must be mighty, ready for instant action, so that no political aggressor may be tempted to risk his own destruction.' But things had gone too far. America's military establishment and arms industry, he declared, have 'total influence' on every aspect of American society: their 'economic, political, even spiritual' influence 'is felt in every city, every State house, every office of the Federal government'. Eisenhower warned: 'In the councils of government, we must guard against the acquisition of unwarranted influence, whether sought or unsought, by the military-industrial complex. The potential for the disastrous rise of misplaced power exists and will persist.' (Eisenhower was particularly concerned that American science would be corrupted by 'government contract[s]' and 'project allocations'; and that universities would become handmaidens to military research, losing their historic role as 'the fountain-head of free ideas and scientific discovery'.)[13]

What Ike had not exerted himself to dismantle while in power was not altered by his cautionary message on leaving office. The Cold War had reached its peak and American science was reorganised to pursue the arms race more vigorously. A string of protocols were developed that placed science firmly in the hands of the military: scientists had to agree to indirect controls through security clearances and classification of secrets; evaluation of research could be done only through 'peer review' – meaning other scientists working under similar secrecy; the products of research were the province of the military; and the scientists had no obligations to society or their home institution. Scientists were promoted by the military as a race apart, locked in their ivory towers; they had no moral or social responsibility in how their research was used. The military invented a whole string of legal, accounting and economic devices to generate the notion of a free-floating 'pure science' totally detached from its military use. Science was above and beyond democracy; and the conscience of both scientists and the people over such trivial matters as the Bomb was quite irrelevant to pure science. The Department of Defense developed the doctrine that democratic decision-making procedures were irrational, inimical to science. Or as the RAND Corporation put it a decade earlier in its 'Arrow Impossibility Theorem': 'the doctrine of voters' sovereignty is incompatible with that of collective rationality' of science.[14] Thus, the military were legitimately defending the welfare of America's citizens – whose only need should be to worry about free choice in consumer products – and simultaneously looking after national defence. This doctrine of 'double truth' was used by the military to oversee developments in theoretical physics, electronics, computer science and communication technologies – disciplines with clear military applications – but also in abstract subjects such as logic, mathematics and philosophy.

National security, and security from the possibility of enemies within, might be cause for public fear, even paranoia. But translating these concerns into practical effect was the job of the professional military. The birth of the consumer society and the culture of distraction came in the years immediately after the Second World War and enjoyed an innocent childhood through the 1950s. While the mass of the American public concentrated its efforts on getting ahead and having a good time, military preparedness and containment of Communism could not relax. Overtly and covertly, America was assuming the international role of global superpower. Its military budgets steadily rose and its military personnel remained spread across the face of the globe, based conveniently to monitor and contain real or potential threats. America had a network of approximately 1,700 military installations in about 100 countries, what Chalmers Johnson described as 'the characteristic institutions of a new form of imperialism'.[15] Some bases such as Okinawa were a legacy of the Second World War; others were considered strategic necessities as the logic of Cold War rolled around the world. Wherever American troops were based they existed within a legacy of classic 19th-century imperialism. Status of forces agreements (SOFA), contracted with each 'host' nation, meant that these countries could not exercise legal jurisdiction over US military personnel who committed crimes against local people, except in special cases where US military authorities agreed to transfer jurisdiction. The system has an ancient history, going back to the trading outposts in the ancient and early modern world. It was, for example, normal practice in the great trading centres of the Muslim world to grant such measures of self-regulation to traders of different nationalities and religions to facilitate a plural world of exchange and interaction. But its imperialist incarnation was based on a different concept and can be dated to concessions wrung at gunpoint from China in the 19th century. Chinese law was considered too barbaric, and the Chinese too backward, to stand in judgement of 'civilised' white men. That sense of superiority survives in the SOFA, and goes a long way to explaining American reluctance to break this habit by subscribing to the International Criminal Court. Wherever they serve around the world, America's military live in bases that are a world apart from local circumstances, unaccountable and often impervious to their surroundings. The insulated lifestyle, including networks of military golf courses, includes all the comforts of home of the most materially over-endowed nation. Such bases are a source of friction with local populations in numerous countries. Driving accidents, rapes and even murders by US personnel are not infrequent occurrences, and since the military are not subject to local passport and immigration controls, offenders can simply be flown Stateside. On Okinawa, still a military base 60 years after the end of the Second World War, when Japan has become a model developed nation and staunch ally of the US, 'Yanks Go Home' is a popular sentiment because of the perceived arrogance and unaccountability of American forces for their misdeeds, and the lack of transparency in any process of justice.

Military bases are the footprints of military and political power used to intervene in the affairs of foreign nations, overtly and covertly to manipulate the political process: to install and change regimes, to sustain those compliant to American interests, military and commercial. With its network of bases, America has extended an umbrella of 'protection' around the globe. But America's military protection comes with consequences. The military has been used to train local intelligence and counter-insurgency agencies around the world whose record of human rights abuses is notorious. Military aid to friendly nations means contracts for American weapons corporations. It has meant the proliferation of the means of making war, and ensured that conflicts become more brutal and lethal in region after region around the world. Wars between countries, civil wars and local martial law have all been facilitated by the global role of the American military in ensuring America's national security; surrogate wars, repression and denial of human rights becoming a necessary part of America's self-defence.

The end of the Cold War did not roll back America's military presence around the globe. Nor has there been a dismantling of the military-industrial complex. But there has been a mutation in the organisation and management of science in America. The military still plays a major part in shaping American science; but now it shares the management and funding of science with multinational corporations. The function of science is now seen as yielding 'valuable information' that could be used not just for military dominance but also for industrial control. So now American science is largely directed by the dictates of the 'free market'. Most science policy experts agree that these changes evolved during the 1980s, when politicians and corporate leaders became concerned that America was losing the competitive edge in research and development. It had acquired military supremacy but was losing the corporate and market wars. The response was a whole series of new legislation, beginning with the Bayh-Dole Act of 1980. The legislation was designed to reduce government funding of scientific research and facilitate the transfer of research from university laboratories to corporations. What the corporations wanted – and got – was a mechanism to cut their research and development expenses and outsource some of their research to universities – just as they outsourced labour-intensive work – while maintaining control on 'intellectual property' generated from the research. The funding gap left by the military was taken up by pharmaceutical, biotechnology, computer software and entertainment industries. American science now has two masters: the military and the corporations; and Eisenhower's 'military-industrial complex' has now extended to become the 'military-industrial-corporate' complex.

Corporate science, as much as military science, is all about war. It's another name for war on natural resources of the world, appropriation of the indigenous resources of developing countries (such as plant varieties, medicinal compounds, and even the blood of certain indigenous tribes) and patenting of life forms including bits of our human biology. The results of the human genome sequencing were published simultaneously in Britain and the US. The British scientists made their results available free on the Web. But for American scientists, it was the private property of a corporation. Bizarrely, American corporations even claim ownership rights on anything produced by using the scientific concepts or the results of research developed by their scientists. Imagine Newton patenting gravity or Einstein patenting relativity to own the results produced by anyone using these concepts! In a sense, this amounts to a declaration of war on all future scientific knowledge. There is, however, a precedent. It was the practice of American scientist and entrepreneur Thomas Edison, who had a habit of taking out general patents for inventions he had not yet made and then suing anyone who actually realised a workable invention along similar lines. As we saw in Chapter Four, the most notable area to which he applied this practice was the development of cinematograph technology. The story of how cinema began is the endless round of litigation by which Edison sought to intimidate competitors who came up with useful inventions for film cameras or projectors, often ending with Edison buying them up and marketing them as his own.

The alliance of science and the military not only stretches around the terrestrial globe, it also reaches into space – 'the final frontier', as the opening narration of *Star Trek* always claimed. John F. Kennedy's lunar landing programme was aimed as much at lifting civilian morale as promoting military research. Space research in the 1960s and 70s generated as much military hardware as consumer products – from Teflon to anti-ballistic missiles, satellites to guided weapons, desktop computers to stealth bombers. Ronald Reagan swept aside the 1967 Outer Space Treaty to institute the 'Star Wars' programme and militarise space. Even though many American scientists declared that it was unworkable, it did produce a useful outcome: the GPS system which gives complete monopoly and ultimate control of every satellite to the Pentagon – right down to route planners in cars. With President George W. Bush's 'Man on Mars' programme, along with his enthusiastic support for further development of 'Star Wars', we can expect further weaponisation of space and blurring of the distinction between civilian and military space programmes, NASA and the US Department of Defense. The new X-43A, part aeroplane and part spacecraft, now being built by NASA, will produce not only a new generation of space vehicles but also new types of missiles. Powered by Scramjet, which relies on the speed of the engine itself to compress incoming air, X-43A travels at over 5,000 mph – it could be used to produce missiles that can reach anywhere on Earth in less than two hours! As Jean-Jacques Dordian, head of the European Space Agency, has said: 'for the United States, space is an instrument of domination.'[16]

Science has become a commodity, an essential element of a war economy. Military preparedness, as much as fighting wars and supporting surrogate wars and regimes as self-defence, comes at a cost. The staggering recent increase in the military budget has its internal consequences. According to Paul Rogers:

> The 2001 budget was originally pitched at $289 billion – nearly ten times the size of Britain's defence budget – but eventually ended up at $315 billion. The 2002 budget started at $328 billion but was hiked up after 11 September by another $3.5 billion and will now rise by an estimated $20 billion to give an eventual figure of $351 billion. The 2003 request shoots that up to $379 billion. This means that the original figure for 2001 has gone up by $64 billion in two years – almost double the size of Britain's entire defence budget.[17]

Astronomical as these figures are, they are mere snapshots of a continuous stream of annual expenditure. Real defence spending since 1955 has averaged $281 billion per year in 2002 dollars. And this does not include the notable spikes in spending occasioned by the Korean War, the Vietnam War and Ronald Reagan's huge investment in weapons systems such as the stealth bomber and Star Wars. Defence spending reached the $450 billion mark in 1989 and was a major contributory factor in the huge deficits Reagan bequeathed to the American economy. The real story is the cumulative total of national wealth that has, year on year, been devoted to militarised, weaponised national security. The figure is in the range of hundreds of trillions of dollars. And accurate totals are not easy to come by, since there is little transparency in military budgets. Lyndon B. Johnson insisted that Robert McNamara bury the cost of the escalation of the Vietnam War in his annual defence budget. Chalmers Johnson argues: 'From the Korean War to the first years of the twenty-first century, the institutionalisation of these huge defense expenditures fundamentally altered the political economy of the United States.'[18] It is part of normal political horse-trading for members of Congress of all political persuasions to try to ensure that some defence contracts end up in their districts. But the culture of war, the ethos of national security, the militarisation of the American worldview, and the popular acceptance of pervasive threat from ever-present enemies, does not allow a general debate to question what might have been for America and the world if so much wealth had been invested in other ways. The argument that peace and mutual security could be better served by sustainable global development has advocates but no compelling lobby in a nation dominated by the military-industrial-corporate complex.

And it is not only in the wider world that a different set of priorities could make a difference. These astronomical sums of money could, of course, be used to address the poverty of urban America, the healthcare needs of the poor and support programmes for the elderly and veterans. One in three Americans lives in urban poverty. More than 43 million Americans have no health insurance and the US has the highest proportion of children born in poverty in the developed world. When we consider that the Bush government, like the Reagan administration, has chosen to help the rich by cutting taxes, awarding subsidies and contracts to corporations, lowering standards of pollution and safety in the work place, and generally enriching all those in the weapons, oil, mining, logging, construction and pharmaceutical industries, we can see an altogether different war in operation: a war on the poor. One option the poor do have is to join the military – their only chance to escape poverty. Hence, African-Americans, who are 12% of the nation's population, make up 26% of the army. The numbers are similarly slanted for Latinos and Native Americans. Of the six soldiers who raised the flag on Iwo Jima, one, Ira Hayes, was a Pima Indian who until he enlisted had spent his entire life on the Gila River Reservation where he was born. Being plucked from obscurity and thrust into the forefront of a public relations exercise for the military and the war effort horrified Hayes. 'It was supposed to be soft duty, but I couldn't take it. Everywhere we went people shoved drinks in our hands and said "You're a hero!" We knew we hadn't done that much but you couldn't tell them that.' For Hayes the real heroes were his 'good buddies' buried back on Iwo Jima. After the war, Ira Hayes alternated between living among the institutional neglect and poverty of the reservation and being sought out as an icon. Reluctantly, in 1954 he attended the dedication of the Iwo Jima Memorial in Arlington National Cemetery, a re-creation in statuary of that famous photograph. Three months later he was found dead, drowned in a puddle after a night of drinking. The irony of his life and death are the subject of 'The Ballad of Ira Hayes', written by Pete LaFarge and recorded by both Bob Dylan and Johnny Cash:

> Down the ditches for a thousand years
> The water grew Ira's peoples' crops
> 'Till the white man stole the water rights
> And the sparklin' water stopped.

> Now Ira's folks were hungry
> And their land grew crops of weeds
> When war came, Ira volunteered
> And forgot the white man's greed.

It is not quite the emphasis brought to the Hollywood treatment of the Ira Hayes story in the 1961 biopic film *The Outsider*.

The American military has always appreciated the power of public relations. The strategic collaboration formed during the Second World War has outlived the Office of War Information and the Hays Office to become vested in the Pentagon's public relations apparatus. The constant need to earn public and congressional support for those huge defence budgets is not the least imperative driving the strategic alliance with Hollywood. The mechanics of the relationship are just what they were in the Second World War: 'Hollywood wants something from us: equipment, access to installations, stories, personnel. And we have the opportunity to tell the public something about the military', Philip Strub, Department of Defense, Hollywood Liaison, said in the 1997 documentary *The Military in the Movies*, made by the Center for Defense Information.[19] What 'the Pentagon won't tell is how big their PR apparatus is', comments Joe Trento of National Security News Service in the same documentary: 'Suffice it to say, we're talking about many millions of dollars, perhaps hundreds of millions of dollars spent polishing the image, polishing the appearance of the Pentagon and the military services.' Or as the narrator explains: 'The Defense Information School at Fort Meade, Maryland, equips 3,800 personnel a year with a broad array of public relations and media skills. But the image factory of Hollywood is where the military has the most profound effect on public consciousness.' The collaboration saves Hollywood producers millions of dollars in production costs. The scrutiny of storylines and scripts remains a quid pro quo for improving their bottom line.

As Peter Biskind showed for 1950s films, war and the military are themes that permit latitude. When the military is seen as the central organisation and agency of the nation, a metaphor for 'we the people', military/war films can become a forum for debating social issues and presenting contrasting visions of society and ideology. But metaphors have their limits, as Vietnam was to prove. Films such as *The Deer Hunter* (1978), *Apocalypse Now* (1979) and *Platoon* (1986), critical of the war and questioning of militarism, received no support from the Pentagon. Whereas *The Green Berets* (1968), which revived the traditional form and structure of Second World War films, 'received unlimited cooperation from the Army following a personal letter from [its star John] Wayne to President Johnson'.[20] In war films, John Wayne is most notable for playing the tough, hard-bitten commander, the stern father figure attuned to the rigours of combat, focused on doing the job in hand whatever it may be, and seeing his role as serving national security and the American Way. The nature of war and military technology has changed immeasurably since John Wayne's wars. But the screen persona he fashioned is father to the evolution of the genre.

The evolutionary process that begins with Sergeant Stryker on Iwo Jima has become one of the most familiar figures in film and television. But the hard man tasked with making tough fighting men has mutated. Marine training has become a cliché, but a cliché with increasing overtones of acceptable brutality. 'War is hell', war is brutal, war is the unrelenting necessity by which security is attained. But the metaphor of Marine training reiterates something more. The process itself is brutalising and its aim is to produce unquestioning submission to authority, the good soldier who will do what he is told and not stop until the job, however nasty, is done. It is a military ethos neatly summed up as 'theirs not to reason why, theirs but to do and die', as Tennyson so quotably wrote of the archetypal military disaster, the Charge of the Light Brigade. But the lack of reason to question is more than a function of training: it is a consequence of the conflation of the military with the nation. When the military is the vessel of national purpose, and national purpose is not only security and defence but the expansion of universal ideals – freedom, liberty, democracy – identified as self-evident and the special possession of the nation itself, what space is there to stop and ask questions? What has evolved since the Second World War is a complex ideology, widely expressed through popular culture, in which not only is the military indispensable, but the possession of overwhelming military power makes all situations capable of military solutions. As in the war films of the 1940s and 50s, the nature of the enemy and the presentation of war has remained consistent. The issues are always simplified into a confrontation of good versus evil, the enemy remains forever cruel, barbaric and implacably opposed to everything that defines us – the US. So the nature of the enemy conditions why the military, the organisation that is the vessel for 'we the people', must always be trained and prepared. In other words, we have an ideology that comprehensively establishes the ninth law of American mythology: war is a necessity.

War enters the consciousness of Americans almost the day they are born. From infancy to adolescence, in the toys and games they play, the comics they read, the television shows and films they watch, American children are instilled, drilled and shaped with the language and morality of the military. There is Action Man, complete with a whole range of military gear. There is GI Joe, ready to take on evil-doers the world over. And there is a whole range of soldiers, in all variety of combat situations, brought together as 'Special Forces: Showdown with Iraq'. Not to mention the George W. Bush doll, dressed in the US pilot regalia he wore when he landed on the USS *Abraham Lincoln* in May 2003. And his nemeses: the Saddam Hussein doll and the Osama bin Laden doll. And in between, a veritable army of war-like creatures, aliens, monsters, gladiators, generals, commanders and, believe it or not, fatigue-clad hamsters that dance to military music!

When they learn to read, American kids – like kids everywhere – turn to comics. And what do they read there? The golden age of American comics begins immediately after the Second World War and incorporates all the characteristics of the military mentality. The iconic Captain America, for example, was created to fight the Nazis; basically a human, he has only modest superhero attributes. His real power is insatiable thirst and will for total victory: he represents the unchallenged adherence to American values, and it is his conviction of the eternal nature of these values that helps him to succeed. Dressed with the US flag, and embodying the spirit of America, he leads a team of superheroes – 'the Invaders' – against all those with nefarious designs over America, fighting for liberty, democracy, justice and social rights. But even though these values are seen as universal, they are subject to contingency and political expediency. Captain America has gone through many transformations, each as aggressive and warlike as the other. In the 'Authority' series of comics, he is a perfect soldier, following orders in every detail even if it means destroying hospitals or killing children, and is quite unabashed about bullying or an occasional (homosexual) rape. In the Marvel 'Ultimate' series, he is an old soldier, a true Republican, a sort of John Wayne of our times. In yet another version, he is a genetically enhanced Marine, inclined to use maximum prejudice. If Captain America is supposed to be a metaphor for the US, then different versions present different self-perceptions of America. Neo-conservative Republicans will probably opt for the traditional Captain America, with his colourful Stars and Stripes costume and constant declarations of the supremacy of American values. American liberals would be just as comfortable with the Republican 'Ultimate' version, an out-of-place-and-time entity, someone who is rather shameful but nevertheless represents true American spirit, someone you would like on your side when things go wrong. But to the rest of the world, the various Captain Americas look part and parcel of a non-negotiable programme of military bullying hell-bent on world domination.

Of course, many comic heroes have much more complex moralities: Wolverine of the X-Men (like Captain America, he too fought in the Second World War); The Question, a Golden Age character who talks poetically, was prone to violence but became a Zen warrior after a near-death experience; and Lobo of the Justice League, DC Comics' answer to Marvel's Wolverine, an alien with an indestructible body and a hunter with a tendency to carnage. The post-Gulf War comic heroes, such as Punisher and Electra, reflect America's role as the (bad) policeman of the world. Some even have their origins in evil, like Ghost Rider and Demon. Spawn is an amalgam of all the morally ambiguous military heroes. A former hit man for the CIA, Spawn died on a mission and went to hell where he was transformed into a hell soldier to fight in an ongoing, perpetual war against heaven. He lives in a New York alley with a group of homeless characters, nourishing his deep thirst for revenge. Although he has enormous magic powers, he prefers to fight like a soldier with big weapons and to engage in direct, hand-to-hand conflict. His body, which is in perpetual semi-decomposed condition, gets damaged quite frequently; he can heal it with his powers but he chooses to wear enormous scars (some of them with the stitches still on), displaying them as medals of his battles. Violence is his language, weapons are his grammar; and he engages in grotesque violence without reason. The underlying message is simple and direct: violent force is good and legitimate. If you have power you have the right to use it, and the more spectacular the violence the better.

From comics, children graduate to the violent spectacle of video games. Most video games are designed with a specific intention to promote the culture of war with an accent on shooting, killing and blowing things up. In games like *Mortal Kombat*, *Missile Command*, *Battlezone* and *Comanche Maximum Overkill*, which contain horrific scenes of violence, the object is simply to kill or hunt your opponent; *Doom* and its various sequels involve nothing more than relentless and perpetual digital killing. The women in these games, if there are any, are either simply cyber-bimbos, electronic renderings of Barbie dolls, or as psychotic as the male characters. There is an intimate relationship between video games, virtual reality and the military. The dress rehearsal for 'Smart Bombs', the kind that frequently missed their targets in the Gulf War, was carried out in cyberspace. So it is not surprising that the software games market is saturated with 'shoot-em-up' scenarios, flight simulators, jet fighters and virtual re-enactment of historic wars, not simply because people like playing such games, but because weapons guidance and research for military use has become an integral part of video games. Indeed, the US Marines were so impressed with *Doom* that they produced their own version, available as a free download: *Marine Doom*. Not surprisingly, it has a dual purpose: it is used for recruiting as well as for training. The American military now works very closely with the games industry to develop software geared to preparing young men for a life of armed conflict and perpetual warfare. With *America's Army*, one of the most popular recruiting games, young people can learn how to kill enemy soldiers while still in their pyjamas having breakfast, and then find the address of their local army recruitment centre to enrol. In *Kuma: War*, developed by the Department of Defense and Kuma Reality Games, you can prepare yourself for actual missions based on real-world conflicts. The game uses satellite technology to update itself regularly, provides authentic military intelligence, and recreates the 'reality' of what may actually be happening in a particular zone of conflict. So players can simulate real news stories such as the American raid in Mosul, Iraq, in which Saddam Hussein's two sons, Uday and Qusay, were killed, or the raid on the Tora Bora Mountains in Afghanistan in the hunt for Osama bin Laden – all from the comfort of their living rooms.

Games frequently become films. Think of *Mortal Kombat*, *Final Fantasy* and *Resident Evil* and their various sequels. Films in turn become computer games: *Terminator*, *Hannibal* and *The*

X-Files. There are films that are little more than glorified advertisements for the American military: *Top Gun* (1986) and *Behind Enemy Lines* (2001), for example. Then there are television shows that promote the military and the ethos of its various institutions: *JAG* and *NCIS*. We can extend the 'military-industrial-corporate complex' to 'military-industrial-corporate-entertainment complex'. As Henry Giroux notes: 'combat teaching games offer a perfect fit between the Pentagon, with its accelerating military budget, and the entertainment industry, with annual revenues of $479 billion, which include $40 billion from the video game industry. The entertainment industry offers a stamp of approval for the Pentagon's war games and the Defense Department provides an aura of authenticity for corporate America's war-based products. While collaboration between the Defense Department and the entertainment industry has been going on since 1997, the permanent war culture that now grips the United States has given this partnership a new life and greatly expanded its presence in popular culture.'[21]

In schools too, American youth are infused with military culture. Indeed, the presence of the military in schools is as strong as in the entertainment industry, as both teachers and recruiters. The military's Junior Reserve Officers Training Corps (JROTC) is now an essential part of secondary education right across America. Under President George W. Bush's educational reforms, schools that do not provide full access to military personnel and recruiters risk losing all federal aid. Schools themselves are beginning to resemble prisons, giving as much emphasis to 'security' as education: surveillance cameras, regular searches for guns and drugs, armed guards, barbed-wire fences and lockdown drills being rather common. Far from developing critical thinking, students are being educated to accept the military ethos of regimented discipline, control and surveillance and unquestioning acceptance of authority. This is known as tough love! The kind of tough love Sergeant Stryker began handing out back in the old days. Once they leave school, youngsters are targeted by custom-made Hummers, football jerseys and base-ball caps. The yellow Hummer, spray-painted with two black men in military uniform, is the vehicle of choice for the US Army's 'Take It to the Streets' campaign which is aimed specifically at young African-Americans. The more fashion-conscious young end up buying the latest in military designer fashion from Army-Navy stores: camouflage jackets, aviator sunglasses, night-vision goggles, gas masks, army boots and commando gear. And, of course, they drive the Humvee, which became popular after its use in Desert Storm, to complete their fantasy of military glamour.

The necessity of war is deeply entrenched in American mythology. This is why the military has so easily moved out of the barracks and taken over so much of American life, society and culture. It is only natural for *Time* magazine to declare 'The American Soldier' as the 'Person of the Year' for 2003. But why limit him to a single year? The American Soldier is in fact the Person of the American Century.

As war films of the 1950s demonstrated, national security must always tackle not only external enemies but the enemies within. And this internal, homeland war is even more pervasive. The conventional distinction between military, police, and crim-inal justice has become blurred. During the last three decades, 'counter-terrorist' squads have been established within the mili-tary, and paramilitary units set up within police forces. So the police now work closely in collaboration with the army, main-taining strong operational, training and ideological links. Military units play a major role in 'internal security', while police units are trained and armed like the military, with, for example, SWAT teams modelled on the Navy Seals. Everyday policing now routinely integrates and uses paramilitary tactics – we saw its first use in the 1999 anti-globalisation protests in the 'Battle of Seattle'. The domestic version of the pre-emptive strike on a sovereign state is to be found in the post-9/11 legislation that gives police and security forces power to detain, imprison, and hold without legal representation, charge or trial, anyone they might suspect to be a terrorist or have information about terrorism. The traditional notion of innocent until proven guilty is replaced by an idea lifted straight from the science-fiction movie *Minority Report*, in which a pre-crime unit investigates and punishes crimes *before* they happen. As in the film, the 'Total Information Awareness' programme, which was later renamed 'Terrorist Information Awareness', collects data on movements and ordinary activities of citizens (credit card charges, library book withdrawals, university course enrolment). Citizens are urged to spy on their neighbours' behaviour, watch for suspicious-looking people, and supply data to government sources, while security computers in airports are provided with names of millions of ordinary citizens who, because of their ethnic background or particularities of their name or appearance, are seen as potential terrorists, including demonstrators and pacifists. Critics of all types are warned to 'watch what they say', and lists of 'traitors' are posted on the internet. The atmosphere of perpetual war generated by such procedures taps into the infinite reservoir of American innocence and brings Laws 1 and 3 of American mythology into play: fear is essential; and ignorance is bliss. The patriotic response they generate requires unquestioning approval for 'security' policies, however dubious they may be from the perspective of law and morality. Of course, just as the war waged on foreign lands has a strong profit motive, the war for 'homeland security' too has an economic rationale. As Henry Giroux notes:

> the United States is refashioning authoritarianism as a form of rabid patriotism. This is coupled with anti-terrorist legislation that legitimizes limiting civil liberties and basic freedoms while sanctioning the surveillance of dissenters and the arrest, if not torture, of those marked as a threat to the collective safety ... However, government and corporate elites do more than translate collective fears about uncertainty into privatized concerns about individual safety. They also create

the conditions for a 'fear economy' that fuels corporate profits. In addition to being frisked, searched, monitored, scanned and interrogated, the populations of the United States and its allies will also be subject to the pressure of venture capital that will make 'germ warfare sensors and threat profile software', along with 'discrete technologies of surveillance, environmental monitoring and data processing ... into a single integrated system'. 'Security', in other words, will become a fully-fledged urban utility like water and power.[22]

In American self-perception, all its wars are a product of its benevolent dispensation. As Sidney Lens notes, the myth has it that the US 'has always tried to avoid war; when it has been forced to take the military road, it has seldom done so for motives of gain or glory. On the contrary, its wars were fought only for such high principles as freedom of the seas, the right of self determination, and to halt aggression. In thought, as in deed, the United States – so the myth goes – has been anti-war, anti-imperialist, anti-colonialist. It has not sought an inch of anyone else's territory, and the few colonies it acquired were treated with kindness and liberated as quickly as circumstances permitted.' In reality, 'America the benevolent' is a delusional mirage: it 'does not exist and never has existed'. Contrary to popular belief and manufactured myth, 'the urge for expansion – at the expense of other peoples – goes back to the beginnings of the United States itself'[23] – as does the love of war for its own sake and for the benefits it brings.

CHAPTER SIX

Universal Soldier: America as Global Narrative

It is night. Cautiously, a soldier makes his way through the devastation of a village in the jungle. Bodies of his fellow soldiers with their ears sliced off are lying among dead villagers. The sound of whimpering is heard. In a ruined building he finds two villagers, a young girl and a boy, bound and kneeling before his sergeant who is preoccupied, stringing his trophies – the ears of his soldiers – into a necklace. What happened here? This village had been cleared, the soldier admonishes his sergeant, these people were all innocent. With a crazed expression, the sergeant shakes his amulet of power, his necklace of human ears, and explains: They wouldn't listen. They are all traitors, his men, the villagers, all ready to rise up and stab you in the back. 'How did this shit happen?' 'It just happened', says the sergeant. The soldier tries to be conciliatory. 'My tour is up. I just want to go home. Let's just go', he says. But the sergeant has a mission: 'You're just like the others, you just want to leave like none of this happened. Well it happened and it doesn't just go away. It happened. Do you hear me?' the sergeant insists. He rounds on the soldier, ordering him to prove he is not a traitor by shooting the prisoners as spies. When he will not, the sergeant coolly shoots the boy in the head. The soldier lashes out, knocking the sergeant to the ground, grabbing at the distraught girl, pulling her away from the corpse. They run off, but are pursued. The sergeant takes aim and shoots his insubordinate subordinate in the leg; as he falls he yells at the girl to run. The sergeant lobs a grenade at her retreating form and she crumples in the explosion. Enraged at this wanton slaughter, the soldier turns his weapon on the sergeant; in a hail of bullets they kill each other.

By the dawn's early light a helicopter comes in to land. An American officer climbs from the whirling machine and enters the devastated village where a clean-up operation is under way. A medic has found the body of the sergeant, and timorously examines the necklace of human ears: 'I'd hate to be the poor schmuck who's got to explain this shit back home to Ma and Pa', he says. 'How do we write this up?' asks another. 'Nothing happened here at all', the officer replies; 'Write them up as MIA [missing in action] – you didn't find anyone.' As the officer departs, we overhear him radio a 'Code Zebra' for ten bodies and give instructions for them to be bagged and packed in ice. So begins Roland Emmerich's 1992 film *Universal Soldier*.

After the premise, headlined 'Vietnam 1969', the scene shifts to 'the present day' to provide the pitch, the idea on which the film's narrative is hung. A cargo plane lands in the desert and delivers a huge, ominous truck onto the tarmac, where a guard of soldiers is waiting. The truck hisses and swells before our eyes. Soldiers in desert fatigues exit the truck. They line up for inspection before a technician who tests the integrated mechanical eye-piece and headset worn by each soldier to ensure they are relaying clear pictures and telemetry to the monitors within the vehicle. As the troops pass for inspection we recognise the two soldiers we last saw kill each other in the village in Vietnam. Instantly, we are transported from the horrors of conventional war into the realms of science fiction and prepared for the unfolding of the picture's tagline: 'The future has a bad attitude.' Regenerated, these men have been reconstructed as universal soldiers, unisols. And we witness them doing what is beyond the powers of ordinary troops or police. At the Hoover Dam, terrorists are holding hostages whom they will kill, one by one, until their colleagues are released from prison. But the terrorists are no match for the superior technology and awesome powers of the unisols. A helicopter flies in at speed. Effortlessly, the unisols jump from the 'copter into the waters below, swim the mile and a half to the dam in less than four minutes, scale the towers like spiders on a string, and then abseil Australian fashion – facing forward – down the retaining wall as if it were a level pavement. All their actions are controlled and monitored by the scientists back in the truck. The unisols take out the guards posted by the terrorists and enter the dam. When one of these future soldiers is mown down by the bad guys he bleeds from his wounds and falls, apparently slain. But that is not the kind of science fiction construct a unisol is. When his attackers are reassured by his apparent demise, his dead hand moves to grasp a weapon and he efficiently takes out the terrorist controlling the bomb, the advantage that prevented conventional forces from rescuing the hostages. A few more shots taking out the last of the terrorists and the situation is resolved. A press conference is quickly assembled for the awaiting press corps. A uniformed military officer announces: 'This is the third success for the universal soldiers – without casualties, without injuries. As to the identity of the unisols, that's classified.'

It has always been the case that genre movies have a dynamic of their own, and yet they succeed not only as diversion but because they encode, refer to and infer the values, ideals and experience of America. So *Universal Soldier*, for all its preposterous elements, also has a clear perception of the most haunting dilemmas of American empire. What are the uses and consequences of power? When the deterministic doctrine of power becomes the dominant force, what are the human consequences? Brutality is inherent in conflict: how does this impact on one's own troops; what does it mean in human, economic and political terms in the places 'over there' for other people? In the logic of the American Empire there is always an inherent tension in

201

trying to tell friend from foe, as well as the constant fear of betrayal. The power that underpins empire relies on technological superiority; it comes at vast expense, and it requires wholesale organisation of the nation and its economy. And the power of the imperium means exercising its muscle to influence events far removed from its homeland, having the power to command by remote control in ways that are neither known nor obvious to ordinary Americans. In the movie, the tension and effects of the logic of empire are embodied in the central characters: Sergeant Andrew Scott, the crazed killer whose purpose, as he later explains, is just 'winning this war'; and his antagonist, Luc Devereaux, the good soldier who just wants to go home. Can the dilemmas produced by the exercise of power be left behind – is it possible to just walk away? Can the details and consequences of the exercise of empire be kept remote, at a distance from ordinary life, back home in America? And how is it all explained to Ma and Pa? What do they know of the mission statement, and what should they know of the reality of the mission of empire?

Between the ideal and the reality there exists the shadow. In the case of America, the shadow has been war. The condition is as original as it is inevitable. The will to expand, to overspread, to compete and to be pre-eminent is contained within the very idea of America. It is why the land was first settled, and this understanding of history is the cultural commons of its people. Achieving, sustaining and securing the destiny of America has meant conflict, wars of many kinds – hot, cold, internecine, savage wars, frontier wars and brush wars – and has made war a motif deeply woven into the social consciousness of national life, the ideal metaphor for a 'can do' people. But, on the other hand, all the ideals for which America claims to stand, those ideals it projects and takes as self-description, focus on the image of peace, the freedom and liberty to pursue the exemplary abundance of its way of life according to the principles on which the nation is founded, of, by and for its people. It is in the nature of settler colonies to inculcate the 'get up and go' spirit; local difficulties are the impetus to move on, to find a new place undisturbed by troubles. A settler colony of continental proportions can exist and expand by war and allow the vast majority of its people to live in peace. Such a settler colony is implicitly imperial and entirely provincial – simultaneously.

America's myths and legends centre on war, on feats of arms, the force that made the nation in geographical extent and political existence. Power and its uses have always been at the heart of the American experience. The ideology extracted from these tales expounds the virtues of domestic peace and tranquillity, alert to the need, and ready for, self-defence, yet dedicated to the quiet enjoyment of getting on. America is unique in being a nation defined by ideas and their symbols, not by a specific territory or people. The settlement of America began as a project of empire. The nation that declared its independence was conceived as, and from the first termed, an 'empire'. It took over the mantle of the imperial power it deposed by conceptualising itself as the proper meaning of nation and empire. By declaring themselves a nation based on defining principles that were the ideal and perfect form of human aspiration, the newly confederated states could properly take on the mission of empire-building as their Manifest Destiny. A nation of immigrants whose population expands by attracting new waves of immigration is not a people. The making of the American people is a conscious process of inculcating and appropriating the defining ideas and symbols on which the nation bases its identity. The shared experience of the American people is acquired by coming to America. The bulk of the American population came to America at the closing of the western frontier. As we saw in Chapter Four, between 1870 and 1900 more than eleven million immigrants made their way to America, and by 1900, 60% of the residents in America's largest cities were either foreign-born or first-generation Americans. American history was a learned experience, consciously constructed and acquired through the medium of popular culture and its mythic narratives, the most easily digested form of ideological education for people becoming Americans. The power that held the nation together was a melting pot of ideology, the ideological ideals of American self-description. Central to this ideology is the notion that American tradition and history are universal narratives applicable across all time and space – Law 10 of American mythology.

America is the refuge, a haven where the imperfections of the old world are to be redeemed. War, persecution, tyranny and corruption – these were the scourges of peaceful existence that the settlers of America sought to escape. The positive values they came to enact were peaceful freedoms, the liberty for each individual to determine for themselves the best way of life unconstrained by oppressive governments and monarchs of all kinds. Life, liberty and the pursuit of happiness – what more unifying concepts could there be for those leaving their old life behind and imagining what would be better in the new land destined to be their home? Domestic tranquillity to build a better life is the heart of the American Dream. It has been expressed in Biblical terms from the outset – America is Canaan, the land of milk and honey, peopled by New Israelites. Those who reached this land of promise are people ready to live in peace, peace-seeking and peace-loving people – a refrain beloved of President George W. Bush who used it repeatedly in speeches after 9/11, the date from which he began to prepare America for war and became, as he also constantly reminded people, a wartime president.

The idea of America, as much as America's ideals, is conceived in global terms as a universal human principle. The Declaration of Independence and the Constitution use elegant prose to express grand concepts, truths that are self-evident and inalienable as universal human precepts. Expressed and understood in their ideal, perfect form, these principles stand beyond context and circumstance and take no cognisance of local detail. America has not only been peopled by immigrants from the world, in its essence and meaning it is the world and humanity's finest aspirations. It is the refuge of hope of all mankind yearning to be free. Therefore, it is natural for Americans to understand their myths and historic narrative as The Grand Narrative, a global story of how all the world would and should be, if only it could. America is a messianic dream of global dimensions; its mission is to be the human future. When America is threatened – under attack, defending itself or pre-emptively engaged in conflict – it is no mere historic civilisation, one in a succession of such earthly powers, but the most fundamental human ideals that are in peril and must be defended. In a profound and direct sense, then, to oppose America is to be against all that is good and best in human aspiration. Most importantly, America's self-image as global narrative finds confirmation in being the most affluent and powerful nation ever known in human history. Quite simply, America must be what all history and human effort was striving to attain, the grand pattern made manifest. For the whole world to progress, there can be no other or better formula than to follow the American way. Together, these powerful themes serve as justifications for the role American power must assume on the world stage.

The same mythic tradition, the familiar narratives and motifs extracted from American history, seamlessly transfer from the western frontier to the global frontier. The unifying self-image of America moves from history to the present and into the future with remarkable consistency, an ideological fit that makes it difficult to stop and ask questions. America's mission is the world's mission, for what else is the rest of the world striving to achieve? The mythic tradition that is the cultural grooming of all Americans is framed and expressed in terms that make consistent ideological sense of any and all situations. America is the world as it should be, and the world would be America if only it could. What more is there to say? In fact, a great deal more about the detail of history, culture, circumstance and the consequences of power in history and the present. But the world in all its complexity is far from the lives of ordinary Americans who are insulated from the rest of the world by the absorbing competitive needs of maintaining the affluence of their lifestyles and the consoling explanations of the enveloping presence of America's mythic vision.

However limited and self-serving it may be as history, Americans accept the oft-repeated assertion that they have won two world wars, saving Western civilisation from itself. Having won the Second World War and emerged from that conflict as the world's strongest power, its economy primed by wartime production and unscathed by attack on the homeland, America was a superpower. Reality, idealism and ideology all united to confirm the logic of America assuming the responsibilities and duties created by wartime action and accumulated power. As the world's leading power, it was its role to order the global system according to its own values for the benefit of all nations. A new global frontier was a reality, and like the western frontier it came complete with a global enemy, an ideological enemy that was the antithesis of the idea of America, that sought to thwart and subvert American ideals everywhere. In the aftermath of the Second World War America was demobilised, at peace and intent on pursuing consumer abundance at home, and at the same time at war everywhere, confounding enemies within and 'over there'.

In the sustaining myths so easily translated from western frontier to global frontier the central character, the hero, is a particular type. In the Western genre, as we pointed out in *Why Do People Hate America?*,[1] the hero is an equivocal character, a man capable of and licensed to use violence, to be as hard and brutal as those who are lawless or savage and who oppose and threaten the peaceful expansion of settlement, the outposts of future civilisation. In the same vein, the ethic of war is a stern taskmaster, as repeated in so many war films by all those hard-bitten sergeants who train Marines, or those uncompromising officers who must press their men to do what it takes to win. To be secure, in extremis, civilisation must match violence with violence – that is what self-defence means. It must use the knowledge and strategy of the enemy to defeat them. The hero enables the mass of the people, the homesteaders, the innocent villagers, to live in peace, to be and to think of themselves as peaceable people, while their enemies are annihilated. War is the necessary bulwark against the fear of being overrun by enemies who are savage, brutal and implacably hostile, envious and evilly intent on overthrowing the peaceful progress that is the meaning of the American Dream. The doctrine of meeting opposition and force with overwhelming destructive power by using 'strategies of annihilation' is embedded deep in the conventions of American myth. The course of war has been the story of harnessing the stern resolve and hard-bitten outlook of the Western hero to the ever-developing technology of military might.

In the Second World War, technology, the militarisation of science and its application to strategies of annihilation, produced a distinctive American way of using power, as Michael S. Sherry argues:

> American war making displayed a 'technological fanaticism' – a zeal to inflict technological destruction on its enemies – that contrasted with the apparent human fanaticism of geno-cidal Nazis and crazed Japanese. By virtue of their economic and technological superiority, Americans could act out war's destructive impulses while seeing themselves as different from their enemies. Rarely witnessing the human costs to the enemy, scientists could press new technologies on the armed forces, air force crews could incinerate enemy cities, and battle-ships could pummel Japanese-held islands from miles off-shore. The intricate technology of war provided physical and psychic distance from the enemy.[2]

And most importantly, as Sherry goes on to say, 'for Americans alone, the attractions of technological warfare were not challenged by being on the receiving end of it'. War 'over there' was the prelude. The elements that brought victory in world war continued to operate as America formed its distinctive imperium arrayed along the global frontier. And physical and psychic distance was provided not only by technology, whose aim was both annihilation of the enemy and making American soldiers as invulnerable as possible, but also by the insulation of ideological self-justification, the remoteness of the rest of the world from the daily life of ordinary Americans; the insulation of a lack of interest in the rest of the world, untroubled by a culture of information and media inquiry. Empire, power, war and its harsh brutal realities have the common consoling characteristic of being 'over there', exercised by remote control, remote from 'we the people' who nevertheless are beneficiaries of their operation.

The regenerated human cyborgs, the unisols of *Universal Soldier*, are an apt metaphor for the philosophy of war America has devised. They have been designed to be indestructible agents of awesome power and to 'follow orders at all times'. And after each mission their memory is erased by chemical injection. But as in all science fiction movies, there is a problem. Specifically, the problem is 'aggressive traumatic recall'. The good soldier, Luc Devereaux, begins having flashbacks. Two Asians cowering among the hostages rescued by the unisols bring back memories of the village in Vietnam; he remembers Sergeant Scott and recognises him as his fellow unisol. It soon becomes apparent that Scott is having 'aggressive traumatic recall' of his own. The condition causes both to lock onto their overriding thought at the point of death. For Luc, this is going home; for Sergeant Scott, completing the mission and ensuring orders are obeyed. The problem is compounded by the intrusion of an investigative reporter anxious to learn more about the universal soldiers.

The reporter and her cameraman must be captured to prevent them telling what they have learnt about the unisols. When Sergeant Scott catches up with them – once again, a man and a woman kneeling before him, identified as traitors – he again cold-bloodedly executes the man. The scientists back in the control vehicle are horrified. 'We just killed an innocent man', says

Dr Woodward. 'We can't just cover this up – we have a moral obligation to tell the truth about this.' The military commander rounds on him: the whole programme is a covert operation and must be kept secret. Covert operations, secret wars, huge expenditures without the radar of public scrutiny spent on such endeavours and on developing whole new technologies of war – these are not solely the stuff of science fiction. They work as plot devices in science fiction because they echo reality. Vietnam, the 'dirty little war' in the lyrics of the musical *Hair*, was the setting for numerous examples of covert dissembling. But then Chile, Honduras and Nicaragua all came after. Maintaining and operating empire is constantly bedevilled by questions of what can be explained to the people back home. What they are permitted to know exists in tension with the other haunting question: how much do they really want to know about actions undertaken in their name but without full disclosure?

The good soldier, Luc, once again rescues the woman and they make a getaway. The reporter asks Luc what he wants to do. 'My tour is up. I just want to go home, but I can't until you're safe', he replies. So together they try to uncover the secret of Luc's real identity and evade the determined pursuit led by Sergeant Scott, still intent on completing his mission of dealing with the traitors and winning the war. When Luc stops at a seedy motel, the television is playing: 'Now we return you back to *Nixon and the War Years*, Part Seven', says the announcer. Luc watches President Nixon: 'We will keep America the strongest nation in the world and we will couple that strength with firm diplomacy, no apologies, no regrets.' This clear mission statement of American empire is followed by a sound-bite, only half heard because interrupted by the continuing action, referring to the pardon issued to Nixon on his resignation in the wake of the covert Watergate break-in and his administration's attempts at a cover-up. From that point on, the film follows the conventions of the car chase formula, with plenty of fights, shoot outs, crashes and spectacular stunts. But its narrative line is also a metaphor – an answer to the questions it has intimated. The characters cannot just walk away from what happened 'over there'; the climax of the film brings the consequences home to be played out, literally, before Ma and Pa Devereaux on their homely farm in Louisiana. To the very end, Sergeant Scott is utterly determined to fulfil his mission: he keeps injecting himself with muscle strengtheners to be stronger, more powerful, indestructible, relentless and inevitable in his pursuit of winning the war he cannot escape. In the last extreme, the only way Luc can overcome this force is to feed Scott's impaled body into a shredding machine and grind it to bits.

In the metaphor of *Universal Soldier*, Devereaux and Scott are both products of empire, but they embody alternate responses to its pressures and consequences. One is committed to the logic and dictates of whatever it takes to win the wars that maintain the empire, while the other, Luc, is ready to walk away and be done with war, to erase his memory of reality even before his memory is erased by his controllers. At the heart of the American psyche there is a fissure bridged by a preference for disassociation, willingness to look the other way – to look at the big picture of the grand ideals and forget, ignore or merely deny the troubling realities. It produces a readiness to accept the logic that makes war and calls it self-defence or peace, the pacification of bringing civilisation into being. What has been true of America at home in its history has characterised its actions abroad. The American Dream is a motif imposed upon history as much as it is a product of history. America is not a simple narrative; it is immensely complex and contradictory – it exists across severe tensions. The tensions are the alternate pulls of ideals and reality. The laws of American mythology exist to subsume and overlay the harshest reality with the balm of idealism, to justify means by the distraction of high purpose and good intent. The rhetoric of American life is eulogy, unstinting praise for the values and ideals of the nation in their pure and perfect form. Reality 'out there' exists to be reconfigured, made to conform to legend. But there are times when this approach to reality becomes a discernible lie. Reality is a storyline that can be spun to leave the ideals in place and parade shocked innocence about undesirable real events. America is a nation that is forever losing its innocence without finding a reformative impulse. The current champions of American empire appeal directly to the notion of American innocence, intrinsic goodness and the universal nature of American narrative. There is no awareness here that the ideals of the Republic are way past their 'sell by' date – that, at the end of the day, it is American mythology itself that needs to replaced with something more life-enhancing.

Consider, for example, Michael Ignatieff, the Canadian apologist for American imperialism and Professor at Harvard University, who describes the American Empire as a new kind of 'burden': 'America's empire is not like empires of times past, built on colonies, conquest and the white man's burden. We are no longer in the era of the United Fruit Company, when American corporations needed the Marines to secure their investments overseas. The 21st century imperium is a new invention in the annals of political science, an empire lite, a global hegemony whose grace notes are free markets, human rights and democracy.' The new burden means that the US is 'the only nation that polices the world throughout five global military commands; maintains more than a million men and women at arms on four continents; deploys carrier battle groups on watch in every ocean, guarantees the survival of countries from Israel to South Korea; drives the wheels of global trade and commerce; and fills the hearts and minds of an entire planet with its dreams and desires'.[3] So the empire may now be 'lite', but it is still a universal soldier and does what good old heavy empires always did: occupies foreign lands, rapes their economies and cripples their minds!

Apart from being 'lite', the empire is also 'benevolent'. In a much-quoted article in *Foreign Policy*, Robert Kagan, a senior associate at the Carnegie Endowment for International Peace, declared that 'the truth about America's dominant role in the world is known to most clear-eyed international observers'. And it is this: 'the benevolent hegemony exercised by the United States is good for a vast portion of the world's population.' A world without US hegemony, he suggests, would be more violent, more chaotic, less democratic and economically stagnant. And he spells out 'the unique qualities of American global dominance': despite overwhelming military and economic superiority, the American people chose not to 'set the crown of world empire on their brows'; instead, they chose a '*strategy* to risk nuclear annihilation on [their] otherwise unthreatened homeland in order to deter attack, either nuclear or conventional, on a European or Asian ally'. Moreover, 'the identification of the interests of others with its own has been the most striking quality of American foreign and defence policy'. Americans may be self-interested, selfish, arrogant, and occasionally ham-handed, 'but *excusez-moi*', Kagan asks in a mocking tone:

> compared with whom? Can anyone believe that were France to possess the power the United States now has, the French would be less arrogant, less selfish, and less prone to making mistakes? Little in France's history as a great power, or even as a medium power, justifies such optimism. Nor can one easily imagine power on an American scale being employed in a more enlightened fashion by China, Germany, Japan, or Russia. And even the leaders of that least benighted of empires, the British, were more arrogant, more bloody-minded, and, in the end, less capable managers of world affairs than the inept Americans have so far proved to be. If there is to be a sole superpower, the world is better off if that power is the United States.[4]

So, what can we expect in this wonderful world of benign American power? Kagan suggests quite explicitly that America should not hesitate in drawing its mighty sword and slaying anything and anyone that gets in its way. Like the deranged villain in *Universal Soldier*, he laughs out loud at Europe and her multilateralism. A Europe that has achieved integration peacefully and multilaterally, by negotiations and without militarism, has moved 'beyond power into a self-contained world of laws and rules and transnational negotiations and cooperation', and thus has no understanding of the brute realism of empire-building. In contrast to Kant's 'Perpetual Peace' that is the lot of Europe, Kagan suggests in *Paradise and Power*, the United States is all about taming an anarchic Hobbesian world where war is a necessity. America is thus ever ready to visit violence to any corner of the world both to maintain and to expand its empire.[5]

What both Ignatieff and Kagan amply demonstrate is a monumental ignorance of history. As Sidney Lens notes in reference to Ignatieff: 'only someone blind to the history of the United States, its obsessive drive for control of oil, its endless expansion of military bases around the world, its domination of other countries through its enormous economic power, its violations of the human rights of millions of people, whether directly or through proxy governments, could make that statement.'[6] Robert Jensen, Associate Professor of Journalism at the University of Texas in Austin, describes 'benevolent empire' as the 'third American holocaust' (the first two being the genocide of Native Americans and slavery), the product of a foreign policy that is 'relentlessly barbaric'.[7] But something very specific is at work in Ignatieff and Kagan's views; something that we also find in Paul Berman's notion of 'liberal imperialism'[8] and Stanley Kurtz's 'Democratic Imperialism',[9] as well as in the works of a string of right- and left-wing champions of the American Empire.[10] And that something is the deterministic re-formulation of history in the universal soldier framework. History – of democracy, liberalism, cultures, civilisations and great powers – is being presented as universal destiny: the histories of all nations and peoples, states and empires, merge into the universal narrative of American history and culminate to produce a global, benevolent American

Empire. This is what the world was created for. This is the sum of all human experience. This is the aggregate of all the yesterdays of humanity. This is the theory that Philip Bobbitt tries to demonstrate in his monumental study *The Shield of Achilles*.[11] Subtitled 'War, Peace and the Course of History', the book suggests that all the wars of all histories and all the peaceful states of the world produced a 'course of history' that ends up with a very special state: a state that is immensely powerful *and* democratic *and* committed to human rights – the global United States of America. It is thus the only power that has not only might but historic right on its side – and hence, can attack any country it wishes. This historic imperative, this natural and universal destiny, also gives the US, says Bobbitt, the right to take pre-emptive action against any nation, and places it above international law. This is the new 'constitutional theory' that Bobbitt wants the rest of the world to embrace.

In its most complete and articulate form, this thesis is expressed by Francis Fukuyama in his *The End of History and the Last Man*.[12] Ignatieff, Kagan, Bobbitt and others are simply borrowing a leaf from Fukuyama, former Deputy Director of the US State Department's Policy Planning Staff and a signatory to the infamous policy paper 'Rebuilding America's Defenses: Strategy, Forces and Resources for a New Century', cobbled together by the neo-conservative think-tank, The Project for the New American Century.

Fukuyama developed his thesis immediately after the fall of the Berlin Wall. The end of the Cold War, he argues, not only means the end of Communism, it also signifies the unabashed victory of American economic and political liberalism. American 'liberal democracy', he suggests, is the 'end point of mankind's ideological evolution', the 'final form of human government', and as such constitutes the 'end of history'. From the American Declaration of Independence onwards, there has been a trend towards democratic governance that demonstrates that there is 'a silent and mysterious inner process at work' underneath the perturbations of history, somewhat similar to the 'invisible hand' of the market. This suggests that:

> There is a fundamental process at work that dictates a common evolutionary pattern for *all* human societies – in short, something like a Universal History of mankind in the direction of liberal democracy. The existence of peaks and troughs in this development is undeniable. But to cite the failure of liberal democracy in any given country, or even in the entire region of the world, as evidence of democracy's overall weakness, reveals a striking narrowness of view. Cycles and discontinuities in themselves are not incompatible with a history that is directional and universal, just as the existence of business cycles does not negate the possibility of long-term economic growth.[13]

Thus, for the past 300 years all histories, all cultures have been evolving, by the sheer force of nature and deterministic history, towards a single goal: to become part and parcel of a universal American narrative.

> History was not a blind concatenation of events, but a meaningful whole in which human ideas concerning the nature of a just political and social order developed and played themselves out. And if we are now at a point where we cannot imagine a world substantially different from our own, in which there is no apparent or obvious way in which the future will represent a fundamental improvement over our current order, then we must also take into consideration the possibility that History itself might be at an end.[14]

All of us are thus as free as we will ever get, and the status quo is the best we can ever hope for. The United States of America, with its principles of 'Liberty' and 'Democracy', is the apex of human evolution and all of us are propelled towards the Great

Republic. But since 'history' – that is, history of non-Western culture which Fukuyama has cannibalised – incorporates the world-views of all other people, their value systems, their cultures, what we may call their total modes of being, the termination of history also terminates the very being, the very identities, of all Others. So other people, quite incidental to American 'Universal History', can now be truly declared dead and buried: 'it matters little what strange thoughts occur to people in Albania or Burkina Faso', as their culture is not part of the 'the common ideological heritage of mankind'. Indeed, they are not people at all!

The early attempts to write 'Universal History', Fukuyama tells us, 'were undertaken in conjunction with the establishment of the scientific method in the sixteenth century'. Scientific method, as introduced by Galileo, Bacon and Descartes, established the possibility of both accumulative knowledge and dominion over nature. It was the success of modern natural science which engendered the 'modern notion of progress' and enabled 'Francis Bacon to assert the superiority of modernity to antiquity on the basis of inventions like the compass, printing, and gunpowder' – none of which, by the way, were Western inventions but developments of knowledge accumulated in the East in entirely different cultural contexts. Nevertheless, the possibility of mastering natural sciences was not 'a universal feature of all societies, but had to be invented at a certain point in history'. Once this scientific method was discovered, 'a qualitative change occurred in the relationship of scientific knowledge to the historical process'; it provided a 'mechanism' for the direction of history by creating 'a fundamental, non-cyclical division of historical time into periods before and after'. Henceforth, this directional mechanism could be used to explain all historical developments. What are the basic components of the mechanism unleashed by modern science? Fukuyama explains:

The first way in which modern natural science produces historical change that is both directional and universal is through military competition. The universality of science provides the basis for the global unification of mankind in the first instance because of the prevalence of war and conflict in the international system. Modern natural science confers a decisive military advantage on those societies that can develop, produce, and deploy technology most effectively, and the relative advantage conferred by technology increases as the rate of technological change accelerates. Zulu spears were no match for British rifles, no matter how brave individual warriors; mastery of science was the reason why Europe could conquer most of what is now the Third World in the eighteenth and nineteenth centuries, and diffusion of that science from Europe is now permitting the Third World to regain some of its sovereignty in the twentieth. The possibility of war is a great force for the rationalization of a society, and for the creation of uniform social structures across cultures. Any state that hopes to maintain its political autonomy is forced to adopt the technology of its enemies and rivals. More than that, however, the threat of war forces states to restructure their social systems along lines most conducive to producing and deploying technology.[15]

So, the master narrative of America is a product of its science- and technology-based military muscle – its ability to perform the functions of universal soldier. But what else is responsible for the global domination of the US? The triumph of the idea of America, argues Fukuyama, is demonstrated by the 'unquestionable relationship between economic development and liberal democracy' (colonialism and the global economic structure, of course, have nothing to do with it) and the spread of consumerism around the world. The force that was moving history forward was not the American quest for power and territory but the need of the individual for the Platonic idea of 'thymos' or 'that-which-demands-recognition-in-others'. Or more appropriately, 'megalothymia', the desire to be recognised as superior to all other people. This desire is fulfilled by American consumerism, which not only provides the free and respected individual with all the 'thymos' he or she needs, it also sublimates 'megalothymia' and directs it towards harmless activities like playing with junk bonds or going hang-gliding in California, thanks largely to a happy combination of (right-wing) Christianity, military science and technology, 'democratic liberalism' and benign imperialism. 'Apart from fast-disappearing tribes in the jungles of Brazil or Papua New Guinea', the whole of humanity is linked through 'the universal nexus of modern (American) consumerism':

> Societies which have sought to resist this unification, from Tokugawa Japan and the Sublime Porte, to the Soviet Union, the People's Republic of China, Burma, and Iran, have managed to fight rearguard actions that have lasted only for a generation or two. Those that were not defeated by superior military technology were seduced by the glittering material world that modern natural science has created. While not every country is capable of becoming a consumer society in the near future, there is hardly a society in the world that does not embrace the goal itself.[16]

Thus Fukuyama, and other proponents of American empire, give the rest of the world three stark choices: disappear, without a trace and complete with your culture and values, from history and the future; be subdued by American military technology and become a colony of the benevolent empire; or embrace American consumerism in its totality and be reduced to a cipher. But Fukuyama not only terminates history, which he sometimes uses as a synonym for progress, on the basis of military might and the spread of consumerism, he also measures contributions to world history in terms of a people's participation in consumer society. Japan, for example, is said to make an important contribution to 'world history by following in the footsteps of the United States to create a truly universal consumer culture, both the symbol and the underpinning of the universal homogenous state'. Thus a state becomes 'homogenous' not on the basis of a single culture, national aspirations, religion or worldview, but on the basis of American universal consumer culture.

Is there an escape from the homogeneity of the American Empire? Fukuyama suggests that America's universal soldier narrative is up against three 'ideological competitors': nationalism, culture and religious fundamentalism. Nationalism is dismissed as irrelevant since it can be 'modernised', reframed within the master narrative of America. Culture, in the form of resistance to American values and consumerism, provides a bigger threat. It is the link of culture with religion which makes culture a stubborn form of resistance to the spread of American imperialism. The real danger to American hegemony comes from fundamentalism in general and Islamic fundamentalism in particular. However, while Islamic fundamentalism may have won a few victories, it does not have much of a future. For Fukuyama, just as for other champions of American imperialism, the only form of Islam that exists is 'Islamic fundamentalism', which he equates with the entire history of Islam. When it comes to the real crunch, he argues, Islam's history and civilisation, worldview and culture, will stand no chance against Hollywood, American television and the celebrity and pop industries. Moreover, when the 'oil runs out' and Muslim countries are forced to make it 'on their own', they will face a stark choice between Islam and modern consumerism. The elementary point that oil-rich countries are already living in the midst of consumer culture, while non-oil-rich countries lack the cash and, therefore, the choice to buy into consumer culture, does not occur to Fukuyama. Nor does the fact that both have already chosen 'Islam' – in its various, somewhat corrupted, modern forms.

Fukuyama raises self-congratulation to the status of a theology, generating a rational philosophy to beat all philosophies and a worldview to live by. His thesis, as indeed the very idea of a benevolent American Empire, is a form of pathological fundamentalism. As Stuart Sim notes, the echoes of Christian Right fundamentalism in Fukuyama's work are clear and distinct: 'In true fundamentalist fashion, Fukuyama looks forward to "the homogenization of mankind". No religious fundamentalist could put it better: goodbye difference, goodbye dissent, hello conformity.' One would have expected, suggests Sim, that after 9/11, Fukuyama would have had a few doubts. But he remained adamant, making 'the standard fundamentalist claim: that one's opponents simply haven't seen the light yet. And the standard fundamentalist response: we won't give up, we shall prevail. It's a temperament seemingly impervious to setback.'[17]

Francis Fukuyama was a student of Samuel Huntington, Professor of International Relations at Harvard University. Just after Fukuyama's book, Huntington published his famous article 'The Clash of Civilizations?' in the influential journal *Foreign Affairs*, whose managing editor, Fareed Zakaria, was another former student of the Harvard professor. Huntington argued that future conflicts will not be based on ideology or economy but on culture: 'the fault lines between civilizations will be the battle lines of the future.' There are a number of such 'fault lines', but the most significant is the dividing line in Europe which separates what is essentially Eastern Europe and the Balkans from the Muslim world. The people on the East European side share the common experience of European history and are generally a product of the Renaissance, the Reformation, the Enlightenment, the French Revolution and the Industrial Revolution. On the other side, according to Huntington, we have a people who 'historically belonged to the Ottoman or Tsarist empires and were only lightly touched by the shaping events in the rest of Europe; they are generally less advanced economically; they seem much less likely to develop stable democratic political systems'.[18] This is, of course, the historical divide where civilisation as we know it ends and the wilderness of the other cultures begins; and where the final battle for the empire will be fought. The 'Clash of Civilizations' thesis has been reiterated a number of times; and it has most frequently been reduced to a clash between the West and Islam. But in its original formation, Huntington was concerned not just with the 'bloody borders' of Islam; he was worried about the entire non-West rising up against the US. 'Confucian, Japanese, Islamic, Hindu, Slavic-Orthodox, Latin American and possibly African civilizations', Huntington wrote, are rediscovering their civilisational identities and 'have the desire, the will and the resources to shape the world in non-western ways' (God forbid!). He singled out the 'Confucian-Islamic connection' as the most lethal, consisting of 'weapons states' – as though America was not a 'weapons state' – eager to take on a homogenous West led by the US. To thwart the lurking dangers, Huntington recommended that the West, meaning America, should: '"limit the expansion of the military strength of Confucian and Islamic states" (that is, continue with imperialism); "exploit the differences and conflicts among Confucian and Islamic states" (that is, divide and conquer); "support in other civilizations groups sympathetic to Western values and interests" (that is, promote insurrection); and "strengthen international institutions that reflect and legitimate Western interests and values" (that is, retrench Western global domination).'[19]

In the more elaborate form of his thesis, *The Clash of Civilizations and the Remaking of World Order*, Huntington provides an extensive list of fault-line conflicts that have taken place on a 'boundary looping across Eurasia and Africa that separates Muslims from non-Muslims': Bosnia, Kosovo, Cyprus, Chechnya and Southern Sudan, for example. But he is forced to concede that while at the 'micro or local level it is between Islam and the others', the real clash of civilisations 'at the macro or global level of world politics' is 'between the West and the rest'.[20] And the issues in this clash are 'classic ones of international politics' such as 'relative influence in shaping global development and the actions of global international organisations such as the UN, IMF and World Bank'; 'relative military power, which manifests itself in controversies over non-proliferation and arms control and in the arms race'; and 'economic power and welfare, manifested in disputes over trade, investment and other issues'.[21] In other words, the conflict between 'the West and the rest' is about issues of injustice and exploitation, the issues at the core of American imperialism.

Unlike Fukuyama, with his one-dimensional, neo-conservative chauvinism, Huntington is a much more complex person. To begin with, he is an old-fashioned Democrat who describes himself as 'a child of Niebuhr'. Reinhold Niebuhr, one of the foremost American Protestant theologians, was an active socialist in the early 1930s. He began to champion traditional Protestant values after the Second World War, and related them to American society in the shape of 'conservative realism'. His *Nature and Destiny of Man: A Christian Interpretation*[22] has made a profound impact on American theology, leading many international relations experts to suggest that he is the father of American political thought. As an Episcopalian, Huntington is attracted to Niebuhr's 'compelling combination of morality and practical realism' which shapes his own ideas of conservatism.[23] Like Niebuhr, Huntington possesses a deep, Christian moral stance that frequently leads him to denounce imperialism and the presentation of American tradition and history as universal narratives. America, Huntington has argued, has perpetuated naked imperialism since the 1950s; and has pursued a deliberate policy of creating a unipolar world after the fall of the Berlin Wall. It has behaved like a 'rogue superpower', forcing the rest of the world to agree to its demands.[24] Moreover, he dismisses the idea that the West, or indeed America, represents a 'universal civilisation'. 'The assumptions, values, and doctrines currently held by many people in Western civilisation' represent nothing more than 'Davos culture': it is the culture of the businessmen, bankers and government officials who gather every year in the Swiss town of Davos at the World Economic Forum. While the Davos people 'control virtually all international institutions, many of the world's governments, and the bulk of the world's economic and military capabilities', not many people share their culture: it exists only at an élite level.[25] So: 'what is universalism to the west is imperialism to the rest';[26] indeed, imperialism is a logical product of the very idea that American culture is universal.

But Huntington's apparent anti-imperialist stance does not mean that he is against the American Empire. His main concern is to preserve the Christian Protestant identity of the empire. Hence his acute distaste for multiculturalism and his insistence that the United States cannot be a country of many civilisations. To be America, America must have a Protestant cultural core. As he argues in *Who We Are: The Challenge to America's National Identity*, the Catholic American Latinos, multiplying rapidly, are a threat to the nation; indeed, the very mixing of races and cultures in America is a path to national and moral degeneration.[27] Huntington's anxiety regarding the non-West, so clearly displayed in *The Clash of Civilizations*, is essentially the fear of a demographically challenged Protestant morality being swamped by a resurgent and multi-civilisational, expanding non-West. 'What appears to be an outright rejection of universalism', notes Leong Yew, is 'a way of preventing the uniqueness of western culture from getting lost'. Huntington's anxiety, suggests Yew, can be captured in one word: de-westernisation, and all the fear associated with the loss of the Protestant ethics.[28] So 'the old fashioned Democrat' turns out to be an old-fashioned colonialist arguing for both assimilation and differentiation to preserve old-fashioned imperial power relations.

Huntington's other student, Fareed Zakaria, editor of the international edition of *Newsweek*, hides his colonial desires behind similar ambivalence. In his rather pedestrian book *The Future of Freedom: Illiberal Democracy at Home and Abroad*,[29] Zakaria posits two varieties of democracy: a liberal one that resides in America, and an illiberal one that is the lot of the rest of the world. Liberal democracy is based on neo-liberal free trade and totally free markets. In other words, 'democracy' and 'markets' are basically the same things. America represents the ideal democracy because of its 'state-centered realism', meaning it uses its brute power to expand its market and the influence of its empire. Zakaria is unabashed in celebrating both America's military might and its gruesome expansionist past without a hint of irony, or indeed any moral qualms about imperialism or the human and social cost of using brute power. This is an apologia for empire at its most obnoxious.

As Benjamin Barber notes, 'confusing democratization with economic liberalization is to confound the spread of liberty with the spread of McWorld – that seductive compound of American commercialism, American consumerism, and American brands that ... has dominated the globalization process'. The 'ethos of Disney' is not synonymous with 'the ethics of liberty'; and citizens are not the same thing as consumers.[30] Creating consumers for American markets, opening other nations to be taken over by American corporations, does not amount to introducing democracy:

> Privatization does the ideological work of global market economics inside nation-states, privileging the private interests of corporations and banks and delegitimizing the common goods of the community. National government now becomes an instructed instrument of the private sector rather than a participatory assembly of the public sector. In this guise, government is made over into a useful tool of global firms, banks, and markets in such international organizations as the World Trade Organization and the International Monetary Fund – nominally democratic political organizations constituted by sovereign states, but in effect servants of global economic interests that undermine both national sovereignty and democracy. Privatization does not decentralize power; it is not devolution. Rather, it shifts power deployed from the top down that is public, accountable, and transparent to the private sector, where it remains top-down but is now unaccountable and opaque. Privatization effectively gives public power

away, yielding it to private elites beyond scrutiny and control. In the name of liberty, it destroys democracy by annihilating the good of the public (the *respublica*) in whose name democratic republics are constituted in the first place.[31]

Equating democracy with consumerism, argues Barber, produces two fatal errors. Firstly, it misrepresents voluntary choice. Voluntary choice, by definition, must be freely made, without constraints. But how people spend their money in countries under the influence of the empire is not as free as it may seem. There is nothing voluntary in a society where wants, needs and desires are artificially manufactured. 'Freely made choices are subject to marketing, merchandizing, advertising, and packaging influences, all of which (as the billions spent in these sectors suggest) are intended to shape, modify, divert, and even compel choice in the direction of what producers need to sell rather than of what consumers need to buy.'[32] So, asks Barber, during the build-up to the Iraq war, when American consumers rushed to buy, on the recommendation of the Department of Homeland Security, such bizarre products as duct tape, plastic sheeting and gas masks, were they acting voluntarily or was something else motivating their consumption? Secondly, it misunderstands the critical difference between public and private choosing. Capitalism does not manufacture goods that fulfil the needs of ordinary folk, if it ever did. Global capital is focused on manufacturing needs to ensure the sale of surplus goods which no one actually needs or could possibly use. The 'need' for duct tape was generated by the dubious claim of the Department of Homeland Security (which it later retracted) that people could protect themselves from chemical and biological attacks by sealing their windows. Much more dubious is the need for Humvee vehicles, designer water and DVD burners; and 'even consumer capitalism's least sceptical celebrants may admit that the billions spent on marketing to children from one to six years old points to something other than pure market freedom and pristine consumer choice'.[33] Still, if we were to assume, argues Barber, that people freely choose what they really want and need, consumer choice comes down to private choice. And these private choices, manipulated or not, are not a substitute for public choices and do not influence public outcomes. Democratic governance cannot be reduced to private choices, for it is essentially all about public choosing: 'about dealing with the public and social consequences of private choice and behaviour.' Democracy therefore has no real connection with consumerism, let alone with the so-called free market. Its function is to produce conscientious citizens and accountable governance. Linking democracy with free trade and free markets is a formula for expanding the empire.

This formula, as Robert Jensen has argued, is based on two underlying assumptions that are intrinsic to American mythology. First, American market capitalism is not just the only variety that exists in the whole world, it is also the only economic system that is remotely compatible with democracy. Except for occasional disruption by the unions, it is a 'harmonious system in which benevolent owners and hardworking managers labor selflessly to provide for customers and workers'. Second, America is the only country on this planet that values and, in both history and contemporary times, has pursued democracy and freedom – no other country in the world values freedom and democracy like America! Every other nation in the world acts out of pure selfishness but America 'goes forward with a benevolent mission'.[34] The notion of a benevolent empire seems contradictory. However:

an Empire to which the ruled routinely consent is not unusual. This is what we call 'hegemony,' a word which indicates power establishes 'the rules of the game' by which others routinely play. Others may come to approve of the rules as well, so that hegemony is also partly legitimate. But the basis of hegemony is more of a matter-of-fact acceptance of things 'as the way they are.' Then people's own everyday actions help reproduce the dominance without much thought. For example, the US dollar is the world's reserve currency, stable, secure, so foreigners routinely invest in the US economy, subsidizing American consumers and indirectly paying for the US military, without their even being much aware of this. Foreigners see this mainly as the way the global economy works, and so it is also the way they can make profits. In practical terms they consent, though they may occasionally grumble.[35]

Or, as Gore Vidal put it, 'the brilliance of the American political system for 200 years lies in its giving the rich a licence to steal from the poor and making them think they voted for it'.[36] The poor here include not just the poor of America but also the poor of the rest of the world that a hegemonic empire loots and plunders.

The global narrative of empire propagated by its champions is a monolithic one. It operates through a uniform set of propositions, enforced by all the major global agencies, especially the IMF, through a simple one-size-fits-all mantra: democratisation along with privatisation and liberalisation of trade is what the world needs. These are the practical measures to which the ruled are required routinely to consent. But as Amy Chua so cogently argues in *World on Fire*,[37] in the real world, where history and context have meaning, the consequence of this mantra has been proliferating instability. In the complexities of the post-colonial world, new nations are artificial creations of former empires and reflect all the internal tensions of competing imperial powers. Democratisation often empowers élites of one ethnic group only to marginalise another and hence breed internal conflict. Economic élites can often be ethnically defined and distinct from political élites, another recipe for internal tensions which often leads to conflict. Privatisation robs governments of the levers of economic control that might allow these tensions and gross inequalities inherited from the past to be ameliorated and thus reduce the festering animosities leading to conflict. Meanwhile, liberalisation of trade and financial flows opens economies to being bought up by foreign capital and multinational corporations with no allegiance to the internal development of the economy, or the society and its diversity of ethnic and cultural needs. The gross effect has been to undercut what little social advances have been made, painfully, over decades; the future prospects for the poorest across a range of social and economic indicators become worse and worse, and human rights abuses are increased, leading to numerous regional and nationwide outbreaks of ethnic violence, leaving a trail of death and destruction in their wake. As hegemony, it is hardly a happy lot. As hegemony, it is sustainable only as long as the empire has no interest in outcomes beyond its own economic bottom line and is prepared to erase all else from its memory and decreasing attention span.

The new hegemonists, as Charles Maynes notes, are 'almost a parody of the Kaiser and his court at the beginning of this century'.[38] Like the German imperialists, they are drunk with their military and economic might and anxious to impose their will on the rest of the world. And like empires of old, the ruling élite of America have become staggeringly reckless and violent, blatantly breaking every norm and value that they so loudly proclaim. As the empire becomes more and more intoxicated with its military power, America will become more belligerent, more dependent on sophisticated technological warfare and surveillance, and more eager to search out new villains to subdue and new nations to conquer. But the first victims of this paranoid militarism will be American citizens themselves.

The 'war on terrorism', according to James Bovard, is now the biggest political growth industry in the United States.[39] After the atrocities of 9/11, the Bush administration immediately increased the power of federal agencies right across the spectrum and established a new Department of Homeland Security. As Saul Landau asks: 'Why do Americans need yet another security agency? There exists just on the federal level, the CIA, the DIA, the NSA, the FBI, the INS, the AFT, the DEA, and God knows how many other police agencies, alongside the panoply of defence and nuclear security agencies.'[40] So yesterday's evil idea of 'big government' now acquires truly Biblical proportions. The Department of Homeland Security was followed by the Uniting and Strengthening America by Providing Appropriate Tools Required to Intercept and Obstruct Terrorism (USA-PATRIOT) Act, passed by Congress with hardly any questions, which treats every citizen like a suspected terrorist and gives unquestioned power to every federal agent to use against anyone suspected of committing any of the 3,000 federal crimes on the statutes. The new anti-civil-liberties legislation led within a month to the arrest and detention of over 1,200 people, few with the remotest links to 9/11. In the long run, notes Bovard, Americans have more to fear from their government than from the terrorists – terrorists may be here today and gone tomorrow, but power-hungry politicians will always be there. The more proponents of empire recall freedom and democracy, the more individual liberty and public safety will be compromised, the more carefully Americans should count their remaining constitutional rights. The sole beneficiary of the sacrifice of individual liberties is the government which finds it easier to hide its mistakes and abuses; the more lies the administration tells, the less chance the citizens have of controlling it or making it accountable for its abuses.

Thus, a hegemonic empire would have a corrosive effect on America itself. The United States can continue its military adventures, writes Charles Maynes, only through a volunteer army which fills its ranks not just with blacks and Latinos, but also with less internationally-minded people. The US, Maynes suggests, is rapidly developing into two societies: 'not so much black versus white but cosmopolitan versus national, or between those who have directly, even extravagantly, reaped the benefits in recent years from the new globalized economy and those who have paid its price in terms of military service, endangered jobs, and repressed wages.'[41] The beneficiaries, consisting of less than a quarter of the population, are the jet set whose sons and daughters do not serve in the US military. The vast majority, who pay the price of the empire, will be alienated, rapidly leading to further fissures in American society.

Can the global narrative of empire actually sustain itself? Can American foreign policy carry on, to use the words of Michael Mann, simply on the basis of threats, bombings and invasions – 'threats are made almost daily, bombings seasonally, and an invasion every two years'?[42] Can the US continue, as Benjamin Barber asks, forever to 'shock and awe' its enemies, even remove the long-established taboo against the tactical use of nuclear weapons, or even deploy 'the mother of all bombs – the Massive Ordnance Air Blast, (or MOAB), the Defense Department's new 21,000-ton "conventional" bomb'?[43] Will the American Empire dominate the globe for the rest of the 21st century? Or, as billionaire financier George Soros suggests, is American supremacy nothing more than a 'bubble' waiting to burst?

We are living in abnormal times, suggests Soros; right in the middle of a cycle of boom-and-bust, in fact. American power looks formidable but is nothing more than a bubble, not unlike the dot.com bubble. And just as was the case with the dot.com boom, fantasy has totally subsumed any notion of reality. But when the gap between reality and its whimsical interpretation becomes totally unsustainable the bubble will burst – just as it did in the case of infotech. The empire may be able to stabilise the situation for a period – say in Iraq and Afghanistan. But we have moved too far from equilibrium for America to return to the status quo. It is the most hated power in history today; with the exception of one or two 'allies', almost every country in the world is against America. When the bubble bursts the repercussion, for America and others, will be far and wide. Nothing short of a total revision of the very idea of America, the reinterpretation of its mythology, and a new vision will save the day.[44]

In contrast, Emmanuel Todd, writer and researcher at the French National Institute for Demographic Studies in Paris, suggests that the American Empire is already in irreversible decline.

American military power, Todd argues in *After the Empire*, cannot be understood apart from America's economic performance.[45] The US has been exporting soldiers for decades, and importing manufactured goods and immigrants. It is dependent on sweatshop labour, both within its borders and abroad, to sustain its wealth. Take Wal-Mart, for example. America's largest retail chain store is totally dependent on the cheap labour of the People's Republic of China, and contributes a significant chunk to the GDP of the world's fastest-growing economy. Even the Wal-Mart Stars and Stripes flags that Americans wave at every opportunity are made in China. America's huge fiscal and balance of payment debt is crippling. The size of the opponents it chooses is a true indicator of its real power: Afghanistan, a medieval midget; Iraq, an underdeveloped country of 24 million exhausted by over a decade of economic sanctions. In short, America is living on borrowed time. It is not too dissimilar to the last days of the Roman Empire. In contrast, Michael Mann argues that Todd misses the point – the advocates of empire justify the ends through the means of really short and easy wars. They want to fight wars that do not produce American body-bags and that are preferably fought at a distance with overwhelming force. They would not take on China even if they wanted to, simply because of all the devastation that would follow. The real problem for the empire is that even short and easy wars are not delivering the goods that the champions of imperialism desire. 'The American Empire', Mann suggests, will turn out to be 'a military giant, a back-seat economic driver, a political schizophrenic and an ideological phantom. The result is a disturbed, misshapen monster stumbling clumsily across the world.'[46] Its downfall will come not from external threats but from its own internal incoherence.

The empire is unsustainable, argues Charles Maynes, because the world has changed; and the rules that the imperial powers themselves established to enhance imperialism are no longer valid. In particular, Maynes suggests that:

● War no longer pays for the great powers. For most of history, wars have paid. The victor ended up with more land and people. Over time, almost all of the latter accepted the sway of the new occupier. That is how most of the great nations of the world were built. With the rise of modern nationalism, however, it has become more and more difficult to absorb conquered territories without ethnic cleansing. Successful recent examples of seizing territory include the Russian, Polish, and Czech border changes after World War II, which involved brutal exchanges of populations. Unsuccessful examples of seizing territory include those in which the indigenous populations have remained, such as Israel's occupation of the West Bank, Indonesia's occupation of East Timor, and India's incorporation of Kashmir. Moreover, although ethnic cleansing does still take place today in a number of locations worldwide, those carrying out such practices are not the great powers but countries still in the process of nation-building along nineteenth-century lines. For most of the great states, in other words, war is not an option for power or wealth seeking. War is reserved for defense.

● Instead of seeking international power and influence through external expansion, most established powers now seek both through internal development. Postwar Germany and Japan have confirmed that these are more reliable paths to greater international prominence than the ones pursued since 1945 by Britain and France, both of which have relied on military powers to hold their place in the international system only to see it decline.

● The behavior of great states in the international systems that have lost traditional forms of power in recent decades has been remarkably responsible. Postwar Germany and Japan, as well as post-Cold War Russia, have all accepted being shorn of territories with notably few repercussions. A principal reason was the treatment of the first two by their rivals and the hope of the third that the rest of the world would not exploit its weaknesses so as to exclude Russia from the European system, but would instead take aggressive steps to incorporate it. In this regard, a policy of hegemony sends exactly the wrong message, particularly if one of our purposes is to prevent Russia from ever 'reviving' in a way that threatens us.[47]

Whether the rules for building empires have changed, or American global narrative is incoherent, or the empire is in terminal decline, or American power is a bubble waiting to burst, one thing is certain: if the American psyche were a single individual its psychosis would require institutional care and long-term remedial therapy. Robert Lifton, Visiting Professor of Psychiatry at Harvard Medical School, suggests that America is suffering from a 'Superpower Syndrome'; we would argue that the United States is afflicted by 'Empire Psychosis'. Lifton defines 'Superpower Syndrome' as aggregate behaviour that conveys psychological and political abnormality that is profoundly destructive both to the national body and to the world which that body inhabits. At the heart of the syndrome is a powerful fear of vulnerability and victimisation. It is based on the notions of apocalyptic violence ('a form of ultimate idealism, a quest for spiritual utopia') and a prophetic America which sees the world in ontological terms of good and evil, where the empire is always good and innocent.[48] While not totally disagreeing with this diagnosis, we would argue that America's malaise is not a recent phenomenon – as Lifton seems to suggest. The idea that American narrative is benevolent and universal has deep roots in American history. America's efforts to rule the world and to see its own history as the destiny of all humanity are intrinsic to its mythology. Its lethal righteousness, its claim that its model of democracy is the only model, and the linking of democracy to free markets are all an integral part of its worldview. In other words, America has turned its mythology into pathology.

America as global narrative is an intoxicating vision. It draws into itself all the strands of American mythology and projects them onto the world as a whole. It is a self-serving, self-justifying vision that provides an explanation for any and all American actions around the world. It allows successive administrations in Washington, Republican or Democrat, to offer the American people explanations of policy and action defined only in terms of high and good intent. The ideology of empire is the same ideology that made America. To question American empire is fundamentally to question the American self. The result is, quite simply, that America is never ready for the intrusion of reality. The reality of the operation of American empire exists not within the comfort zone of the American Dream, but as the global nightmare of effects. To the American public, the work of empire is by remote control, often covert, in large part operated by and through surrogates, co-opted regimes and élites in country after country around the world. The human rights abuses and brutality that such surrogates use to maintain and sustain themselves in power is backed by the presence of American military bases, aid and covert funding, but comes with deniability for Washington, the deniability that maintains innocence. Empire by remote control offers the prospect of walking away, simply going home and erasing the memory if events take the wrong turn. But as *Universal Soldier* suggests, there can be no certainty that memory-erasing injections are capable of permanently insulating innocence from the nasty and brutal reality that empire means for other people, any more than for Americans who are active agents in its administration and operation. The costs and consequences of empire can and do make their way to the American homeland. The increasing polarisation of America, the red and the blue political map, however, is not indicative of polarised attitudes to empire. The global narrative belongs to both sides of the internal debate; it has its roots in Republican and Democrat thought, strategy and policies. Argument over details leaves the global structures of empire intact. The two political parties offer the American people different styles of operation of the doctrine of empire, not a debate about the ideology of empire itself and whether it serves the long-term interests of America or the rest of the world. The success of the global narrative is that it has created the physical and psychic distance between ideals and reality that leaves the American political process no space to consider the distinction between the American Dream and the Global Nightmare.

The only way Luc Devereaux can stop Sergeant Scott is by feeding him to the shredder. That is a cinematic metaphor. In the real world of politics, the US has not been able to conceive of a way of debating reform that does not look like shredding everything that defines America. So it remains trapped in an earlier sequence of *Universal Soldier*. While on the road, Luc, the good unisol, rediscovers the pleasures of food. He eats plate after plate of food. Eventually, the diner's owner asks whether he can afford to pay for all he has consumed. Luc makes no answer; he is too intent on relishing the delights set before him. The burly chef is called to add menace to the request for payment. Still Luc makes no answer beyond the obvious statement: 'I just want to eat.' A fight ensues. The burly chef is despatched. Other clients of the diner join in. Luc uses his undisputed military power to continue to eat, fighting with chicken leg in one hand and a piece of his adversary in the other. It's all played for laughs. But the analogy with America is no laughing matter, either for the American people themselves or for the rest of the world. Like Luc, America cannot contain its pathological hunger. And like Luc, its military prowess is unquestionable, even in its good, benign persona. But when the empire has had its fill, what will remain for the rest of humanity?

Conclusion: Beyond *Groundhog Day*

'Almost from the beginning', says Neal Gabler, 'something was wrong with America'.[1] What was wrong, as we have argued and tried to show, is the mythology that America created to live by and that defines its self-image. This mythology has proved as lethal for America as for the rest of the world. The American Dream has become a Global Nightmare. The old familiar stories evoking a past full of heroes and high purpose are used to manipulate and justify how and why America acts in the present. America's fidelity to its mythic stories produces a continuous time-loop, shaping conditioned reflexes: the predictability of automatic reaction to events. America repeats its history over and over again, moving within a spiral of bloody sagas, because what it chooses to see, how it tries to understand the world in all its shifting diversity, answers to the popularly held simple stereotypes of myth-ridden thinking. When death and destruction, suffering and injustice are unleashed on other people as well as on their own citizens and society, America has the wrong questions ready at hand, too many obstacles to the sorts of inquiries that might be more relevant and conducive to better solutions. The American condition resembles most closely the dilemmas of *Groundhog Day*.

Groundhog Day is both a fable and a movie. As a myth, Groundhog Day is as old as time itself. Its origins are buried in pagan celebrations, Native American folklore and German tradition. According to fable, if a groundhog comes out of its hole after a long spell of hibernation and sees its shadow, there will be 40 more days of winter. Of course, for the groundhog to see its shadow, the sun must be shining and the spring-determining rodent has to look in the right direction! In its modern American reincarnation, the legend of Groundhog Day centres on the small Pennsylvania town of Punxsutawney – meaning 'the town of the sandflies'– originally established by Delaware Indians in 1723. The Delawares believed that their forebears began life as animals in 'Mother Earth', emerging centuries later as men; they considered groundhogs their honourable ancestors. When German settlers arrived in Pennsylvania they brought with them the tradition of Candlemas Day, 2 February, the mid-point between Winter Solstice and Spring Equinox. On this day, priests blessed candles and distributed them to the laity; the lighted candles were placed in each window of their homes. If the sun appeared on Candlemas Day, German folklore suggested, an animal would cast a shadow, predicting a six-week extension of winter. In their ancestral homeland, the Germans scrutinised a badger for the shadow. In Pennsylvania, the groundhog provided an appropriate replacement. So Groundhog Day is now officially established as 2 February; and the authorised groundhog is Punxsutawney Phil.

This enchanting myth furnishes the movie *Groundhog Day* (1993) with its framework. An obnoxious, self-obsessed weatherman on a Pittsburgh TV station, unsurprisingly called Phil, is forced to make the annual trip to Punxsutawney for the media event that is now Groundhog Day. This is his fourth trip to observe the yearly appearance of the divining Punxsutawney Phil, who will inform the nation if spring has finally arrived. Phil covers the festival and intends to head back to Pittsburgh, but a snowstorm forces him to stay in Punxsutawney. The following day, Phil wakes to see no signs of snow. It's the previous morning and Groundhog Day is beginning all over again. After a full day's work at the festival, Phil wakes up to exactly the same morning: the alarm in his Bed and Breakfast room goes off at

6.00 am, the radio plays 'I Got You Babe', an impending blizzard is announced, he bumps into a hotel guest, asks for an espresso in the breakfast room, meets his nerdy friend from high-school days who tries to sell him insurance, and finds his producer Rita and cameraman Larry preparing to film the festival. Groundhog Day does not end; it repeats itself over and over again in an endless cycle. Every day, Phil's world is inhabited by the same people but only he knows that Groundhog Day is repeating itself, and only he can remember what happened yesterday. After initial confusion, Phil begins to think he is immortal and can get away with anything: he indulges himself freely and even cheats death. But eventually the realisation dawns that to escape the dilemma, he must change his behaviour. Phil begins to thaw his moral winter with charitable deeds, learning to play the piano, and coming to terms with the limitations of his own life. Finally a Groundhog Day dawns when Phil has been transformed so much that even the long-suffering Rita, who stoically endured his infantile and uncouth behaviour, begins to like him.

Like Phil, America too is trapped in Groundhog Day. National history presented as change, energy and movement dissolves to disclose an underlying conformity that is the definition of an enduring American Way. We have pointed to ten laws of American mythology that work together to generate this underlying consistency in action and reaction. Each law, by virtue of being a law, has multiple layers of meaning and diverse applicability. The laws are: fear is essential; escape is the reason for being; ignorance is bliss; America is the idea of nation; democratisation of everything is the essence of America; American democracy has the right to be imperial and express itself through empire; cinema is the engine of empire; celebrity is the currency of empire; war is a necessity; and, lastly, all of American tradition and history are universal narratives applicable across all time and space. Together these laws frame the 'group think', the collective mindset of the nation. They are disseminated through popular culture as well as framing the rhetoric and policy-formation of political life. It is within the familiar terms of these laws that America negotiates with events, reconfiguring their myths only to keep them more firmly in place. Recurrence is the watchword running through America's history.

Clearly, our reading of American history and culture is at odds with the official view. We are not Alexis de Tocqueville. The French liberal philosopher toured America in the 1830s, and in 1835 published the first volume of *Democracy in America*,[2] containing a positive and optimistic view of the new Republic. He commends the democratic spirit of equality, the importance of religion in American life and the 'matchless Constitution' that gives the nation a decentralised government. Each of these principles became central to de Tocqueville's own thinking, and his writings on America offer it as a model for all nations. We can hardly think of a book on America that does not contain a reference or a quote or two from de Tocqueville. His works are widely available on the internet, including numerous sites devoted merely to quotations and student crib notes – a clear indication that he is an essential topic of study for Americans. The epithet that Americans find most conducive to their self-image – 'America is great because she is good, and if America ever ceases to be good, she will cease to be great' – is frequently cited, quoted by presidents and politicians both Republican and Democrat, and is attributed to the ubiquitous de Tocqueville. We find it entirely consistent with our analysis that this statement occurs nowhere in *Democracy in America*, nor anywhere else in de Tocqueville's writings. The apparent source of this 'unverified' quotation turns out to be a 1941 book on religion and the American Dream which quoted the passage as coming from *Democracy in America* but supplied no documentation.[3] A fuller version of the quotation appeared eleven years later, in an Eisenhower campaign speech:

> I sought for the greatness and genius of America in her commodious harbors and her ample rivers – and it was not there

... in her fertile fields and boundless forests and it was not there ... in her rich mines and her vast world commerce – and it was not there ... in her democratic Congress and her matchless Constitution – and it was not there. Not until I went into the churches of America and heard her pulpits flame with righteousness did I understand the secret of her genius and power. America is great because she is good, and if America ever ceases to be good, she will cease to be great.[4]

This was attributed not directly to de Tocqueville but to 'a wise philosopher [who] came to this country'. Thus the passage found its way into circulation and general attribution to de Tocqueville. It was quoted by Ronald Reagan in a 1982 speech, and has been used by Bill Clinton, Pat Buchanan and innumerable other politicians. It is a great quote because it tells Americans what they want to hear, what they want to believe about themselves. It is a great quote because, like so much in American history, it is a fabricated myth.

The 'de Tocqueville factor' is alive and well not only in the recurrence of this quotation. Its spirit is to be found everywhere in America – most specifically in notions that America is an indispensable nation, the ideal democracy, the lone conscience of the world. Consider, for example, a characteristic outburst of the celebrity pundit of cable news Bill O'Reilly. In July 2004 he told his audience: 'The truth is that the USA has freed more human beings in 230 years than the rest of the world combined.' It has, he adds, 'a provable history of freeing oppressed people all over the world [and] in fighting evil dictators'. In a fit of truly Yeatsian 'passionate intensity', O'Reilly continued:

The foreign and defense policies of Ronald Reagan resulted in the dissolution of the Soviet Union and the freeing of approximately 122 million people in Eastern Europe. The state of Israel would cease to exist if not for American protection, and about 5.5 million Jews would be in grave danger.

Nearly 23 million Taiwanese would be denied freedom if not for American protection. More than 48 million South Koreans would be living under a dictatorship if not for American protection. USA action led to the removal of the Serbian dictator Milosevic, who was responsible for the murders of hundreds of thousands of people in the Balkans. The USA and Britain removed the Iraqi dictator Hussein, who was responsible for the murders of hundreds of thousands of people in the Middle East. And we have also removed the terrorist Taliban government in Afghanistan. America is sending $15 billion to Africa to help victims of AIDS … American action in Central America, Grenada, and Haiti has kept millions of people out of totalitarian regimes. Of course, all of this has cost every American taxpayer big. And thousands of American service people have lost their lives protecting people overseas.[5]

Indeed, America is great because it is good. The trouble with this view of world events is that it denies agency to any other people, confirming the view that America is the indispensable nation. Eastern Europeans might legitimately consider that their actions played a major role in securing them their new dispensations, and even trace their origins more to Gorbachev's policy of Glasnost and Perestroika and his announcement that Russian tanks would no longer roll into East European capitals, than to Reagan's policies. It takes a specifically American view of freedom: a human condition defined only by not being under the grip of a Communist regime. The fact that Central America, Taiwan, South Korea, Grenada and Haiti have all known capitalist dictatorships that practised perversions of democracy accompanied by human rights abuses including widespread torture, slaughter and 'disappearances' under the tutelage and supervision of America, is not to be considered. Nor is the complicity of American foreign policy in the coming to power of the Taliban and Saddam Hussein to be taken into consideration.

The ideal always excludes reality; notional freedom always trumps the actual nature of governance and the lived condition.

The occasion for O'Reilly's outburst was a recent, unnamed opinion poll showing that 40% of Canadian teenagers – rising to 64% among French Canadians – 'think America is an evil country'. Canada and France are two particular topics of O'Reilly's animus. The United States, he argued in this instance, gets a relentless pounding in the Canadian media and from its liberal government. According to O'Reilly, Canadian youth are not getting the full picture – because Fox News is not permitted in Canada, while its rival news network CNN is. Worse: the far left in America, symbolised by Michael Moore, are telling everyone what a bad place America is. 'Canada', he argued, 'should be ashamed that so many of its young people are flat out ignorant'. 'It is insulting and dishonest for Americans and Canadians and Europeans to condemn this country because they don't like certain policies. Dissent is good. Slander is unacceptable.'

What space, one wonders, is there for dissent, and what would be acceptable dissent in the face of this venomous tirade and the worldview it describes? It has never been easy to engage Americans in a critical debate about America. It has never been welcome to interrogate the ideas and mythology that form the American psyche and find them flawed, wanting and full of that most human of qualities: imperfection. But such critical engagement is essential and urgent. The evidence is compelling that America is marching across the mythical de Tocqueville threshold. The American Dream has become a Global Nightmare because the consequences of American power are having a devastating effect on the actual condition of people's lives around the world, as well as costing lives uncounted and unconsidered in lands far removed from the United States.

Bill O'Reilly regularly informs his audience that his is the most watched show on cable news, that he is looking out for the interests of ordinary folks and operating a 'no spin zone' dealing in plain facts, not political doublespeak. He is an eager advocate of the conservative position in the culture wars, a trenchant denouncer of rap music, the liberal cabal of Hollywood, judges, social workers and the American Civil Liberties Union. Therefore, he appropriates to himself the power to define what constitutes legitimate dissent, regularly shouting down and shutting out comments that stray beyond his exacting and circumscribed boundaries. Bill O'Reilly is not America, and to represent him as the mainstream would be bizarre. Yet he is part of the proliferation, especially on talk radio, of the new aggressive conservatism. There is an acrimonious argument under way about media bias in America, whether its abundant airwaves are dominated by propaganda of the right or the left. This has the effect of paralysing critical inquiry of any kind. But the real issue has less to do with political orientation than the fact that news and talk is increasingly dominated by comment and opinion that is personal speculation masquerading as information. The democratic spirit of talk radio is that everyone is entitled to an opinion, which of course they are. It just does not follow that everyone knows what they are talking about. The best indicator of this democratisation is the obsessive fascination with celebrity trials. A legal trial in a court of law is a search for fact to arrive at informed, reasonable judgement. Across television and radio, particular celebrity trials grab and hold public attention, providing hours of coverage before charges have been brought, before trials have taken place, as well as during the actual court proceedings. A panel of journalists, defence lawyers and former prosecutors, as well as forensic experts and former policemen, will gather to speculate wildly, with seeming authority, about things they cannot possibly know, poring over every titbit of information, misinformation and spurious detail making the rounds of television, radio and print. The object of the exercise is to encourage everyone to form a fixed opinion. The result is that a fair trial, in the sense of one decided by impartial jury untainted by exposure to the case, becomes virtually impossible. From O. J. Simpson to the Scott Peterson trial, the right of the audience to hold an opinion does not democratise the judicial system – it undermines its very purpose.

Americans are a people who exist by dramatising themselves, and the greatest engine of drama is sensation. The celebrity trials of today and the sideshows they occasion on television, radio and in the press are not new. They are part of the recurrence of American life. The expansion of media outlets merely emphasises a tendency that has always been present. Sensationalism is what works and what sells in the mass. It is the cliff-hanger, the energy that drives narrative form and overrides and obscures reasoning about what is happening and why. Sensation is fun, breathless entertainment, stirring the emotion rather than stimulating questions. Sensation connects with the audience at a visceral level, confirming, reassuring, frightening, terrifying. It provides a vivid portrayal of the sense of self, the 'this is who we are and how we came to be "we the people"'. It is vindication without reflection, and it comes with the elegant get-out clause for avoiding responsibility or awkward questions: it's only entertainment! But in the cause of entertainment, the entire culture of discussion and debate becomes oblivious to the quality of information in circulation. Or as Neal Gabler neatly points out: 'In fact, it was entertainment, and not, as Marx declared, religion, that was the real opiate of the masses.'[6]

Religion in America, however, is a potent force. Since the Great Awakening of the early part of the 19th century that democratised Christianity and Christianised America, religion has had its own connotations of entertainment. The characteristic conventions of evangelical preaching, the sensational response of the congregation and the emotive stirring of popular hymnody, have been entertainment and have become big business. There are two aspects of evangelical thought that are reshaping the American landscape more profoundly than religious theme parks and crystal cathedrals. One is the trend to literalism. Biblical literalism based on the inerrancy of the King James Bible underpins the rise of the Creationist movement, a powerful force in American life. Creationism is the belief in the literal meaning of the six days of divine creation as stated in the Book of Genesis. It stands in stark opposition to scientific Darwinism in all its various forms, based on the concept of evolution. Creationism has become an increasingly sophisticated organisation. But its most notable effects have been to limit debate both within circles of the religious and within science. Literalism has raised the translators of the King James Bible to the status of the only authoritative interpreters of the Word of God, while limiting the understandings that can be placed on the actual words they used in authoring their translation of Biblical texts. 'Six days' must mean six days in the conventional sense of six 24-hour periods of time. Any scientific speculation about evolution over vast periods of time, in the Creationist view, is inherently godless, de-divinising the world. But interestingly, the Creationist abhorrence of scientific Darwinism has no problem with the much older tradition commonly known as social Darwinism. The idea that human social organisation has evolved through various stages is very old and familiar, and sits comfortably within a Biblical framework. Mankind has fallen or risen; theoretically this process is guided by Divine Providence, but the judgements on who are lesser peoples, and why, are made by human beings. And the whole structure of social Darwinism came to centre entirely on the biological concept of race: there were superior or inferior races, which of course is a biological principle.

Scientists have risen up to combat the spread of Creationism. In the process, the biological theory of Darwinism – the principle of evolution with modification – has become a canonical belief system, a scientific religion that is beyond question. Its most ardent supporters insist that science leaves no place for a divine Creator because evolution is an explanation of everything. However, the vast majority of Christians and many scientists have been able to reconcile the concept of evolution with belief in an omnipotent creator God. The publication of Darwin's *On the Origin of Species* in 1859 was not, for the silenced majority, a declaration of war between religion and science, but a challenge to understanding. And the challenge continues. Many Christians, scientists and lay people alike, have critical questions about how the theory of evolution is employed as the basis for general explanations of the world and various aspects of social life. The trouble is that Darwinian orthodoxy within science is rigorously policed because of the existence of Creationism. It makes for a fundamentalist temper within science, and inhibits posing reasonable questions lest people be suspected of being closet Creationists or the thin end of a Creationist wedge. In the process, all those in the middle ground who would prefer to inquire and reason are marginalised.

The second effect of the evangelical temper in American life is the tendency to deify. America began with a sense of religious mission, but that is quite different from asserting that the nation, its Constitution, system of laws and all their works are providential, inspired works of the spirit in the mould of the Biblical Israel itself. Raising the meaning and significance of human agency to inspired works of God is an extension of Biblical literalism. It is a move beyond the general tendency in American history and thought to invest the nation, its history and symbols with an aura of sanctity, to regard them as aspects of a diffuse civic religion. But the moves to insist on public display of the monuments to the Ten Commandments, the sound and fury over the phrase 'under God' in the pledge of allegiance, imply something far more than opposition to radical secularism. The best model we can offer, for the parallels are too clear to be avoided, is the rise of fundamentalism in the Muslim world. In both cases, there is a desire to ground society and thought on literal certainty derived from religion. In both, it is human historical interpretation of religion that is raised up. The opinion of dead good men becomes more important than continued personal wrestling and reasoning with religious text. Meanings and their social implication and action are fixed. The purpose is to stem anxiety caused by rapid social change, social diversity and the new forms of behaviour they generate. In both cases, this search for certainty is offered as a return to a pure and perfect original pattern in action, thought and belief, and in both cases it authors something quite new, a genuine postmodern dispensation. Fundamentalists in America, as in the Muslim world, are most fixated on adherence to a code of personal morality. But in neither sphere do they stop there. To secure their moralist worldview, in both arenas a militant, politicised temper is the natural and logical outgrowth of the search for simple religious certainties. The world becomes a tapestry of good and evil locked in battle; no aspect of life is beyond this conviction.[7] But when this fundamentalist temper is politicised, it becomes panic politics that operates as a pincer movement on the vast majority. Debate becomes more and more constrained; to raise questions too easily can be decried as lacking commitment to essential enduring values. In America, the language of values is everywhere in political debate. But the meaning and practical application and implications of values ceases to be a serious subject of debate. Values are invoked, not interrogated. It is not only the moderate majority that is silenced; the very notion that there might be alternatives, new ideas, new understandings of American society and the world at large, is cowed into silence, marginalised and removed from the political agenda of informed debate.

In the 'war on terror' this militant, politicised religious temper in America finds the perfect adversary. Two factions that intuitively understand each other are ready to engage in apocalyptic battle. It is less clear that the rest of American society, the Muslim world or the world in general can intervene to question the policies and change the course of events to moderate a slide into increasing danger and insecurity for everyone, everywhere.

The state of American debate is a matter of urgent global concern. America has declared an open-ended, ongoing 'war on terror'. Terror is a tactic, not a specific nation, people or political organisation. As a tactic it transcends borders, is resorted to under different conditions with different objectives by a diversity of groups; it exists and operates in many places around the world. A war on terror therefore places no limits on where it may lead. This 'war on terror' has been used to legitimate a new doctrine of international policy, the right of pre-emptive attack defined as self-defence. Under this banner, America launched an illegal war based on false intelligence that has cost tens of thousands of lives and devastated the lives of millions more in Iraq. The aftermath of war has seen international terrorists find bases in Iraq, where none existed before. And Iraq has become a recruiting agent for disaffected would-be terrorists, giving the whole structure and organisation of international terrorism a new lease of life, making it more widespread and harder to eradicate. Iraq has been a demonstration of the limits of American power and capabilities, and this is a proper concern for every citizen of the globe. What Americans know, how America operates its system of governance, what Americans permit to be done in their name, are vital issues for the safety and well-being of people everywhere. Whether the world can join the American debate is the next big question of the human future.

The operation of the ten laws of American mythology works to construct a national psyche and self-image that precludes a serious analysis of power. America is satisfied with its dominant power in the world because it is satisfied with itself. The idea that power can be as corrosive for America as the use of American power is for the rest of the world is unthought. Average Americans have no realistic appreciation of how powerful their nation is, and therefore no sense of how it distorts and controls all relations, situations, actions and circumstances around the world. The greatest accumulation of power the world has ever seen is encouraged to vaunt its muscularity and at the same time fear its weakness and fragility – and both responses are abuse of power, not responsible routes to safety and sustainable continuation, let alone peaceful cohabitation with the rest of humanity.

The war on terror is the ultimate Groundhog Day. By reconfiguring the Cold War motif of an ideological conflict on a global scale with its echoes and footprints everywhere, including within America, it is a far older nightmare that is being rekindled. It has been devised by ardent Cold Warriors anxious for the simple dichotomy of good and evil that made all calculations simplistic, straightforward and enriching for the vested interests they represent so ably. And this new war, the war on terror, has immense advantages over its predecessor. The war is virtual: ever-present everywhere and nowhere, it exists only in the definition, for it is not a war against specific tangible nations but against those who oppose it. In fact, it is the most basic recurrence of the civilised/savage dichotomy, with as much lack of interest as the old one had in the Good Indian's fate. Already thousands of innocent non-combatants, ordinary citizens of Afghanistan and Iraq, have died, been maimed, seen their livelihoods and possessions destroyed. Their numbers are not counted, nor are they remembered or given any memorial in American political debate. American security, the right to life of Americans, is the monotone of political discussion. Are these lost lives less precious, less irreplaceable? To people around the globe, the silence on this issue suggests a callous disregard for the lives of non-Americans, and does nothing to make Americans safer.

The prevailing climate of anxiety, panic and fear being whipped up in the US has stopped Americans from considering the savagery of their civilisation, the brutalising, terrorising power at the command and disposal of those who deem themselves good because of how effortlessly they can destroy without acknowledging, counting or caring about the collaterals – the Good Indians mown down in the crossfire. The mastery of the technology of surveillance and destruction is the basis of America's overwhelming power. It seems never to occur to Americans how intimidating this accumulation of power appears to other people. But most of all, it has not initiated any questioning of the limits of what can be known and achieved by such means. When the idea that war is a necessity has become ingrained, then the counter-thought that war may be incapable of bringing peace, of building the conditions for peace, or is the most inappropriate means of counteracting and defeating an enemy, is pushed off the agenda of debate. America is certain that enemies abound; that is why it has developed a military-industrial complex to deter, contain, intimidate and eradicate real and potential opponents. But what the war in Iraq has demonstrated most clearly is how incomplete, limited and fallible this worldview is. The various investigations and inquiries into how America went to war and how it got things so wrong should raise questions about far more than the limitations and failings of intelligence agencies. What should be brought into question are systemic failings of American self-perceptions and worldview.

There is much food for thought in the evidence given to the Senate Armed Services Committee by Dr David Kay, the former head of the Iraq Survey Group, the body charged with tracking down the weapons of mass destruction that were the source of imminent threat and *casus belli* of the Iraq war. Dr Kay presented a lucid, humane and important analysis into the serial failures of American intelligence. He pointed out that in the Second World War it was generally believed that mass aerial bombing of Germany was destroying the will to fight, as well as removing its production capacity: 'As it turned out, afterwards, the German will to fight increased under the bombing and the war production went up till the last two months of the war; it was still increasing.' In the case of Vietnam, Dr Kay briefly intimated that similar estimates of societal determination and economy turned out to be wrong. For nearly 50 years America talked up the threat of the Soviet Union. But Dr Kay observed: 'After the fall of the Soviet Union, what had looked like a 10-foot power turned out to be an economy that barely existed and a society that had horrible levels of human health problems, of lack of education and all, leading to the current situation.'[8] Just as in the case of Iraq, what was seen as a potent, hostile power was in fact a deeply corrupt and corroded society on the road to total disintegration.

These are tales of major failings, not just of American intelligence but of America's ability to understand the rest of the world. None of these assessments, which were the foundation of American foreign and defence policy, went unquestioned. America has a notorious history of misidentifying the significance and meaning of movements around the world, of committing its military and intelligence resources as well as its diplomatic and economic power to confront straw men. Nationalist movements, movements for social justice throughout the Americas and around the world were defined as Communist, proto-Communist, or fellow travellers to be opposed and eradicated. In the process, countless people have died, been denied their liberty and prosperity, been tortured and maimed. There have always been dissenting voices within America, as there were around the world, arguing that these were faulty judgements that generated injustice and insecurity rather than made either America or the world a safer and better place. The question is not why intelligence agencies failed, but why the entire systemic climate of information and debate failed to take account of, and take seriously, such alternative readings of the world. In his evidence to the Senate Committee, Dr Kay concluded that the failing lay in having under-funded and under-developed 'our human intelligence capability', the capacity for 'understanding the other'. This is the essence of America's problem with itself and with all others.

We have argued that the ten laws of American mythology help to explain the predicament that now faces America and the whole world. Paradoxically, the American Dream makes America a stranger to much of its own self and history, just as it renders it incapable of distinguishing reality from phantasms in the wider world. The entire framework of mythology builds a conviction of American exceptionalism, a certainty that America is not just good but also right, and therefore different and in ineffable ways better than other peoples and nations. It is not anti-American to suggest that this hubris and arrogance is a danger to American lives as much as the lives of people everywhere. America is not the first empire the world has seen. Imperialism is not an incurable disease, but it is a disfiguring one. It disfigures the humane instincts that are necessary to construct a peaceful and sustainable interconnected world with justice and fairness for all. If America is to be liberated from its distorting vision of itself and of others, it has to recover the ability to reason with its fallibility. To argue that America is imperfect is not to be anti-America but rather to uphold the self-evident proposition that Americans are human, and to invite them to see their dilemmas and concerns mirrored in the debates and problems of the rest of the world. We can do no better than commend to Americans the advice of James Madison, one of the architects of the Constitution and the fourth president, 1809–17:

> Attention to the judgement of other nations is important to every government, for two reasons – the one is that, independently of the merits of a particular plan or measure, it is desirable on various accounts that it should appear to other nations as the offspring of a wise and honourable policy; the second that, in doubtful cases, particularly where the national councils may be warped by some strong passion or momentary interest, the presumed or known opinion of the impartial world may be the best guide that can be followed.[9]

To pay due 'attention to the judgement of other nations', America must take two steps. American mythology places America above humanity and above history. So, in the first instance, America must rejoin the human community. The notions that America is an indispensable nation, the ideal democracy, the lone conscience of the world, have to be seriously examined. It is not simply a question of seeing that American democracy is deeply flawed, that American conscience routinely attributes evil to others while overlooking its own hubris, but also of seeing the founders of American mythology as genuinely human. One cannot simply remember, for example, George Washington as a worthy and inspiring chap without remembering that he was also a slave owner who considered the Native Americans to be savages at par with wolves. Mythology loses its value as incentive and inspiration when it paints history in terms of perfect men who built a noble, blameless nation. The narrative of courageous men must be balanced with American history's record of brutality and genocide, on the home continent as well as abroad. Deconstructing the elements of American mythology does not, of course, mean that Americans should not be patriots. All nations value patriotism. But patriotism does not mean loyalty to a myth, let alone a particular interpretation of that myth. For Americans, patriotism has come to mean that 'nothing that is susceptible to accusations of meanness, wrongdoing, and evil' can be laid at the door of America. As the Indian historian Vinay Lal notes, American 'patriotism engenders a more politically satisfying idea of transcendence: thus, the evil perpetuated in the name of the American nation-state can ultimately be overlooked on the assumption that [it does] not violate the core idea of America as the repository of social and cultural goods. Whatever America may do, however much its action may shock the world into resignation, despair, and bitterness, the idea of America cannot be irrevocably tarnished.'[10] It is this notion of patriotism that makes Americans blind to the existing structures of government, administration, law and constitutional arrangements. But institutions created in history cannot last for ever; nothing that is a product of fallible human beings is designed to last for all times and all places. Genuine democracy requires citizens of any state to reject those institutions that are inherently unjust and do not serve their interests.

Genuine democracy also needs an informed citizenry able to engage seriously with politics. In American society, where dissent is dubbed unpatriotic and relegated to the margins, it is becoming increasingly difficult to be serious about anything – politics, arts, literature – which is not in total conformity with the dictates of American mythology. When life itself is a movie, anything outside the purview of film and celebrity is almost invisible. Cinema and celebrity, as we argued in Chapter Four, serve as engine and common currency of empire, as well as reinforce, regurgitate, reiterate and constantly re-establish the American Dream, as we have tried to show throughout this book. Indeed, the propensity of Hollywood to rewrite history in the framework of American mythology has gone from being simply ridiculous to absurdly sublime. The old John Wayne version of *The Alamo* was released in 1960 when the United States was preparing to bomb Vietnam into the Stone Age. The new version is released when the US is busy bringing 'freedom and democracy' to Iraq. The story surrounding the 1836 siege of the Texan fort by the 7,000-strong Mexican army is one of the central fables of American mythology. But neither the official version nor the film tells us that the Americans who died at The Alamo were defending the right of white settlers to steal Mexican land, and resisting the Mexican government's prohibition of human slavery. Hollywood has totally rewritten the history of the Second World War: Americans led *The Great Escape*, captured the Enigma code machine in *U571*, and in *Pearl Harbor* thwarted the Luftwaffe in the summer of 1940. So it is hardly surprising that in *The Few*, Billy Fiske, the American hero of the 'finest hour', who won an Olympic Gold medal for America and died without shooting down a single plane, wins the Battle of Britain single-handedly. Meanwhile, centuries ago an American samurai conquered Japan in *The Last Samurai*; a horseman from the Wild West rode his American mustang to victory in a 3,000-mile Arabian desert race in *Hidalgo*; and in a time before history, Sinbad, an all-American anti-hero, travels the oceans in *Sinbad: The Legends of the Seven Seas*. Such blatant distortions of history and appropriation of other people's culture may be presented as entertainment, but they are an epic form of myth-making. What they actually represent is self-glorification as psychosis.

But this psychosis, with its unquestioning allegiance to the American Dream that has turned into both local and global nightmare, does not augur well for American democracy. 'It is clear', says the novelist J.G. Ballard, that in today's America, 'there are no suppressed dreams, no forbidden nightmares. Every American fear and paranoid anxiety is out in the open, from the ranting of ultra-right shockjocks to *The Day After Tomorrow.*' These are a 'thinly veiled glimpse of the self-destructive urges lurking alongside the hamburger and comic-book culture we all admire. As the nation infantilises itself, the point is finally reached where the abandoned infant has nothing to do except break up its cot.'[11] The infantile mythology of America also promotes a conformist outlook – indeed, despite all the pretensions to individualism and freedom, the US is one of the most conformist countries in the world. 'The neat narrative formulas in which most entertainment is packaged', Neal Gabler tells us, deny 'personal taste or sensitivity or intelligence – anything that might pry the individual away from the undifferentiated lump and thus narrow the appeal of a movie or book or TV show'.[12] Most foreigners find this 'undifferentiated' conformity of America frighteningly dumbfounding. In this conformist modern America, Gabler goes on to say, celebrities are not only 'the protagonists of our news, the subjects of our daily discourse and the repositories of our values, but they have also embedded themselves so deeply in our consciousness that many individuals profess feeling closer to, and more passionate about, them than about their own primary relationships'.[13] Entertainment has thus ceased to be escapist: escape itself has become the reason for being human à la America.

Witness how the entertainment media have acculturated the mass audience to the motifs of the national security state and the military-industrial complex. Films and television vaunt American military might without questioning how that power is used. Special Forces, FBI agents, CIA spies and other covert operators for the government are stock characters of the movies and TV.

The professionalisation of the military, a move that America made only after 1973 in response to the unpopularity of Vietnam, has been domesticated as a security blanket for the American populace. This professionalisation has become a cliché. It began with John Wayne in *Sands of Iwo Jima* – Wayne the heartless, ruthless sergeant drilling his men into a fighting force. It is Clint Eastwood in *Heartbreak Ridge* and innumerable other incarnations. It is the subtext of *A Few Good Men* and so many lesser cinematic scripts. The moral is the creation of superb killing machines who do only what they are told and never question the orders they are given. But what it exemplifies is not a concern for the American public. Just following orders was, after all, exactly the psychosis that the Nuremburg Trials were convened to excoriate and condemn. But hard, trained, unquestioning men doing what a man's got to do to keep the folks safe is not only a celluloid motif – it is the cornerstone of imperial America, the cinematic nightmare that is unleashed on real people in Afghanistan, Iraq and elsewhere. That other regular plot device of Hollywood, the development of the national security state and the military-industrial complex, schools the masses on a very specific lesson. It is the miasma of power that teaches the audience that the citizen cannot bring change, that the good small guy – the guy who has resisted the hypnosis of movies, celebrities, television, videogames, and infotainment masquerading as news, and has broken out of *Groundhog Day* – is just that: small and ineffectual. The good person may be small; but he or she is never ineffectual. It is within the means of the aware and enlightened 'Citizens of the Empire', as Robert Jensen suggests, to change and humanise America.

Traditions constantly adapt to change; indeed, they continue as traditions by reinventing themselves. Americans too need to reinvent their mythology in a broader framework of humanity. American lifestyle, notes Vinay Lal, with its 'characterisation of the competitions fought in its own sporting leagues as "World Series", the abundance of food, water, and natural resources that is taken for granted, the view that access to unlimited oil is a constitutional right, the gargantuan portions served in restaurants, the penchant for the big in nearly every aspect of life – all this and much more point to a country that cannot be assimilated into known cultural and political histories of human societies'.[14] In other words, Americans have to join the human race. Or, as Jensen puts it, Americans have to 'put our faith in each other to stop living on top of the world and start living as part of the world'.[15]

The world itself needs to be rescued from American hegemony. War, markets, entertainment, the basic ingredients of American imperialism, are relentlessly imposed on the rest of the world on the arrogant assumption that what is good for America is good for the whole of humanity. This is, of course, another way of saying that American tradition and history are universal narratives applicable across all time and space – what we have called Law 10 of American mythology. It is all done in the name of freedom and democracy. But the more loudly America praises 'freedom and democracy', the more it violates the basic freedom and democratic aspirations of developing countries. For America, 'freedom' is simply a word invoked to justify its imperial ambition and sanctify itself and its mythology. 'The most dangerous forms of tyranny', writes Benjamin Barber,

> are those that are advanced under the banner of freedom. Hence Pope John Paul II's trenchant warning that 'the human race is facing forms of slavery which are new and more subtle than those of the past, and for too many people, freedom remains a word without meaning.' To take but one egregious example, when freedom is associated with the privatisation of goods as obviously public as the human genome, the pope's fears are vindicated. Freedom must mean something more than corporate profit and consumer choice.[16]

For the vast majority of the inhabitants of the planet, freedom does not equal 'free trade' – a euphemism for corporate plundering. There are, American myths notwithstanding, other ways of being free. And one way to be free is to be free from American cultural domination. No one outside America really buys the idea that market forces should be the sole determinant of cultural patterns. Almost all cultures see themselves as unique and worth preserving, and would fight to defend their cultural heritage from the onslaught of free markets – and Americans would do just the same. Would American officials, asks Barber, 'cling so ardently to their own position regarding international free trade in cultural goods if it turned out that market forces were in fact overwhelming the United States with, say, the culture of the Middle East or Latin America'?[17] Notice, Barber points out, how Americans become disturbed when Latinos insist on speaking Spanish and express a strong desire to hold on to their own cultural heritage. Where do market forces go in this case? Or in the case of the 'English only' movement or the race to install V-chips in home television sets to control what minors may view? The point is that there is nothing special about Americans. Other human beings have the same concerns and aspirations as Americans. And just as Americans do not want to be dominated by others, so other peoples and cultures do not want to be dominated by Americans. American historic experiences and culture are a provincial phenomenon; they are not universal narratives. American mythology must be deconstructed with this realisation so that it can be opened up to other possibilities. The notion that an innocent and virtuous America must save itself from a frightening world, by isolating itself or imposing an awesome hegemony on everyone, is dangerously obsolete.

The 21st-century world is an interdependent world. The realities of interdependence are totally out of sync with American mythology. These realities make their own demands – and global peace is not possible without meeting these demands. These realities insist that the suffering and deaths of others be seen to be as important as those of Americans; and be treated with equal concern and respect. They state that the cultures and traditions of other people, including the Native Americans and Latinos in America, be valued and promoted as much as the dominant culture of America and its history and traditions. They insist that something be done about the plight of those denied food and shelter, as well as their basic human dignity, by exploitative American economic policies and corporate pillage. They assert that attention be paid to the victims of unjust American policies in the Middle East, particularly the Palestinians. They require that urgent attention be focused on global issues such as climate change and the HIV epidemics. They stipulate that global concerns, from media monopolies to international crime syndicates, be actively challenged. 'America may be preponderant', notes Zbigniew Brzezinski, former national security advisor to the president, 'but it is not omnipotent'. It cannot meet the demands of an interdependent world unilaterally. Moreover, the rest of the world cannot function as though it is there simply to provide markets for America, to furnish the United States with its wealth and maintain its over-indulgent, over-consumptive lifestyle. The burdens of an interdependent world 'cannot be shared without shared decision-making. Only by shaping a comprehensive strategy with its principal partners can America avoid becoming mired, alone, in hegemonic quicksand.'[18]

After joining the human community, America must descend to join human history. The Founding Fathers of America were much enamoured of classical civilisation – a motif and rhetorical reference that looms large in American culture. So Americans may like to compare their own destiny with that of ancient Rome. The Roman Republic became a military empire in which the Senate, ensconced on Capitol Hill in Rome, became an irrelevant rubber stamp to the Emperor who controlled and manipulated all power while maintaining the mystique of republican forms and longingly dreaming of a return to the Republic and its values. The populace meanwhile were contented with bread and circuses. America has now made the transition. Its military-industrial complex is the essence of the economy, defence spending the great unquestioned catch-all through which preservation of jobs and wealth is justified. National security has come to mean in effect the security of the empire that America has established, not by direct administration of foreign territory but by dominance of the global economy and the internal affairs of other states through its string of military bases and control of global institutions. America is an empire unlike any other because its mode of imperialism has always been conceived and operated by indirect means. An imperial president has accumulated, without much scrutiny, powers and the operation of levers of powers neither envisaged nor designed by the Constitution; he now has at his disposal serried ranks of militarised institutions from the Joint Chiefs of Staff, National Security Agency and the Pentagon to the FBI, CIA, and the Department of Homeland Security, which are, in fact, parallel reality states. The great irony, for it is no paradox, is that the war on terror was declared by neo-conservatives who cling closely to the rhetoric of adherence to the literal meaning of the Constitution, to small government and lower taxes. The mass of the population have been diverted from these troubling developments by the rise of mass entertainment and the culture of celebrity as the expression of an affluent lifestyle. Rome moved slowly towards dictatorship – just as America is now moving towards an oligarchy of corporate interests and wealthy families. It was only a matter of time before civil war erupted in Rome from conflicts between rich and poor, patrician and plebeian forces. Analogies should not be taken too far. America need not descend into internal strife, even though US politics is totally polarised, reflecting and being fed by a huge cultural rift between individual lifestyles and moral values, and extending from the airwaves to the altar and from bookshelves to the bedroom. America – and Americans – can yet redeem themselves.

When Phil first realises that he is trapped in *Groundhog Day*, he concludes that he has been absolved of all moral responsibilities. 'No tomorrow. That would mean there will be no consequences. No hangovers. We could do whatever we wanted.' But such behaviour, he soon realises, leads to depression and despair. The beginning of the end comes when Phil resolves to change himself. He greets the hotel guest he runs into every morning with words of hope and promise. He takes the beggar he regularly ignores for breakfast; and even tries to save his life by giving him mouth-to-mouth resuscitation. Small acts of self-reflection lead to big things. America needs to follow the example of Phil and realise that it cannot continue to exist within the spirals of its own grandiose, pathological self-perceptions. 'The greatest country that ever existed on the face of the earth' must join the human community to break out of the *Groundhog Day* of its own history and mythology.

Notes

INTRODUCTION

1 Joshua Gamson, *Claims to Fame: Celebrity in Contemporary America*, Berkeley: University of California Press, 1994. Gamson's Introduction is entitled 'Explaining Angelyne'.

2 A film by Alex Cooke, a Mantron/Article Z co-production for the BBC, broadcast on BBC4, Friday 9 January 2004.

3 Nicholas Lemann, 'The Next World Order', *The New Yorker*, 1 April 2002.

4 Available from *www.newamericancentury.org*

5 William Rivers Pitt, 'The Project for the New American Century', 25 February 2003, available from *www.truthout.org*

6 New York: Viking Press, 2003.

7 'Progressive Internationalism: A Democratic National Security Strategy', Washington, DC: Progressive Policy Institute, 30 October 2003; available from *www.ppionline.org*

8 John Pilger, 'Bush or Kerry? No difference', *New Statesman*, 8 March 2004, p. 18.

9 Chalmers Johnson, *The Sorrows of Empire: Militarism, Secrecy and the End of the Republic*, New York: Metropolitan Books, 2004, p. 51.

10 William Pfaff, *Barbarian Sentiments: America in the New Century*, New York: Hill and Wang, 2000, p. 275.

11 Gore Vidal, *The Decline and Fall of the American Empire*, Chicago: Odonian Press, 2000.

12 Paul Krugman, *The Great Unravelling*, New York: W.W. Norton, 2003.

13 Quoted in Morris Berman, *The Twilight of American Culture*, New York: W.W. Norton, 2000, p. 23.

CHAPTER ONE

1 Richard Slotkin, *Regeneration Through Violence*, Norman, OK: University of Oklahoma Press, 2000a, p. 4.

2 Quoted from *Map of Virginia with a Description of the Country the commodities people government and religion Written by Captain John Smith sometimes Governor of the Country*, published Oxford, 1612.

3 For a fuller discussion of Captain John Smith and the Pocahontas legend, see Ziauddin Sardar, *Postmodernism and the Other*, London: Pluto Press, 1998, pp. 87–108.

4 See Roger Bartra, 'Discovering the European Wild Men', in Rasheed Araeen, Sean Cubitt and Ziauddin Sardar (eds), *The Third Text Reader on Art, Culture and Theory*, London: Continuum, 2002.

5 Slotkin, op. cit., 2000a, p. 4.

6 Richard Slotkin, *Gunfighter Nation*, Norman, OK: University

of Oklahoma Press, 2000b, p. 256.

7 John G. Cawelti, *The Six-Gun Mystique Sequel*, Bowling Green, OH: Bowling Green State University Popular Press, 1999, pp. 1–2.

8 Barry Glassner, *The Culture of Fear*, New York: Basic Books, 1999.

9 Daniel J. Boorstin, *The Americans: The National Experience*, New York: Vintage Books, 1965.

10 Neal Gabler, *Life: The Movie*, New York: Vintage Books, 1998.

11 Jonathon Jones, 'The Final Frontier', *The Guardian*, 17 June 2002.

12 Richard Slotkin, *The Fateful Environment*, Norman, OK: University of Oklahoma Press, 2000c.

13 Garry Wills, *A Necessary Evil: A History of American Distrust of Government*, New York: Touchstone Books, 2002, p. 28; emphasis in the original.

14 Ibid., p. 31.

15 *The Emory Wheel*, 25 October 2002; available from *www.emorywheel.com*

CHAPTER TWO

1 Quoted in *The Constitution of the United States: A History*, available on the US National Archives website, *www.archives.gov*

2 Robert Jensen, *Citizens of the Empire: The Struggle to Claim Our Humanity*, San Francisco: City Light Books, 2004, p. 3.

3 Gallup Organisation, 1999, cited in Robert A. Dahl, *How Democratic is the American Constitution?*, New Haven, CT: Yale University Press, 2001, p. 122.

4 Michael Schudson, *The Good Citizen: A History of American Civic Life*, Cambridge, MA: Harvard University Press, 1998, p. 202.

5 Daniel Lazare, *The Frozen Republic*, New York: Harcourt and Brace, 1996, p. 2.

6 Interviewed by Bill O'Reilly on *The O'Reilly Factor*, Fox News Channel, 24 March 2004.

7 Lewis Lapham, *Waiting for the Barbarians*, London: Verso, 1997, p. 220.

8 Lee Greenwood, 'God Bless the USA', song lyrics published by Rutledge Hill Press, 2000.

9 Dahl, op. cit., p. 156.

10 John W. Kingdon, *America the Unusual*, Belmont, CA: Wadsworth, 1999, p. ix.

11 Dahl, op. cit., p. 2.

12 Ibid., p. 115.

13 Wills, op. cit., p. 16.

14 Ibid., p. 57.

15 *Dred Scott v Sandford*, 60 US (19 How) 393 of 1857.

16 Available at *www.FairVote.org*

17 Dahl, op. cit., p. 18.

18 Ibid., p. 18.

19 Ibid., p. 20.

20 Quoted in Gabler, op. cit., 1998, p. 30.

21 Dahl, op. cit., pp. 69–70.

22 Wills, op. cit., p. 19.

23 Ibid., p. 16.

24 Ibid., p. 20.

25 See Bernard Bailyn, 'Realism and Idealism in American Diplomacy', in his collected essays, *To Begin the World Anew*, New York: Alfred Knopf, 2003.

26 Garry Wills, 'The New Revolutionaries', *New York Review of Books*, 10 August 1995, p. 52.

27 Lazare, op. cit., p. 284.

28 Lapham, op. cit., p. 67.

29 Ibid., p. 68.

30 Wills, op. cit., 2002, p. 21.

31 Both the quotation from the Massachusetts delegate and that by Samuel Bryan are from the National Archives and Records Administration article 'A More Perfect Union: The Creation of the US Constitution', available at *www.archives.gov*

32 Gore Vidal, *Inventing a Nation: Washington, Adams, Jefferson*, New Haven, CT: Yale University Press, 2003, p. 46.

CHAPTER THREE

1 Robin Wood, *Howard Hawks*, Berkeley, CA: University of California Press, 1968.

2 Andrew J. Bacevich, *American Empire: The Realities and Consequences of US Diplomacy*, New Haven, CT: Harvard University Press, 2002, p. 8; the Albright quote is from p. x.

3 Jedidiah Morse, *American Geography*, 1789, p. 469.

4 *Boston Herald*, November 1789; quoted in Reginald Horsman, *The New Republic*, London: Longman, 2000, p. 6.

5 John Winthrop, *A Modell of Christian Charity*, 1630; Boston: Collections of the Massachusetts Historical Society, 1838, third series, 7:31–48.

6 Stephen Prothero, *American Jesus: How the Son of God Became a National Icon*, New York: Farrar, Straus and Giroux, 2003, p. 9.

7 *Holy Trinity Church v US*, 143 US. 457, 1892.

8 Theodore Roosevelt, 'Expansion and Peace', in *The Works of Theodore Roosevelt*, vol. 12, New York: Charles Scribner, 1926, pp. 35–6.

9 Quoted in Sidney Lens, *The Forging of the American Empire*, London: Pluto Press, 2003, p. 166 (originally written and published in 1971).

10 Quoted in Lens, op. cit., p. 176, and Bacevich, op. cit., p. 79.

11 Quoted in Bacevich, op. cit., p. 55.

12 Quoted in Lens, op. cit., p. 280.

13 Slotkin, op. cit., 2000b, pp. 101–06.

14 Quoted in Lens, op. cit., p. 175.

15 Quoted in Stuart C. Millar, *Benevolent Assimilation: The American Conquest of the Philippines 1899–1903*, New Haven, CT: Yale University Press, 1982, p. 211.

16 Quoted in Lens, op. cit., p. 178.
17 Quoted in Bacevich, op. cit., p. x.
18 Quoted in Lens, op. cit., p. 195.
19 Kingsley Amis, *Rudyard Kipling*, London: Thames and Hudson, 1975.
20 Quoted in Lens, op. cit., p. 212.
21 Quoted ibid., p. 215.
22 Ernest R. May, *Imperial Democracy: The Emergence of America as a Great Power*, New York: Harper and Row, 1961.
23 Bacevich, op. cit., p. 6.

CHAPTER FOUR

1 Statement of President Coolidge to the Society of American Newspaper Editors, 1925.
2 Gabler, op. cit., 1998; see Chapter One: 'The Republic of Entertainment', pp. 43–52.
3 Robert Sklar, *Movie-Made America: A Cultural History of American Movies*, revised edn, New York: Vintage Books, 1994, p. 22.
4 Ibid., p. 29.
5 *Edison v American Mutoscope Company*, 114 Fed. Rep. 926, 1902, at 934–35.
6 Sklar, op. cit., p. 38.
7 Ibid., p. 40.
8 *The Moving Picture Annual and Yearbook for 1912*, 1913, p. 7.
9 Neal Gabler, *An Empire of Their Own: How Jews Invented Hollywood*, New York: Anchor Books, 1988.
10 Ibid., p. 5.
11 Ibid., p. 4.
12 Ibid., pp. 6–7.
13 'Winning Foreign Film Markets', *Scientific American*, vol. 125, 20 August 1921, p. 132.
14 Edward G. Lowry, 'Trade Follows the Film', *Saturday Evening Post*, vol. 198, 7 November 1925, p. 12.
15 Quoted in Sklar, op. cit., p. 219.
16 *Mutual Film Corporation v Industrial Commission of Ohio*, 236 US. 230, 1915, at 243, 244.
17 Quoted in Sklar, op. cit., p. 148.
18 Introduction to Minnie E. Kennedy, *The Home and Moving Pictures*, 1921, p. 3.
19 Donald Young, 'Social Standards and the Motion Picture', *The Annals of the American Academy of Political and Social Science*, vol. 128, November 1926, p. 147.
20 Hugo Münsterberg, *The Photoplay: A Psychological Study*, New York: Dover, 1916; retitled *The Film*, 1970, p. 30.
21 'The Motion Picture Code of 1930' (Hays Code), available from *www.artsreformation.com/a001/hays-code.html*
22 *Halliwell's Film and Video Guide 2003*, London: HarperCollins Entertainment, 2003.
23 *Propaganda in Motion Pictures*, US Congress, Senate Committee on Interstate Commerce, 1942, p. 423.
24 Quoted in Gabler, op. cit.,

1988, p. 216.

25 Quoted ibid., p. 195.

26 Ibid., pp. 196–7.

27 See Ziauddin Sardar, *Orientalism*, Buckingham: Open University Press, 1999.

28 Gabler, op. cit., 1988, p. 432.

29 Constantin Costa-Gavras, 'Resisting the Colonels of Disney', *New Perspective Quarterly*, 12 (4), Fall 1995, pp. 4–7.

30 As stated in television documentary 'The American Nightmare', Minerva Pictures production, directed by Adam Simon, broadcast on BBC2 on 5 January 2004.

31 Ziauddin Sardar, *The A to Z of Postmodern Life*, London: Vision, 2002, p. 35.

32 *Time*, 19 April 2004.

33 John Walker, *Art and Celebrity*, London: Pluto Press, 2003, p. 16.

34 Irving Rein, Philip Kotler and Martin Stoller, *High Visibility*, Chicago: NTC Business Books, 1997, pp. 14–15.

35 Quoted in Gabler, op. cit., 1988, p. 216.

36 Daniel Boorstin in *The Image, or What Happened to the American Dream*, London: Weidenfeld and Nicolson, 1998, p. 70; quoted by Walker, op. cit.

37 Walker, op. cit., pp. 6–7.

38 Leo Braudy, *The Frenzy of Renown: Fame and Its History*, New York: Vintage Books, revised edition, 1997, p. 599.

39 Ibid., p. 600.

40 We have analysed this episode of *The West Wing* in considerable detail in *Why Do People Hate America?*, Cambridge: Icon Books, 2002, Chapter One.

41 Benjamin R. Barber, 'The Making of McWorld', *New Perspective Quarterly*, 12 (4), Fall 1995, pp. 13–14.

42 Thomas Frank, 'Dark Age', in Thomas Frank and Matt Weiland, eds, *Commodify Your Dissent*, New York: W.W. Norton, 1997, p. 272.

CHAPTER FIVE

1 Editors of *US Camera Magazine*, quoted on
www.iwojima.com

2 Eddie Adams, quoted in 'Fifty Years Later, Iwo Jima Photographer Fights His Own Battle', by Mitchell Landsberg at
www.ap.org

3 Roy Hoopes, *When the Stars Went to War*, New York: Random House, 1994, p. xvii.

4 Garry Wills, *John Wayne's America*, New York: Touchstone, 1998.

5 *The Making of a Nation: 100 Milestones That Define America*, Washington, DC: US News and World Report, 2004.

6 David Ryan, *US Foreign Policy in World History*, London: Routledge, 2000, p. 23.

7 Lens, op. cit., p. 35.

8 Slotkin, op. cit., 2000b.

9 Ibid., p. 89.

10 Peter Biskind, *Seeing is Believ-*

ing: *How Hollywood Taught Us to Stop Worrying and Love the Fifties*, New York: Owl Books, 1983.

11 Julian Smith, *Looking Away: Hollywood and Vietnam*, New York: Charles Scribner, 1975, p. 43.

12 F.A. Long, 'Growth characteristics of military research and development', in *Impact of New Technologies on the Arms Race*, ed. B. Feld et al, Cambridge, MA: MIT Press, 1971, pp. 271–303.

13 Martin J. Medhurst, *Dwight D. Eisenhower: Strategic Communicator*, Westport, CT: Greenwood Press, 1993, p. 191.

14 Kenneth Arrow, *Social Choice and Individual Values*, New York: Wiley, 1951, pp. 59–60.

15 Johnson, op. cit., p. 32.

16 James Wilsdon, 'Mission to Planet Rumsfeld', *The Guardian*, 1 March 2004.

17 Paul Rogers, *A War on Terror*, London: Pluto Press, 2004, p. 83.

18 Johnson, op. cit., p. 56.

19 *The Military in the Movies*, Centre for Defense Information. A full transcript of the documentary is available from *www.cdi.org*

20 Ibid.

21 Henry Giroux, 'Living in the Shadow of Authoritarianism: Proto-Fascism, Neoliberalism, and the Twilight of Democracy', *Third Text*, 69, vol. 18, no. 4, July 2004.

22 Henry Giroux, 'Global Cap-
italism and the Return of the Garrison State', *Arena Journal*, 19, 2002, pp. 141–60.

23 Lens, op. cit., pp. 1–2.

CHAPTER SIX

1 Ziauddin Sardar and Merryl Wyn Davies, *Why Do People Hate America?*, op. cit.

2 Michael S. Sherry, *In the Shadow of War: The United States Since the 1930s*, New Haven, CT: Yale University Press, 1995, p. 81.

3 Michael Ignatieff, 'The American Empire: The Burden', *New York Times Magazine*, 5 January 2003, Section 6, p. 22.

4 Robert Kagan, 'The Benevolent Empire', *Foreign Policy*, Summer 1998, pp. 24–34.

5 Robert Kagan, *Paradise and Power*, New York: Alfred A. Knopf, 2003.

6 Lens, op. cit., p. xii.

7 Jensen, op. cit., pp. 6, 9.

8 Paul Berman, *Terror and Liberalism*, New York: W.W. Norton, 2003.

9 Stanley Kurtz, 'Democratic Imperialism: A Blueprint', *Policy Review*, April/May 2003, pp. 3–20.

10 See, for example, Ivo H. Daalder and James M. Lindsay, eds, *America Unbound: The Bush Revolution in Foreign Policy*, Washington, DC: Brookings Institution Press, 2003; and various pro-empire essays in Jim Garrison, ed., *American Empire: The Realities and Consequences*

of US Diplomacy, Cambridge, MA: Harvard University Press, 2002.

11 Philip Bobbitt, The Shield of Achilles: War, Peace and the Course of History, London: Allen Lane, 2002.

12 Francis Fukuyama, The End of History and the Last Man, London: Hamish Hamilton, 1992.

13 Ibid., pp. 48–50.

14 Ibid., p. 51.

15 Ibid., p. 73.

16 Ibid., p. 126.

17 Stuart Sim, Fundamentalist World, Cambridge: Icon Books, 2004, pp. 151, 152.

18 Samuel P. Huntington, 'The Clash of Civilizations?', Foreign Affairs, 72 (3), July/August 1993, pp. 22–49 (p. 30).

19 Ziauddin Sardar, op. cit., 1998, p. 84.

20 Samuel P. Huntington, The Clash of Civilizations and the Remaking of World Order, London: Simon and Schuster, 1997, p. 255.

21 Ibid., p. 208.

22 New York: Charles Scribner's Sons, 1948.

23 Robert D. Kaplan, 'Looking the World in the Eye', The Atlantic Monthly, December 2001.

24 Samuel P. Huntington, 'The Lonely Superpower', Foreign Affairs, 78 (2), 1993, pp. 35–49.

25 Huntington, op. cit., 1997, p. 59.

26 Ibid., p. 187.

27 Samuel P. Huntington, Who We Are: The Challenge to America's National Identity, New York: Simon and Schuster, 2004.

28 Leong Yew, The Disjunctive Empire of International Relations, Aldershot: Ashgate, 2003, p. 141.

29 Fareed Zakaria, The Future of Freedom: Illiberal Democracy at Home and Abroad, New York: W.W. Norton, 2003.

30 Benjamin R. Barber, Fear's Empire, New York: W.W. Norton, 2003, p. 156.

31 Ibid., pp. 161–2.

32 Ibid., p. 163.

33 Ibid., p. 164.

34 Jensen, op. cit., p. 70.

35 Michael Mann, Incoherent Empire, London: Verso, 2003, pp. 11–12.

36 Gore Vidal, speech at 1995 Washington, DC dinner party at Marcus Raskin's house.

37 Amy Chua, World on Fire, New York: Doubleday, 2003.

38 Charles William Maynes, 'The Perils of (and for) an Imperial America', Foreign Policy, Summer 1998, pp. 36–47.

39 James Bovard, Terrorism and Tyranny: Trampling Freedom, Justice, and Peace to Rid the World of Evil, New York: Palgrave Macmillan, 2003.

40 Saul Landau, The Pre-Emptive Empire, London: Pluto Press, 2003, p. 29.

41 Maynes, op. cit.

42 Mann, op. cit., p. 15.

43 Barber, op. cit., 2003, p. 164.

44 George Soros, *The Bubble of American Supremacy: Correcting the Misuse of American Power*, New York: Public Affairs, 2004.

45 Emmanuel Todd, *After the Empire: The Breakdown of the American Order*, Cambridge: Cambridge University Press, 2003.

46 Mann, op. cit., p. 13.

47 Maynes, op. cit.

48 Robert Jay Lifton, *Superpower Syndrome: America's Apocalyptic Confrontation with the World*, New York: Nation Books, 2003.

CONCLUSION

1 Gabler, op. cit., 1998, p. 11.

2 Alexis de Tocqueville, *Democracy in America*, New York: Everyman Library, 1994.

3 See John J. Pitney Jr, 'The Tocqueville Fraud', *The Weekly Standard*, 13 November 1995, available at *www.tocqueville.org*

4 Ibid., at *www.tocqueville.org*

5 Bill O'Reilly, 'Hating America', Talking Points Memo on The O'Reilly Factor, Fox News Channel, 7 July 2004, available at *www.foxnews.com*, posted on 8 July 2004.

6 Gabler, op. cit., 1998, p. 17.

7 See Malise Ruthven, *Fundamentalism*, Oxford: Oxford University Press, 2004.

8 Hearing of the Senate Armed Services Committee, 28 January 2004; full transcript at *www.ceip.org*

9 James Madison, in *The Federalist*, Franklin Centre, PA: Franklin Library, 1977, F63, p. 423 (original 1961).

10 Vinay Lal, 'Empire and the Dream-Work of America', *Global Dialogues*, 5, Winter/Spring 2003, pp. 1–2.

11 J.G. Ballard, 'In Modern America, No Nightmare is Forbidden', *The Guardian*, Review, 14 May 2004, p. 9.

12 Gabler, op. cit., 1998, p. 19.

13 Ibid., p. 7.

14 Lal, op. cit.

15 Jensen, op. cit., p. 135.

16 Barber, op. cit., 2003, p. 167.

17 Ibid., p. 38.

18 Zbigniew Brzezinski, 'Hegemonic Quicksand', *The National Interest*, no. 74, Winter 2003–04, pp. 5–16.

Select Bibliography

Achcar, Gilbert, *The Clash of Barbarisms: September 11 and the Making of the New World Disorder*, trans. Peter Ducker, New York: Monthly Review Press, 2002.

Amis, Kingsley, *Rudyard Kipling*, London: Thames and Hudson, 1975.

Araeen, Rasheed, Cubitt, Sean and Sardar, Ziauddin, eds, *The Third Text Reader on Art, Culture and Theory*, London: Continuum, 2002.

Bacevich, Andrew J., *American Empire: The Realities and Consequences of US Diplomacy*, New Haven, CT: Harvard University Press, 2002.

Barber, Benjamin R., *Fear's Empire*, New York: W.W. Norton, 2003.

Berman, Morris, The Twilight of American Culture, New York: W.W. Norton, 2000.

Berman, Paul, *Terror and Liberalism*, New York: W.W. Norton, 2003.

Biskind, Peter, *Seeing is Believing: How Hollywood Taught Us to Stop Worrying and Love the Fifties*, New York: Owl Books, 1983.

Blitz, Michael and Krasniewicz, Louise, *Why Arnold Matters*, New York: Basic Books, 2004.

Blum, William, *Rogue State: A Guide to the World's Only Superpower*, Monroe, ME: Common Courage Press, 2000.

Bobbitt, Philip, *The Shield of Achilles*, London: Allen Lane, 2002.

Boorstin, Daniel J., *The Americans: The National Experience*, New York: Vintage Books, 1965.

Boorstin, Daniel, *The Image, or What Happened to the American Dream*, London: Weidenfeld and Nicolson, 1998.

Boot, Max, *The Savage Wars of Peace: Small Wars and the Rise of American Power*, New York: Basic Books, 2002.

Bovard, James, *Terrorism and Tyranny: Trampling Freedom, Justice, and Peace to Rid the World of Evil*, New York: Palgrave Macmillan, 2003.

Braudy, Leo, *The Frenzy of Renown: Fame and Its History*, New York: Vintage Books, revised edition, 1997.

Brzezinski, Zbigniew, *Choice: Global Domination or Global Leadership*, New York: Basic Books, 2004.

Bush, George W., *We Will Prevail*, New York: Continuum, 2003.

Cawelti, John G., *The Six-Gun Mystique Sequel*, Bowling Green, OH: Bowling Green State University Popular Press, 1999.

'Celebrity', special issue of *Mediactive*, Issue 2, London: Barefoot Publications, 2003.

Chomsky, Noam, *Hegemony or Survival: America's Quest for Global Dominance*, New York: Metropolitan Books, 2003.

Chua, Amy, *World on Fire*, New York: Doubleday, 2003.

Clarke, Richard, *Against All Enemies*, New York: Free Press, 2004.

Constitution of the United States: A History, available on the National Archives website, www.archives.gov

Costa-Gavras, Constantin, 'Resisting the Colonels of Disney', *New Perspective Quarterly*, 12 (4), Fall 1995, pp. 4–7.

Cubitt, Sean, *The Cinema Effect*, Cambridge, MA: MIT Press, 2004.

Daalder, Ivo H. and Lindsay, James M., eds, *America Unbound: The Bush Revolution in Foreign Policy*, Washington, DC: Brookings Institution Press, 2003.

Dahl, Robert A., *How Democratic is the American Constitution?*, New Haven, CT: Yale University Press, 2001.

Ferguson, Niall, *Colossus: The Price of America's Empire*, London: The Penguin Press, 2004.

Frank, Thomas and Weiland, Matt, eds, *Commodify Your Dissent*, New York: W.W. Norton, 1997.

Fukuyama, Francis, *The End of History and the Last Man*, London: Hamish Hamilton, 1992.

Gabler, Neal, *An Empire of Their Own: How Jews Invented Hollywood*, New York: Anchor Books, 1988.

Gabler, Neal, *Life: The Movie*, New York: Vintage Books, 1998.

Gamson, Joshua, *Claims to Fame: Celebrity in Contemporary America*, Berkeley, CA: University of California Press, 1994.

Garrison, Jim, *America as Empire: Global Leader or Rogue Power?*, San Francisco: Berrett-Koehler Publishers, 2004.

Garrison, Jim, ed., *American Empire: The Realities and Consequences of US Diplomacy*, Cambridge, MA: Harvard University Press, 2002.

Gehring, Verna V., ed., *War After September 11*, Lanham, MD: Rowman and Littlefield, 2003.

Giroux, Henry A., 'Global Capitalism and the Return of the Garrison State', *Arena Journal*, 19, 2002, pp. 141–60.

Giroux, Henry A., 'Living in the Shadow of Authoritarianism: Proto-Fascism, Neoliberalism, and the Twilight of Democracy', *Third Text*, 69, vol. 18, no. 4, July 2004.

Glassner, Barry, *The Culture of Fear*, New York: Basic Books, 1999.

Halliwell's Film and Video Guide, 2003, London: HarperCollins Entertainment, 2003.

Hardt, Michael and Negri, Antonio, *Empire*, Cambridge, MA: Harvard University Press, 2000.

Hauerwas, Stanley and Lentricchia, Frank, eds, *Dissent From the Homeland: Essays After September 11*, Durham, NC: Duke University Press, 2003.

Hoopes, Roy, *When the Stars Went to War*, New York: Random House, 1994.

Huntington, Samuel P., *The Clash of Civilizations and the Remaking of World Order*, London: Simon and Schuster, 1997.

Huntington, Samuel P., *Who We Are: The Challenge to America's National Identity*, New York: Simon and Schuster, 2004.

Ignatieff, Michael, 'The American Empire: The Burden', *New York Times Magazine*, 5 January 2003, Section 6.

Ikenberry, G. John, ed., *America Unrivaled: The Future of the Balance of Power*, Ithaca, NY: Cornell University Press, 2002.

Jensen, Robert, *Citizens of the Empire: The Struggle to Claim Our Humanity*, San Francisco: City Light Books, 2004.

Johnson, Chalmers, *Blowback: The Costs and Consequences of American Empire*, London: Time Warner, 2002.

Johnson, Chalmers, *The Sorrows of Empire: Militarism, Secrecy and the End of the Republic*, New York: Metropolitan Books, 2004.

Joxe, Alain, *Empire of Disorder*, trans. Ames Hodges, ed. Sylvère Lotringer, Cambridge, MA: MIT Press/Semiotext(e), 2002.

Kagan, Robert, 'The Benevolent Empire', *Foreign Policy*, Summer 1998, pp. 24–34.

Kagan, Robert, *Paradise and Power*, New York: Alfred A. Knopf, 2003.

Kingdon, John W., *America the Unusual*, Belmont, CA: Wadsworth, 1999.

Krugman, Paul, *The Great Unravelling*, New York: W.W. Norton, 2003.

Kupchan, Charles, *The End of the American Era: US Foreign Policy and the Geopolitics of the Twenty-first Century*, New York: Knopf, 2002.

Kurtz, Stanley, 'Democratic Imperialism: A Blueprint', *Policy Review*, April/May 2003, pp. 3–20.

Landau, Saul, *The Pre-Emptive Empire*, London: Pluto Press, 2003.

Lapham, Lewis, *Waiting for the Barbarians*, London: Verso, 1997.

Lazare, Daniel, *The Frozen Republic*, New York: Harcourt and Brace, 1996.

Lens, Sidney, *The Forging of the American Empire*, London: Pluto Press, 2003 (originally published 1971).

Lewis, Jon, ed., *The End of Cinema as We Know It*, London: Pluto Press, 2001.

Lifton, Robert Jay, *Superpower Syndrome: America's Apocalyptic Confrontation with the World*, New York: Nation Books, 2003.

Magdoff, Harry, *The Age of Imperialism: The Economics of US Foreign Policy*, New York: Monthly Review Press, 1969.

Mahajan, Rahul, *Full Spectrum Dominance: US Power in Iraq and Beyond*, New York: Seven Stories Press, 2003.

The Making of a Nation: 100 Milestones That Define America, Washington, DC: US News and World Report, 2004.

Mann, Michael, *Incoherent Empire*, London: Verso, 2003.

May, Ernest R., *Imperial Democracy: The Emergence of America as a Great Power*, New York: Harper and Row, 1961.

Maynes, Charles William, 'The Perils of (and for) an Imperial America', *Foreign Policy*, Summer 1998, pp. 36–47.

Mead, Walter Russell, *Mortal Splendor: The American Empire in Transition*, New York: Houghton Mifflin, 1988.

Mearsheimer, John, *The Tragedy of Great Power Politics*, New York: W.W. Norton, 2003.

Medhurst, Martin J., *Dwight D. Eisenhower: Strategic Communicator*, Westport, CT: Greenwood Press, 1993.

Millar, Stuart C., *Benevolent Assimilation: The American Conquest of the Philippines 1899–1903*, New Haven, CT: Yale University Press, 1982.

Miller, Mark Crispin, *The Bush Dyslexicon*, New York: W.W. Norton, 2001.

Münsterberg, Hugo, *The Photoplay: A Psychological Study*, New York: Dover, 1916, retitled *The Film*, 1970.

Pfaff, William, *Barbarian Sentiments: America in the New Century*, New York: Hill and Wang, 2000.

'Progressive Internationalism: A Democratic National Security Strategy', Washington, DC: Progressive Policy Institute, 30 October 2003; available from www.ppionline.org

Prothero, Stephen, *American Jesus: How the Son of God Became a National Icon*, New York: Farrar, Straus and Giroux, 2003.

Rein, Irving, Kotler, Philip and Stoller, Martin, *High Visibility*, Chicago: NTC Business Books, 1997.

'Rebuilding America's Defenses: Strategy, Forces and Resources for a New Century', Washington, DC: Project for the New American Century, September 2000, available from *www.newamericancentury.org*

Rogers, Paul, *A War on Terror*, London: Pluto Press, 2004.

Roosevelt, Theodore, *The Works of Theodore Roosevelt*, New York: Charles Scribner, 1926.

Ryan, David, *US Foreign Policy in World History*, London: Routledge, 2000.

Sardar, Ziauddin, *Postmodernism and the Other*, London: Pluto Press, 1998.

Sardar, Ziauddin, *Orientalism*, Buckingham: Open University Press, 1999.

Sardar, Ziauddin, *The A to Z of Postmodern Life*, London: Vision, 2002.

Sardar, Ziauddin and Davies, Merryl Wyn, *Why Do People Hate America?*, Cambridge: Icon Books, 2002.

Schudson, Michael, *The Good Citizen: A History of American Civic Life*, Cambridge, MA: Harvard University Press, 1998.

Sherry, Michael S., *In the Shadow of War: The United States Since the 1930s*, New Haven, CT: Yale University Press, 1995.

Sim, Stuart, *Fundamentalist World*, Cambridge: Icon Books, 2004.

Singer, Peter, *The President of Good and Evil*, London: Granta, 2004.

Sklar, Robert, *Movie-Made America: A Cultural History of American Movies*, revised edition, New York: Vintage Books, 1994.

Slotkin, Richard, *Regeneration Through Violence*, Norman, OK: University of Oklahoma Press, 2000a.

Slotkin, Richard, *Gunfighter Nation*, Norman, OK: University of Oklahoma Press, 2000b.

Slotkin, Richard, *The Fateful Environment*, Norman, OK: University of Oklahoma Press, 2000c.

Smith, Julian, *Looking Away: Hollywood and Vietnam*, New York: Charles Scribner, 1975.

Smith, Neil, *American Empire: Roosevelt's Geographer and the Prelude to Globalization*, Berkeley, CA: University of California Press, 2003.

Soros, George, *The Bubble of American Supremacy: Correcting the Misuse of American Power*, New York: Public Affairs, 2004.

Todd, Emmanuel, *After the Empire: The Breakdown of the American Order*, Cambridge: Cambridge University Press, 2003.

Vidal, Gore, *Inventing a Nation: Washington, Adams, Jefferson*, New Haven, CT: Yale University Press, 2003.

Vidal, Gore, *The Decline and Fall of the American Empire*, Chicago: Odonian Press, 2000.

Walker, John, *Art and Celebrity*, London: Pluto Press, 2003.

Wallerstein, Immanuel, *The Decline of American Power: The US in a Chaotic World*, New York: New Press, 2003.

Williams, Gwyn A., *Madoc: The Legend of the Welsh Discovery of America*, Oxford: Oxford University Press, 1987.

Williams, William Appleman, *The Roots of the Modern American Empire*, New York: Random House, 1969.

Wills, Garry, 'The New Revolutionaries', *The New York Review of Books*, 10 August 1995.

Wills, Garry, *John Wayne's America*, New York: Touchstone, 1998.

Wills, Garry, *A Necessary Evil*, New York: Touchstone, 2002.

'Winning Foreign Film Markets', *Scientific American*, vol. 125, 20 August 1921.

Wood, Ellen Meiksins, *Empire of Capital*, London: Verso, 2003.

Wood, Robin, *Howard Hawks*, London: BFI Publishing, 1968.

Woodward, Bob, *Plan of Attack*, New York: Simon and Schuster, 2004.

Yew, Leong, *The Disjunctive Empire of International Relations*, Aldershot: Ashgate, 2003.

Zakaria, Fareed, *The Future of Freedom: Illiberal Democracy at Home and Abroad*, New York: W.W. Norton, 2003.

Zimmerman, Warren, *First Great Triumph: How Five Americans Made Their Country a World Power*, New York: Farrar, Straus and Giroux, 2002.

Index

Other political titles available from Icon Books

Why Do People Hate America?

Ziauddin Sardar and Merryl Wyn Davies

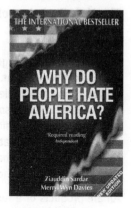

The economic power of US corporations and the virus-like power of American popular culture affect the lives and infect the indigenous cultures of millions around the world. The foreign policy of the US government, backed by its military strength, has unprecedented global influence now that the USA is the world's only superpower – its first 'hyperpower'. America also exports its value systems, defining what it means to be civilised, rational, developed and democratic – indeed, what it is to be human. Meanwhile, the US itself is impervious to outside influence, and if most Americans think of the rest of the world at all, it is in terms of deeply ingrained cultural stereotypes.

This best-selling book explains exactly why America is so hated. It is an important contribution to a debate which needs to be addressed by people of all nations, cultures, religions and political persuasions.

'Required reading' *Independent*

'Contains valuable information and insights that we should know, over here, for our own good, and the world's' Noam Chomsky

'Packed with tightly argued points' *Times Higher Education Supplement*

'Original and thought-provoking' *New Statesman*

Ziauddin Sardar is a writer, broadcaster and cultural critic. He is a regular contributor to the *New Statesman*, and is co-author of *American Dream, Global Nightmare* (Icon, 2004).

Merryl Wyn Davies is a writer and anthropologist. Her most recent books are *Darwin and Fundamentalism* (2000) and *American Dream, Global Nightmare* (Icon, 2004).

UK £7.99 ISBN 1 84046 525 5

Fundamentalist World
The New Dark Age of Dogma

Stuart Sim

The collapse of the Argentinian economy, the rise of the far right, 9/11, suicide bombings in the Middle East, campaigns against multiculturalism, anti-abortion terrorism, the militia movement in America, teaching creationism in schools, riots at Miss World: what ties these seemingly unrelated phenomena together?

All are products of a fundamentalist mentality, determined to crush all opposing ideas. Belief in these kinds of universal theories was, until recently, assumed to be in decline. Stuart Sim argues that this is far from true.

Fundamentalism is no fringe enthusiasm, but an increasingly mainstream and powerful influence. Whether it's religious, political, imperialist, nationalist or even market fundamentalism, believe it: we live in an increasingly fundamentalist world.

'Stuart Sim deserves the most rousing congratulations for having the courage and skill to tackle the most pressing issue of our age. His book is bold, original and immensely thought-provoking' Francis Wheen

'Highly successful in setting modern fundamentalism in its historic context' *Financial Times*

'Sim's direct style makes this worthy and weighty thesis accessible to the general reader' *The List*

'Accessible and compelling writing ... an all-embracing take on the phenomenon' *The Age*

Stuart Sim is Professor of Critical Theory in the English Department at the University of Sunderland. He is the author of *Derrida and the End of History*, *Lyotard and the Inhuman* and *Irony and Crisis: A Critical History of Postmodern Culture*, all published by Icon. His work has been translated into nine languages, and he is a Fellow of the English Association.

UK £12.99 ISBN 1 84046 532 8

Trust ... From Socrates to Spin

Kieron O'Hara

Who do we trust and why? Do we trust the government to act responsibly? Do we trust experts to be accountable? Do we trust corporations to work within the law? Do we trust newspapers (and books) to tell the truth? Should we be less trusting – or more?

A crisis in trust is currently gripping the West. Polls record an all-time low in levels of trust in politicians, businessmen and scientists. In this exhilarating ride through recent news events, literature, philosophy and history, Kieron O'Hara examines the vital questions of how trust is built up and how it collapses.

From Aristotle to Nick Leeson, from Machiavelli to Naomi Klein, from the Book of Job to Blairite newspeak and from Enron to nanotechnology, *Trust* explores the impact of this crisis on our daily lives, offering few easy answers but seeking out the questions we should all be asking.

'Absorbing ... a fascinating read' *New Scientist*

'Very refreshing' *Guardian*

'A timely study of a crucial aspect of public life' *Observer*

'O'Hara succeeds precisely because he casts such a bracingly jaundiced eye over the issue of trust' *Independent*

'An effervescent discussion' *Financial Times*

Kieron O'Hara is a Senior Research Fellow at the University of Southampton. He is involved in the Office of Science and Technology's Cybertrust and Crime Prevention Programme, is the author of *Plato and the Internet* (Icon, 2001) and has contributed to many journals and magazines including the *New Statesman*.

UK £12.99 ISBN 1 84046 531 X

50 Facts that Should Change the World

Jessica Williams

- In Kenya, monthly bribery payments add a third to the average household budget.

- The US spends $10 billion on pornography every year. In 2001, the US spent $10 billion on foreign aid.

- Landmines kill or maim at least one person every hour.

From the inequalities and absurdities of the so-called developed West to the vast scale of suffering wreaked by war, famine and Aids in developing countries, this book paints a picture of shocking contrasts. YOU need to know these facts.

Each fact from this eclectic range is followed by explanation and lively analysis. Some facts will make you rethink things you thought you knew. Some illustrate long-term, gradual changes in our society. Others concern local issues that people face in their everyday lives. All of the facts remind us that our world is deeply interconnected – and that civilisation is a fragile concept.

'A fearless and compelling work. You need to know what's in this book' Monica Ali

'A research handbook for the *No Logo* generation' *Guardian*

'Lucidly written, excellently researched, and with detailed referencing, the world won't look so rosy when you've put it down' *The Ecologist*

'A book to surprise, enrage and inform, it is a powerful antidote to apathy which offers information on how to make a difference. A gem of a book' *Agenda*

Jessica Williams is a journalist and television producer for the BBC, where she has researched and produced interviews with such disparate figures as the political philosopher Noam Chomsky, President Paul Kagame of Rwanda, Sir David Attenborough, Northern Ireland First Minister David Trimble, and the American academic Edward Said.

UK £9.99 ISBN 1 84046 547 6

Why Blame Israel?
The Facts Behind the Headlines
Neill Lochery

For a surprising number of people, Israel has become a pariah state, a threat to world – not just regional – peace and security. Israel gets the blame for half a century of Middle Eastern violence, for inciting Islamic-based terrorism throughout the world, and for stealing land whose historical right of ownership is at best contentious. This book examines the true history of the conflict and asks: should Israel shoulder this blame, or are the realities of the conflict far more complex?

This is the first up-to-date, detailed account of the history of the state of Israel, and the resulting Arab–Israeli conflict, from an author who comes from outside the fray.

'A superb book ... a useful antidote to grotesque distortion' *Mail on Sunday*

'Incisive, informed, well-written. An unusually fair and accurate account from someone who is neither Jew nor Arab' Tom Gross, *Wall Street Journal* Middle East commentator

'A timely, erudite study that deserves to be read' *Good Book Guide*

'A necessary book. This scrupulous, well-written and eminently sane book will go far to set things right.' Bret Stephens, Editor-in-chief, *Jerusalem Post*

Neill Lochery is currently Lecturer in Modern Israeli Politics and Director of the Centre for Israeli Studies, University College London. He has written numerous articles and books, as well as filing weekly pieces for UPI, *The Scotsman*, the *National Post*, the *Chicago Sun-Times* and the *Jerusalem Post*, among others.

UK £12.99 ISBN 1 84046 530 1